Guide to Better

English

Spelling

Guide to Better

English

Spelling

Edna L. Furness

National Textbook Company
NTC a division of *NTC Publishing Group* • Lincolnwood, Illinois USA

ACKNOWLEDGMENTS

Every effort has been made to acknowledge sources of material in the Notes in the last section of the book. Oversights which are brought to the attention of the author will be gratefully rectified in subsequent editions. Special thanks are due to the following:

Barron's Educational Series, Inc., for permission to paraphrase the information from Joseph Mersand's *Spelling Your Way to Success,* which appears in Chapter II.

The Bruce Publishing Co., *The English Journal and The Clearing House,* for permission to use mnemonic devices credited in Chapter VI.

Dell Publishing Company, for excerpt from *How to Spell It Right.* Copyright © 1970.

Donald Publishing Co., for permission to quote the limerick in Chapter VI and the word lists in Chapter VIII from A. H. Lass's *Business, Spelling and Word Power.*

Doubleday & Company, Inc., for permission to paraphrase the material in Chapter VIII from Sylvester Mawson's *The Dictionary Companion.* Copyright © 1932 by C. O. S. Mawson.

Harvard University Press, for permission to adapt the phonetic symbols credited in Chapter IX to *Linguistic Science and the Teaching of English* by Henry Lee Smith, Jr. Copyright © 1956 by the President and Fellows of Harvard College.

John R. Malone, for permission to use the single-sound, or Unifon, alphabet in Chapter II. Copyright © 1962 by the Foundation for Compatible and Consistent Alphabet.

Oxford University Press, for permission to adapt the lists of prefixes and suffixes credited in Chapter VIII to W. Powell Jones's *Practical Word Study.*

Roberta Baldridge, for calling my attention to the mnemonic devices of Arnold Lazarus, Donald S. Klopp, Mrs. G. I. Pennington, Hudson F. Wilcox, Mary Lane, Rubie Jessen, Sylvia Likens, Bobbie Godluve Clark, Don Edwards, Edna Cannam, and Harry Shaw.

Everett E. Robie, for permission to use material from *Word Division, or When to Hyphenate* in Chapter VI.

Scripps Howard, *National Spelling Bee,* "Words of the Champions." Used with permission.

William Collins and World Publishing Company, for permission to quote and adapt material from *The New World Dictionary of the American Language* in Chapter VII. Copyright © 1974 by William Collins, and World Publishing Company.

Tom Talman, "I'd Better Just Whisper It," reprinted from *The Saturday Evening Post,* © 1952 The Curtis Publishing Co.

To the memory of my parents,
Franklin Anthony Furness
Nellie Swanson Furness

Contents

Foreword   11

Introduction   13

Part One: *Why* Spell?   15

    I. Spelling Is Important   17
   II. Spelling Is Here to Stay   24

Part Two: *How* Does One Learn to Spell?   41

   III. What Psychologists Know About Spelling   43
   IV. Do Teachers Really Teach?   55
    V. The Problem for Parents   70
   VI. Two Basic Methods   79
   VII. The Dictionary: Anatomy of an Ally   97
  VIII. Structuring: Another Method   120

Part Three: *What* Words and *How* to Spell Them?   155

   IX. Phonemes and Graphemes: A Final Approach   157
    X. Facing the Demons   172
   XI. A Nostalgic Touch: The National Spelling Bee   196
   XII. Ten Tests of Spelling Success   207

Appendix   221

   A. Answers   221
   B. Notes   225
   C. Other Demon Lists   231

References   240

Glossary   242

Index   246

Guide to Better

English

Spelling

Foreword

In this book Edna Furness does much more than offer interested readers a few tips on spelling English words correctly. She is after bigger game. In fact, her real subject is the English language, as it manifests itself over the years in the curious quirks and turns of English spelling. She shows us why we spell as we do, why spelling is for so many people a difficult problem, how the gap between sounds and letters became so great, and why reform of the alphabet is doomed to failure. Dr. Furness describes the impact of history and of dictionaries on the spelling of English.

Master teacher that she is, Edna Furness employs a descriptive, rather than prescriptive, approach to language. Instead of laying down laws, she believes that by informing readers fully and accurately, they will be led naturally to making the right choices. Dr. Furness shows parents and teachers what they can do to improve the spelling of their children and their students.

For anyone interested in language, this book offers lucid, often witty, insights into its operation. I am happy to welcome this new edition, *Guide to Better English Spelling*, into print.

Wendell Schwartz
Chair, CSSEDC
National Council of Teachers of English

Introduction

Like Caesar's Gaul, this book is divided into three parts. The first part raises the basic question "Why Spell?" and then attempts an answer in the chapter, "Spelling Is Here to Stay." This part—and, indeed the rest of the book—is based on the assumption that learning to spell is an essential phase of literacy. However, it is also the aim of this book to help readers expand their vocabularies, learn how language develops, become familiar with word origins, and acquire the habit of reading, an essential survival skill in a rapidly changing age of high tech.

The second part of *Guide to Better English Spelling* describes recent research in the fields of psychology and linguistics. Psychologists say that the ability to spell depends upon the senses—sight, hearing, and even touch. Linguists say that one can learn to spell by becoming acquainted with etymology, with phonemes and graphemes, and with the structure of language. All these topics are covered in this part. In addition, there is a chapter on what a parent needs to know to help a child learn to spell.

The final part of this book deals with words taken from everyday life that cause spelling problems, words that are frequently used and frequently misspelled. Working from scientifically compiled lists, this book categorizes over 600 spelling demons. Finally, there is a nostalgic look at the National Spelling Bee, an event that has regained popularity and is deserving of attention.

Guide to Better English Spelling is the distillation of one educator's experience over the years, teaching English, Spanish, and Latin in high schools and comparative literature and linguistics in colleges and universities.

Edna L. Furness

PART ONE
Why Spell?

CHAPTER I

Spelling Is Important

It is a pity that Chawcer, who had geneyus, was so unedicated. He's the wuss speller I know of.

Is it worthwhile to spell well? When Artemus Ward made his joke about Chaucer, he pretended to ignore a fact that is familiar to anyone who has studied the famous medieval poet. Chaucer, of course, knew how to spell the English of his day, and his spelling, as difficult as it is for us to read now, appeared perfectly correct to his fourteenth-century readers. But in satirizing the bad spelling of his own day, Mr. Ward touches on another point. That is the fact that bad spelling is bad communication. When a reader has to stop and puzzle over a misspelled word, or to smile over it, he has stopped thinking about what the writer is trying to say; he is thinking only of the illiterate way he says it. For a moment the line of thought is lost, and the reader's only thought is that someone should correct this poor fellow's spelling.

Misspelled words mar a page. They're as noticeable and as unfortunate as a run in a pair of nylons or a fumble on the football field. They defeat you. When you take the trouble to write something, you do so because you feel it's worth reading. These are your own thoughts, and you want these thoughts understood and appreciated. But misspelling, either part or most of the time, undermines your purpose, and your writing becomes a hindrance and an embarrassment. Good spelling, on the other hand, looks right. It seems clear and easy to read. It's good form. In short, good spelling communicates, a fact to be treated later.

The idea that good spelling is good form has been with us for quite

17

a while. During the eighteenth century [1] Lord Chesterfield wrote to his son: "Mind your diction in whatever language you either write or speak: contract a habit of correctness and elegance." In another letter he said: "Orthography is so absolutely necessary for a man of letters, or a gentleman, that one false spelling may fix ridicule upon him for the rest of his life; and I know a man of quality, who never recovered the ridicule of having spelled wholesome without the w." [2] And more recently one twentieth-century mother inscribed this little limerick on the flyleaf of her son's dictionary:

> When words have you puzzled or hesitant,
> Look here where the spellings are resident,
>   And remember, my son,
>   When there's script to be done,
> You should rather write right than be President. [3]

Spelling defined. Just what does the word *spelling* mean? Originally the word *spell,* derived from the Middle English *spellen,* meant "to read out" or "convey meaning." Spelling, according to the *New World Dictionary of the American Language,* is the act of naming, writing, printing, or signaling in the proper order the letters of a word. Ability to spell requires accurate recall and reproduction of the letters in their proper order. In some cases the recall is more difficult, and in some cases easier. One of the easy cases is that of the boy who said, "I can spell *banana* all right, only I don't know when to stop."

In the layman's view, spelling means hearing, pronouncing, or writing the letters of a word in the accepted order. A successful speller is the individual who recognizes the importance of spelling, who holds a positive attitude toward spelling, and who has sufficient knowledge about language to spell words independently.

Spelling and your friends. Good spelling is a sign of literacy. We may even say that spelling and social status are related. Take the case of phonetic spelling—for example, spelling *duz* for *does.* This may be useful to an advertiser trying to capture and hold the attention of the buying public. But in normal situations, phonetic spelling becomes equivalent to spelling incorrectly. He who writes *neet* for *neat, ded* for *dead,* and *rote* for *wrote* will find that his friends notice such spellings. They may be amused. Or they may be ashamed. Writers do occasionally write the exact words of people whose speech is incorrect or corrupt. They even purposely misspell their words to let the reader know the speaker's social level. Mickey Spillane and John

Steinbeck are authors who use this realistic spelling device in such sentences as "Elvira done tole me that nobuddy has gone to the crik." But it is one thing for a famous writer to use a special literary device; it is quite another to create the impression that you are one of the characters he's writing about.

There is a closely related practice called *eye-dialect*. Eye-dialect may be defined as the phonetic respelling of words (for example, *eye-talian*), not in order to show a mispronunciation, but to burlesque the words or their speaker. Now we all pronounce *says* in the same way. But if we spell it *sez*, we imply the person quoted is one who would use a vulgar pronunciation if there were one. Other spellings in eye-dialect tradition are *cum* for come, *lissen* for listen, *enny* for any, and *enuff* for enough.

Spelling has come to be a sign or indication of a person's educational attainments. The poor speller is like the slipshod dresser. He may have excellent qualifications for success if his prospective employer can see beneath the surface indications. But in both cases, the employer has a circumstantial suspicion of him. This can be prevented by the correction of the surface defect. The able applicant who dresses in good taste and speaks politely has inevitably highlighted his other fine qualities in the employer's mind. The man who spells well has disclosed a first indicator of his general education, refinement, and sensibility.

Spelling and your career. Spelling is a matter of accuracy, which is imperative in business and professional life. In the world of journalism there are few copy desks that would take seriously Mark Twain's objection "to a uniform and arbitrary way of spelling words." The police reporter must check on the spelling of names, ages, and addresses in the reports submitted by policemen, who are not experts in spelling and handwriting. After all, inaccuracy may do worse than cause embarrassment—it may involve the newspaper in a libel suit.

One straight-faced editor gets down to classification of the feature writers he has observed for more than twenty-five years. He says, "I have found that they, good or bad, fall into two classes: (1) those who can spell well; (2) those who write 'sargent,' meaning a military man with stripes, and 'vetaren,' meaning a man who has lost his stripes."

Business and professional men know that the abilities to read and spell well are valuable career assets. An illuminating episode is related in a pamphlet published by a large corporation. The top engineer telephones: "I have before [me] . . . a brief report from one of our young engineers. I have to guess . . . what the fellow is driving at. I am no English shark, but I find myself getting a little angry when I see four sentences tied into one with four commas. He has 'principle' for 'principal' and he has also misspelled 'accommodate' and 'Cincinnati.' What if some of this fellow's bad sentences get into the hands of our customers?" [4] When an executive of a corporation that makes diesel locomotives, turbines, generators, jet engines, refrigerators, and two hundred thousand other electrical products considers English and spelling vitally important, then it is time for young engineering students to pay attention.

"That's preposterous," you say. "An executive of a big business does not need a knowledge of spelling. He hires a secretary who knows how to spell." The experience of the angry top engineer is sufficient to underline the fact that the executive is at the mercy of his employee's education and accuracy. And if the boss himself cannot spell, how can he detect errors in his secretary's work? And will the clients who receive the letter hold only the secretary to blame and exonerate the boss? Obviously not. As for the secretary, we all know that an employer does expect his secretary to spell—even on her first job. If she has a spelling handicap, she might as well face harsh reality and realize that her value as a secretary is limited. Uncorrected, such a limitation might cripple her whole career.

Proper spelling is becoming increasingly important in the world of science too. In a paper entitled "Reading and Science Instruction," [5] zoologist Kenneth B. M. Crooks expressed concern for students who cannot pronounce, read, write, or spell well enough to get the full benefits of a science course. High-school students with such deficiencies are frightened away from science. "Pupils who cannot read or spell," he states, " 'escape' science courses, for they fear the 'new' words, the 'big' words, and the 'hard' words, which they cannot read, pronounce, understand or spell. Poor readers are often poor spellers; and poor spellers, poor readers."

Spelling and communication. Some individuals may contend that the evidence thus far presented in favor of good spelling is discriminatory, that spelling is a status symbol, and that attention to spelling is connected with pedantry, with a nonfunctional neurosis about detail. However, one inescapable fact is that good spelling is connected with communication and its corollary, consideration for others.

Good spelling does communicate, and communication is important. After all, communication is a way by which man understands his fellowman, his actions and thoughts. Rollo May, a practicing psychotherapist in New York and a training and supervisory analyst in the William Alanson White Institute, draws an interesting analogy with respect to communication. When communication breaks down, one is like a man dreaming about wandering in a foreign land where he cannot understand what is being said, where he feels nothing, and where he is truly isolated. Particularly startling is Rollo May's observation that aggression and violence occur when the possibilities for communication break down.[6]

This observation corroborates an idea that George Orwell expressed in his book 1984. In this era when Big Brother can use technology for snooping, certain tendencies are loose—that is, the debasement of the language and the debasement of thought.

Despite the dejection and dissatisfaction of college presidents, editors, businessmen, academicians, parents, and teachers, the poor spellers are increasing. The schools continue to graduate poor spellers (so do the colleges, for that matter). Everywhere in academia, errors in spelling persist, and life goes on as if all were well. Some view the spelling decline as a phase of the general decline in standards in our time—in dress, in manners, in reading, in public morality, in academic standards, and in communication. Others view the problem as a temporary decline, as a form of the so-called generation gap, as a kind of youth rebellion against conformity and the Establishment. Many consider it part of modern alienation, such as that seen by social critic and author Vance Packard, who diagnosed America in his book *A Nation of Strangers* as "a society of torn roots," a society victimized by a malaise of loneliness, reflected in songs and poetry.[7]

Concern from the literary, the business, the communication, the professional and education worlds supports the fact that it is indeed worthwhile to spell well. Good spelling enhances your attractiveness in social life and in your career. Good spelling facilitates studying and increases your chances of getting and holding a responsible job. And, after all, learning to spell well isn't as hard as you might think. Let's take a look at the first four steps.

The first step. Your first step toward learning to spell is taken when you grasp the fundamental importance of spelling in the eyes of the world at large—social, business, professional, and scientific. Actually, if you've read this far, you've already accomplished the first step and are ready for the second.

Anyone having the mentality to master the usual high-school subjects has the mental qualifications to learn to spell. Psychologists are fairly well agreed that learning to spell is not strictly a matter of having a high IQ. They say too that there is no such thing as a spelling handicap for persons who can learn the basic facts of mathematics, grammar, and science. In brief, you don't have to be an Einstein or a Schweitzer to learn to spell. To be sure, some people find spelling easier than others, but some people find arithmetic easier, too. All things being equal, we say that the person who is willing to expend time and effort and to study systematically and scientifically has a fair chance (from 98 percent to 100 percent) of being successful. But the study must be systematic, and it must be scientific.

The second step. Your second step then is to take a positive mental attitude. When you can say, "Spelling can be mastered, and I, a normal being, can learn to spell," you have already gone a long way toward success. A self-help program in spelling is a very demanding one. You will need dedication and discipline of the highest order. But if you prove yourself equal to the rigors of a systematic and scientific program, you will have the first reward in the satisfaction of mastering ordinary words that every educated person is expected to know. You will have another reward in vocabulary expansion. The scientific principles that you will learn in studying spelling will enable you to grasp quickly and easily the new words you wish to know and use. And, as an enthusiast for words, you will be doubling and tripling your vocabulary. Instead of always saying *best,* for example, you will have at your command such possible substitutes as *marvelous, excellent, unexcelled, matchless,* and *superb.* You will learn to draw legitimate, accurate, and otherwise desirable synonyms from the great treasure house of English words. And as you learn new words in business, names of new inventions, words used in new relationships, you will inevitably experience the exhilaration of increasing your spelling power.

The third step. If all this appeals to you, you have now taken the first two steps. Number one, you realize and acknowledge the importance of spelling in the social, business, and scientific worlds. Number two, you are cultivating a positive attitude toward spelling, and you acknowledge that you too can learn to spell. What comes next? The third step is to adopt a simple three-point framework for all your dealings with hard-to-spell words. Call them the three L's: look, listen, and learn. Any word will be easier to handle from the first if you:

1. *Look.* Carefully observe the spelling of words you use.
2. *Listen.* Listen to the way words are pronounced. (Do you hear

hafta for *have to, cancha* for *can't you, didja* for *did you, doncha* for *don't you, singin* for *singing, rigah* for *rigor?*) Concentrate on clear, correct pronunciation.

3. *Learn.* Keep a list of words you misspell and then study them. Consult the dictionary for the words you cannot spell.

The fourth step. Finally, a very important step involves becoming aware that you are living in a world of rapidly expanding knowledge. Every ten years the store of knowledge doubles. In the last fifty years more words have entered the language than during any similar, previous period. To survive in the twenty-first century, you will need a larger vocabulary and a greater knowledge of spelling.

Taken together, then, these four steps are vital to the career of anyone who wishes to function effectively in society. Keep them in mind as we discuss the history of spelling in the next chapter. You will consolidate your first four steps in the conquest of spelling.

CHAPTER II

Spelling Is Here to Stay

Simplified spelling is all right; but,
like chastity, you can carry it too far.

MARK TWAIN

Why people can't spell. One of the most serious obstacles to the art of spelling well is the simple fact that English spelling is extremely illogical. Sounds are spelled in an amazing variety of ways, and words that sound alike, and presumably *should* be spelled alike, come out entirely different. If you've had trouble with spelling in the past (and who hasn't, by the way?), you've no doubt caught yourself wishing the whole system could be made over into something simpler and more clear. Why can't all the sounds be spelled the same way? you've probably asked. Why can't words *look* the way they *sound*? Why use five letters to make a sound in one word and only one letter to make the same sound in another? In short, why can't the whole thing be logical?

If you've been asking yourself these questions from time to time, rest assured that legions of scholars and teachers have shared your exasperation through the centuries. Many reformers have attempted to adjust our methods of spelling to our language. But by and large they have made very slow progress, not because new methods are impossible to devise (a number of simple and feasible proposals for spelling reform have been made, in fact), but, oddly, because the great English-speaking public continues to prefer the cumbersome, inconsistent spelling of modern English. In short, the public doesn't *want* change. Why? Isaac Pitman, who is famous for his system of shorthand, and who devoted much of his life to forming a Simplified Spelling

Society, writes these words in his own "spelling system" to explain it: "We instinktively shrink from eny chaenj in whot iz familyar; and whot kan be mor familyar dhan dhe form of wurdz dhat we hav sen and riten mor tiemz dhan we kan posibly estimat?" In this chapter, let's look a little more deeply into the history of the language itself, and into the attitude of the general public toward spelling reform. Some clues to the mysteries of good spelling can be found in this problem.

Why English spelling is unphonetic. In 1954 the *Saturday Review* carried an entertaining article in which Harvey Kinsey Boyer [1] touched upon spelling reform. One look at Mr. Boyer's list of different ways to designate the long *a* is sufficient to arouse sympathy with people who can't spell and with people who dream about spelling reform. This is the list:

toda (as in aerial, aorta)	todaye (as in aye, meaning always)
today (as in pay)	todeh (as in eh?)
todey (as in they)	todée (as in fiancée, matinée)
todei (as in veil)	todé (as in fiancé)
todea (as in great)	todet (as in bouquet)
todai (as in rain)	toder (as in déjeuner, really French)
todeig (as in feign)	todau (as in gauge)
todeigh (as in neighbor)	

Take a look at one phoneme e,* which may be represented by ten spellings:

e	let	eo	leopard
ea	weather	oe	foetid
ae	aesthetic	ai	said
ei	heifer	a	many
ie	friend	u	buried

Of the languages which are in most general use, English and French are both exceptionally unphonetic in their spelling systems. Both languages have made numerous and vast alterations in their sound structure, but have not modified their spelling to accord with these changes.[2] French shows a great cleavage between sound and symbol, but English takes the prize for irregularity and arbitrariness. To understand why, you have only to note the four hundred different spellings we have for forty or forty-five sounds.

---

*In the language of linguistics, a phoneme is defined as any single, particular sound. It is a minimum feature of the expression system of any spoken language. In English there are about forty phonemes. The e sound in *let* is represented by the special phonetic letter ə.

A review of known facts about our language will help to account for the cleavages between sound and symbol in English spelling. English writers have characteristically preserved the historical spelling of the principal languages contributing most to the English language, ancient and modern. The principal contributors are the Celts, the Anglo-Saxons, the Romans, the Greeks, the Scandinavians (mostly Danes), and the Normans.

The Celtic influence upon Old English (Anglo-Saxon) was slight. It is found in place names such as Aberdeen, Thames, Bryn Mawr (*bryn* meaning "hill" and *mawr* meaning "great").

We know about the arrival of the Anglo-Saxons in England in the fifth century A.D. The Angles settled in Northumbria (the north), East Anglia (the east), and Mercia (central England), some Saxons in Wessex (kingdom of the West Saxons), some Saxons in Essex (kingdom of the East Saxons), and some in Sussex (kingdom of the South Saxons). We know more, though, about the pronunciation of Anglo-Saxon words. For example, the *k* in *knight, knit,* and *knot* and the *g* in *gnaw* and *gnarl* were pronounced centuries ago. Moreover the *gh* in *right, sight,* and *tight* were once pronounced. Through the centuries these sounds disappeared, but the letters have remained. On the other hand, sounds in many Anglo-Saxon words, such as *cow, sheep, calf,* and *swine,* have been retained even though the spelling has been changed.

When Saint Augustine and his fellow missionaries converted the Anglo-Saxons to Christianity in 597, the converts borrowed Latin words, some of which were of Greek origin. To what was then Anglo-Saxon, or Old English, were added many words (some are ecclesiastical terms) we use today, such as *alms, anthem, martyr, priest, temple, wine.* The Latin influence is found in place names, which include *castra* ("camp"), in its derivatives Chester, Winchester. Though the spelling of some loan words is changed slightly, some Latin and Greek loan words, among them *bona fide, alibi, comma, drama, verbatim,* and *atlas* retain their original spelling. Some Greek words have silent first letters, which were pronounced in Greek. Examples are *psalm, phthisical, psychiatry, pneumonia, mnemonic,* and *ptomaine.* Many words contain Greek prefixes (*hypo-* and *hyper-*) and Latin (*inter-, sub-, super-*) which lend themselves to forming hybrid words.

The third influence upon the English language is Scandinavian. During much of King Alfred's reign (ninth century) and until the eleventh century, men of the North, or Norsemen, "went a viking," which meant that they went sailing in curious dragon-prowed ships and that they embarked on expeditions of piracy and plunder. These bold men of the North slew unarmed monks, looted monasteries, plundered libraries. Many of the Vikings landed in the north and east of England, plundered, and then stayed. The linguistic result of the Viking ruthless raids was a considerable exchange between the languages of the rival peoples. Our pronouns *they, their, them* are of Danish origin. Our suffix *-by*, the Danish word for "farm" or "town," appears in places names such as Derby, Granby, and Rugby. English nouns of Scandinavian origin are *sky, skull, scrub, scare,* and *skirt;* verbs are *die, give, hit,* and *want;* and adjectives are *low, meek, ugly,* and *wrong.*

Only recently have the Scandinavian borrowings in English been fully appreciated. Stuart Robertson and Frederic Cassidy write, "Aside from Greek, Latin, and French, only Scandinavian, the language of the people whom the Anglo-Saxons called 'Danes,' has made a really substantial contribution to the English vocabulary." [3]

The fourth influence upon our spelling system is Norman. Some Norsemen, migrating from Scandinavia, settled in northern France in the tenth century and adopted the French language, known as Old French, which is the ancestor of the modern French language. In 1066 the Normans (no longer considered Vikings or Norsemen) crossed the English Channel and eventually became the cultural masters of England.

The result of the Norman Conquest was that the Old English vocabulary was enriched by the addition of many new words from French, especially during the fourteenth century, when the social barriers between the Normans and the English were breaking down and Englishmen were at last rising on the social scale. Curious though it may be, the French-speaking Frenchmen were laughing at the French-speaking Englishmen. In the Prologue to the *Canterbury Tales* Chaucer, sometimes called "the father of the English language," makes a gentle joke about the Prioress who spoke a French patois of "Stratford atte Bowe" for she knew not the French of Paris.

Whereas some Latin words came directly into English, some Latin words came into English through Old French, the language spoken by Normans. Let's take, for example, the word *penny,* a *cent.* The Romans of two thousand years ago used the word *centum* for "one hundred," and they pronounced the *c* as a *k—kentum.* Now this same word has survived in Italian as *cento* and is pronounced *chento.* The same is true for the pronunciation of other Italian words and names, in which *c* precedes *e* or *i*—for example, Da Vinci. In modern French, though, *cent* is pronounced *saunt,* while the spelling is *cent.* Because the word *cent* came into English from the medieval French, our word is *cent,* and it retains the Old French pronunciation of *sent.* [4] It has changed semantically in that it is now a hundredth part of something, namely the dollar. Numerous other Old French words, such as *piece, chime, example,* and *bonnet,* have retained their medieval spelling in Modern English and often their medieval pronunciation.

Between 1100 and 1500 words of all types, of all parts of speech, from every level of life, came into English, some from Norman, some from Parisian French. In many cases the English word was preserved along with the French, but often on a somewhat less dignified plane. Thus English has vocabulary doublets: English *cow* on the hoof, French *beef* on the table; English *sheep* but French *mutton;* English *hog* but French *pork;* English *work* but French *labor.*

Others who contributed to English are the American Indians, who added *hominy* and *wigwam;* the Mexicans, *tomato* and *coyote;* South Americans, *quinine;* Africans, *voodoo;* Hebrews, *kibbutz* and *shalom;* Arabs, *zero, alfalfa,* and *sugar;* Dutch, *cookie* and *spa;* Chinese, *tea* and *typhoon;* Scandinavians, *ski* and *slalom;* Japanese, *kimono;* Irish, *slew, blarney,* and *shillelagh.*

Often you will find in a sentence words derived from several languages. Take, for example, "The algebra class now assembles in front of the window of a private auditorium on the famed River Thames." The origin of *algebra* is Arabic; *window* is Old Norse and Latin; *private* is Latin; *auditorium* is Latin; *River* is Old French and Latin; and *Thames* is Celtic.

Knowing that the English language is a linguistic grab bag helps us understand why spelling and pronunciation are so far apart. One reason is that sometimes the spellings of loan words were modified to conform to English spellings. Many times they were not. Another reason has to do with the Great Vowel Shift. In the fifteenth century all the long vowels gradually began to be pronounced higher in the mouth. Those that could not be raised became diphthongs. For example, in Chaucer's time, long *a* was pronounced as in *father,* long *e* as in *May,* and the pronoun *I* as in *he.* By Shakespeare's time, *a* was pronounced as in *name,* and the pronoun *I* became a diphthong, as in *die.* In some areas the *e* had already shifted to the vowel sound in *sweet,* the sound it has today. The original *e* sound still survives in words like *break, great,* and *yea* and in certain Irish names like *Yeats* and *Reagan.*

The beginnings of standardized English spelling. Language experts and laymen have long been bothered by the irregularities and inconsistencies of English spelling. There are rumors of an early-thirteenth-century attempt to regularize English spelling, but the details are vague.

About all we know is that a monk named Orm attempted to clarify English spelling by doubling the consonant after short vowels, thus indicating pronunciation somewhat more accurately.[5] English spelling was phonetic as late as the time of Shakespeare, in intention at least. But although people still tried to write as they spoke, the inherited imperfections of their orthography made it more and more difficult for them to do so. Hence already in the sixteenth century a number of spelling reformers had made their appearance. Among them were Sir John Cheke, John Hart, and Richard Mulcaster, who vied in "improving" the quality of the written language. If we are tempted to underrate their efforts, let us be grateful that they left us generally with one irrational spelling for words that had previously had several.[6]

Mulcaster, in his *Elementarie* (1582), which "entreateth chefelie of the right writing of our English tung," attempted to codify current usage. Among the spelling changes he suggested is the addition of a silent final e to indicate a preceding long vowel (for example, *made*). Another reformer, Sir Thomas Smith, Secretary of State to Queen Elizabeth, published a *Dialogue Concerning the Correct and Emended Writing of the English Language*. Still another reformer was Dr. Alexander Gill, headmaster of St. Paul's School in London, who has left us extracts from Spenser's *Faerie Queene* in phonetic spelling. But his alphabet, as well as the other alphabets proposed at the time, was too intricate and cumbersome to win popular favor.

There were attempts to reform in the eighteenth century. Jonathan Swift and Dr. Samuel Johnson both put a premium on correct spelling. As reformers, Swift and Johnson seldom hesitated to assert their own authority, even if it ran contrary to the practices of the greatest writers. Although they themselves did not always follow a definite pattern for their own spelling, they set about to fix, regulate, and establish the English language for their contemporaries and for posterity. With the publication of Dr. Johnson's great dictionary in 1755, the English had a real guide to spelling.

When English spelling became regulated and "fixed for all eternity," words were spelled according to their origin and not according to their sound. The following summary of fixed features of English spelling may be helpful:

1. With the Norman influence the guttural sound represented by the h and g in original spelling softened and disappeared; however, it remains in many words spelled with a gh—*night, light, dough, plough, thought*—and sometimes turned into an *ff* sound—*rough, enough.*

2. The k has become silent, as in *knock, know, knave, knead.*

3. The g has become silent, as in *gnat, gnarled, gnostic.*

4. The *w* often merges with the vowel following it, as in *toward* (now pronounced in three ways: *to-ward*, *t'ward*, and *to'ord*) or has become silent, as in *sword, two, whole, who, wry, answer.*

5. The *b* has become silent, as in *lamb, comb, plumb, thumb.*

6. The *l* has become soft or disappeared, as in *salve, calm, half.*[7]

America was quick to show its reverence for "right writing," especially in the New England colonies. Many a villager won prestige and position in the local spelling bee by mastering words of six or more syllables. When it came to the longer and more difficult ones, the preacher and the pedagogue vied with one another on such sesquipedalian demons as *testator, euroclydon,* and *antitrinitarian.* Benjamin Franklin, always a reformer, wrote *A Scheme for a New Alphabet and Reformed Mode of Spelling.*[8] In a letter defending his proposals, he remarked:

Whatever the difficulties of reforming our spelling now are, they will be more easily surmounted now than hereafter; and some time or other it must be done; or else our writing will become the same with the Chinese as to the difficulty of learning and using it.

Instead of trying to make pronunciation follow spelling, he proposed a phonetic alphabet, in which spelling might be altered to suit the prevailing pronunciation. This radical reform, however, came to nothing, for Franklin, now past his prime, felt "too old to pursue the plan."

Another American who crusaded against the spelling system we inherited from Dr. Samuel Johnson and his colleagues was Noah Webster. Webster, a schoolteacher in his youth, attempted to make English spelling more consistent and more phonetic in his *Blue-Backed Speller* published in 1783–87. While Webster recognized the fact that "the body of the language is the same as in England," he recommended many spellings that met with peppery opposition. Some of his proposed spellings were later discarded. However, he did succeed in taking the *u* out of *color, favor, honor, flavor, labor, mold,* and so on, in dropping the *k* from *music, critic, relic, public, poetic,* in changing the French-derived *centre, litre, theatre,* to *center, liter, theater,* and in writing single *l* (or other consonant) in such words as *traveled* and *traveling.* He also replaced the earlier *axe, tsar, plough, waggon* with the spellings *ax, czar, plow,* and *wagon.*

Why English spelling is conservative. As we see, there has been at least slow progress since Dr. Johnson's day toward the reform of English spelling, and some attempt has been made to keep our orthography apace with our changing pronunciation. But strangely, through habit, custom, or the heavy hand of tradition, the English-speaking people have never seemed terribly concerned by the irrationalities, inconsistencies, and complications of their system. Because they have not cared to revise their old-fashioned usages, English spelling has always changed more slowly than pronunciation. One wonders why this is true and what can be the counterforces which have worked against spelling reform through the centuries.

One of the first conservative forces, oddly, was the printer. This revolutionary, who first appeared on the English scene in the late fifteenth century, might have been an important agent in the creation of a standard and rational system of spelling, since it was in his interest that reading be encouraged and that language be uniform throughout England. However, he had certain problems of his own, which resulted in exactly the opposite effect. He certainly achieved one reform, which was a general standardization. Before the advent of printing, you might spell *button* any way you fancied, writing it *button, butowne,* or *botheum,* as you preferred, or inventing your own spelling if you liked it better. For dinner you might eat *mutton, moltoun, motone, mottone, motton, motoun, motene, mouton, motown, muttoun,* or *mutten.* At least the printer eventually established that it was *button* and *mutton.*

But though the standardization made correct spelling easier for a time, it also had the effect of freezing spelling so that it no longer kept up with the continuing changes in pronunciation. The centuries that followed the advent of printing (about 1440) witnessed many changes in the pronunciation of English, and when the reform movement finally came in the eighteenth century, it came a bit too late. Dr. Johnson, whose dictionary became the standard for the English language, found it less awkward to list a printer's standard—but old-fashioned—spellings in the dictionary than to initiate new forms of the words. In short, though printing made widespread reading and standardized spelling possible, it also tended to freeze these spellings in outmoded forms.

Printers committed worse sins too. They weren't so scholarly as the scribes they replaced, and they had less respect for refinements of spelling and style. They often varied their spellings in order to fit words onto a line, and readers would find words spelled several ways on a single page. One of the more interesting irrationalities we inherit comes down to us from William Caxton, the most important early printer of English. Caxton, in his search for good craftsmen, hired German printers, who had practiced the art for some time. They didn't know English well, and, following analogies from their own language, they supplied such spellings as *ghost, gherkin, ghospel, ghossip, ghess,* and *ghest*. As time went on, some of these *gh* words kept the unnecessary *h*, as *ghost* did; some, such as *gospel*, dropped the *h*; others were changed, by analogy with French, from *gh* to *gu*—for example, *guest*.[9]

But if printing tended to freeze English spelling in old-fashioned forms, there were other forces also at work to make it irrational. During the sixteenth and seventeenth centuries, the influence of the classical languages encouraged scholars and writers to change the spelling of words to conform with what they thought were their correct etymological sources in Latin, Greek, and Old French. Words which had come from Latin through Old French or Vulgar Latin had often changed considerably in transit, and the scholars restored certain silent or "parasite" consonants to indicate their origins. Thus the *b* in *debt* indicates its Latin ancestor, *debitum;* the *b* in *doubt* shows its parent, *dubitum;* and the *p* in *receipt* reveals its source in the Latin *recipere*. Other words were respelled simply because changes were fashionable. The letter *s* was inserted in *island,* even though the Middle English *iland* was not derived from the Latin *insula* or the French *isle,* but from an Old English word, *igland*. Words such as *sovereign* were changed erroneously. *Sovran* (as spelled by Milton) comes from the Latin *superanus,* from *super* (above), but it was associated mistakenly with the Latin *regnare* (to rule). Hence the *g* in *sovereign* is the result of mistaken analogy, as is the *g* in *foreign*.[10]

But even if the ideas of printers and linguistic scholars were counterforces to the reform of English spelling, there must also have been larger forces at work to preserve the vast collection of outmoded and illogical forms that constitute spelling. If the English-speaking peoples had really wanted spelling reform, it's hard to believe that somehow or other it couldn't have been achieved. But innate conservatism, a fondness for idiosyncrasy, and a kind of tribal insularity have created in the English-speaking peoples an affection for their ancient forms of spelling and a strong reluctance to reform spelling any faster than seems perfectly natural. Linguistic authority Mario Pei reports: "English-speaking people, particularly Americans, take a perverted pride in the intricate and mysterious anomalies of the spelling of their language; it makes them feel superior to foreigners." [11] This tribal insularity is no doubt one factor. Another clearly is the prestige which attaches to the mastery of the difficulties of spelling. According to Thorstein Veblen, an American economist, "Spelling ability is the first and readiest test of reputability in learning, and conformity to its ritual is indispensable to a blameless scholastic life."[12] To a surprising degree spelling proficiency has become a status symbol. A mis-spelled word in a letter of application can militate against a teacher applying for a job. This high status of spelling is mainly due to the many phonetic irregularities in our language. On the other hand, little or no status is attached to spelling achievement in phonetically regular languages such as Spanish and Italian, where a person can spell almost any word he can pronounce.

A public reaction typical of the attitude of the English-speaking peoples toward spelling reform took place in 1906. President Theodore Roosevelt, with characteristic impetuosity, officially aligned with the reformers by ordering public printers to use new spellings of certain words in government documents. Congress, by a vote of 142 to 25, threatened to withhold the appropriation for the printing of execu-tive-department publications if the order was not countermanded. The uproar in the press ranged from furious denunciation to satire, subtle and not so subtle. *The New York Times* wrote about the "arro-gant and outrageous attempt to disturb the natural evolution of the English language." One newspaperman wrote: "Nothing escapes Mr. Rucevelt. No subjekt is to hi fr him to takl." The upshot of the affair was that Roosevelt was forced to limit his reform to White House correspondence. Yet, paradoxically, a study by W. L. Werner shows that out of the three hundred reformed spellings that Roosevelt tried to introduce in 1906, more than half are now preferred and only forty-four are not listed in *Webster's Collegiate Dictionary*.[13] The spell-ing reform movement does move—if slowly.

Modern spelling reform. There have been continuous efforts in the past century to promote reform. In 1875 the American Philological Association appointed a committee to consider spelling reform. From this grew the Spelling Reform Board, which was founded in 1906 by Andrew Carnegie. The Simplified Spelling Board took the position that our difficult and cumbersome spelling places a very real burden upon every user of English and "wastes every year millions of dollars, and effort worth millions more." The scholars and publishers who made up the board claimed that "the anomalies and perversities" of English spelling are obvious enough, and call for reasonable regulation. Like converts to a new religion, they set out to regulate spelling. And they fought a valiant but nevertheless losing fight to reform our mud-dled English spelling. Andrew Carnegie died in 1919, and did not provide financially for spelling reform. Since then the activities of the Simplified Spelling Board have dwindled to almost nothing, though it still maintains a nominal existence.[14]

In 1930 the Simplified Spelling Society of Great Britain and the Simpler Spelling Association of America approved a system of simplified spelling, which, it is claimed, will save at least one year out of the first four years of school, with superior results. In their system the first few sentences from the story of the little red hen would look like this: [15]

dhe litl red hen

wuns upon a tiem litl red hen livd
in a barn widh hur fiev chiks. a pig,
a kat and a duk maed dhaer hoem
in dhe saem barn. eech dae litl red
hen led hur chiks out too look for
fuud. but dhe pig, dhe kat and dhe
duk wood not look for fuud.

The Foundation for a Compatible and Consistent Alphabet has proposed a new "single-sound" alphabet which looks like this: [16]

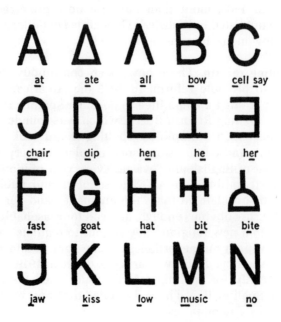

A	Δ	Λ	B	C
at	ate	all	bow	cell say
Ɔ	D	E	Ɪ	Ǝ
chair	dip	hen	he	her
F	G	H	Ⱨ	⌂
fast	goat	hat	bit	bite
ᒎ	K	L	M	N
jaw	kiss	low	music	no

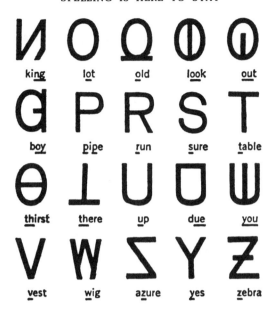

When this alphabet is applied according to a few simple rules, the story of the little red hen then goes like this:

⊥U L⊣TL RED HEN

ⱲUNC UPⱯN U TⴚM L⊣TL RED HEN L⊣VD

⊣N U BORN Ⱳ⊣θ HƎR FⴚV ᴐ⊣KC. U P⊣G

U KAT AND U DUK MⴚD ⊥ER HᴖM

⊣N ⊥U CⴚM BORN. IᴐᴐDA L⊣TL RED

HEN LED HƎR ᴐ⊣KC ᴖT TO LᴖK FⴧR

FᴐᴐD. BUT ⊥U P⊣G, ⊥U KAT, AND ⊥U

DUK WᴖD NOT LᴖK FⴧR FᴐᴐD.

The foundation claims that the Single Sound Alphabet is preferable to the Roman alphabet because it is the only alphabet designed for both machine and human reading, that it alone is designed for simple manual lettering by very young children, and that it is very nearly consistent with the Latin conventions of most European spelling. Time alone will tell whether the Single Sound Alphabet will perish or prevail.

Other reform measures fervently and repeatedly advocated by such distinguished men of letters as George Bernard Shaw have made little headway with the general public. Shaw, who was thoroughly dissatisfied with our alphabet and our spelling system, complained, "We are all over the shop with our vowels because we cannot spell them with our alphabet." In fact he was so exasperated that he left a large legacy to anyone who would improve our antiquated, chaotic array of letters. He unraveled his plan. "Design 24 new consonants and 18 new vowels, making in all a new alphabet of 42 letters, and use it side by side with the present lettering until the better ousts the worse." His far-famed legacy is still getting attention, also dust. And we are still beholden to the twenty-six letters of our alphabet.

Such slight changes as *thru* for *through,* and *tho* for *though* have had a cold reception. The American spellings *labor, color,* and *honor* are not accepted in England, despite the recommendation of H. W. Fowler in his *Dictionary of Modern English Usage.*

For nearly four hundred years, language experts and laymen have struggled with the apparent irregularities of English spelling. Chaucer, in his poem *Troilus and Criseyde,* lamented, "And for ther is so gret diversite in Englissh and in writyng of oure tonge." At the turn of the twentieth century, Thomas R. Lounsbury, an authority on spelling reform, wrote, "English spelling is consistent in inconsistency."[17] Clearly, this consistency in inconsistency has persisted and promises to persist.

But the case for simplified spelling isn't over yet—not by a long shot. Upton Sinclair once wrote a letter to President Kennedy proposing that public documents be printed in a form of simplified spelling and that a spelling commission be subsidized. To support his case he engaged in a little play on five words which are spelled with the same endings, and with which one can have some fun: "A rough cough and a hiccough plough me through." Is it "A ruff cuff and a hiccuff pluff me thruff?" Or is it "a roo coo and a hiccoo ploo me throo?"[18]

But the evidence of the past only leaves us with nagging doubts that Mr. Sinclair's proposal will have any greater success than those we have passed in review. What if Mr. Sinclair did think that it would not be long before the public gets over the shock? There is still the general public that resists legislation—and especially legislation about language. Why? If there's any answer at all, perhaps it can be found in the feelings expressed in this poem by T. S. Watt, which appeared in *The Manchester Guardian:* [19]

I take it you already know
Of TOUGH and BOUGH and COUGH and DOUGH.
Others may stumble, but not you,
On HICCOUGH, THOROUGH, LOUGH, and THROUGH.
Well done! And now you wish, perhaps,
To learn of less familiar traps.

Beware of HEARD, a dreadful word
That looks like BEARD and sounds like BIRD.
And DEAD—it's said like bed, not BEAD.
For goodness' sake, don't call it DEED!
Watch out for MEAT and GREAT and THREAT:
They rhyme with SUITE and STRAIGHT and DEBT.

A MOTH is not a MOTH in MOTHER,
Nor BOTH in BOTHER, BROTH in BROTHER,
And HERE is not a match for THERE,
Nor DEAR and FEAR for PEAR and BEAR.
And then there's DOSE and ROSE and LOSE—
Just look them up—and GOOSE and CHOOSE,
And CORK and WORK and CARD and WARD,
And FONT and FRONT and WORD and SWORD,
And DO and GO, then THWART and CART.
Come, come, I've hardly made a start.

A dreadful language? Man alive,
I'd mastered it when I was five!

Finally, and for the sake of completeness, we may mention voices defending present-day English spelling against the accusations usually brought against it. The voices are those of distinguished language authorities, Noam Chomsky and Morris Halle, who maintain that the English orthography, in fact, "turns out to be an optimal system for spelling English, because it [English spelling] turns out to be rather close to the true phonological representations." By this latter term Chomsky and Halle mean the so-called underlying phonological forms, from which the actual phonic form of the word may be produced

in accordance with rules. For example, our word *taim,* generated from
tim and spelled *time,* follows the "diphthongization rule," which was
characteristic of the well-known historical process of the Great Vowel
Shift of Late Middle English and Early Modern English.[20]

Let's take another example of the phonological basis of standard
orthography, as clarified by Noam Chomsky and Morris Halle in *The
Sound Pattern of English.* One is the use of *s* and *ss* in English spelling.
In such cases, *s* in *resemble* and *resent* is pronounced as *z* and *ss*
in *dissemble, dissent* as *s.* In case of a reform, one thing that would
be lost would be the representation of *-semble* central not only to
dissemble and *resemble* but also to *semblance* and *assemble.*

A third authority, Fred Brengelman, holds a view similar to the
Chomsky–Halle theory. He maintains that a command of English spelling is contingent upon mastery of general spelling principles rather
than upon mere ability to spell (correctly, of course) the relatively
few words a student encounters in his career. Effective spelling instruction, according to Brengelman, is based on the fact that speakers
of English have knowledge of underlying phonological forms and that
our spelling system is related to this knowledge rather than to the
actual pronunciation of words.[21]

Before going on to the next chapter, take a moment to apply what
your knowledge of the history of English has taught you about silent
letters. In each word below supply the missing silent letters. Note the
language from which the word has come into English. Then write
the whole word correctly.

	GREEK	ANGLO-SAXON	OLD FRENCH	LATIN
1.	-nome	lis-en	de-t	-sychology
2.	r-ythm	-nee	recei-t	nas-ent
3.	diaphra-m	glis-en	dou-t	fas-inate
4.	-salm	throu--	rei-n	-onest
5.	-seudonym	thou--t	forei-n	-erb
6.	-neumonia	ni--t	soverei-n	-our
7.	-neumatic	-now	impu-n	-onor

8. r-inoceros	hei--t	dei-n	r-ombus
9. -tarmigan	-nat	arrai-n	s-ientific
10. -nemonic	nei--bor	mor-gage	sc-olar
11. -nostic	i-land	vi-tuals	coales-e
12. dra--m	-nock	solem-	as-end
13. hemorr-oid	-rite	r-ubarb	plum-er
14. hemorr-age	-ni--t	pi-cher	lim-
15. paradi-m	sho-er	colum-	collog--
16. -tosis	cou-d	s-issors	-sittacosis
17. -neumatology	chris-en	fei-n	-umble
18. r-izotomy	hi--	escro-	r-etoric
19. r-yton	g-astly	ro-n	C-esar
20. -tomaine	wa-k	emba-m	r-initis

Mention of effective spelling instruction leads us to ask, "What do psychologists know about the teaching of spelling?" They bring to light some rather important information about the spelling process, as we shall discover in the next chapter.

PART TWO
How Does One Learn to Spell?

CHAPTER III

What Psychologists Know About Spelling

Men get opinions as boys learn to spell, by reiteration chiefly.
ELIZABETH BARRETT BROWNING

When Elizabeth Barrett Browning wrote these words, the teaching of spelling was theorized on the assumptions that there is little or no relationship between the pronunciation of words and spelling and that spelling each word calls for a separate act of learning. Thus spelling competence was contingent upon the ability to recall and to reproduce the letters in their accepted order. Learning to spell was indeed "by reiteration chiefly." Most spelling authorities agreed that the spelling of the English language was irregular and inconsistent, that it was an exercise in futility to develop the power of translating the phonemes in the hearing-pronouncing-spelling vocabulary of prospective spellers into appropriate symbols.

This chapter on spelling and the mind offers you a behind-the-scenes look at the psychological approach to spelling. Many books, monographs, and articles have been written on this thorny and controversial question. One recent writer, impatient with new methods of teaching, has presented the case for a return to the good old days when spelling was taught with reading, and when a person learned to spell by pronouncing each and every letter. This early method is all very good as far as it goes, but it is a little more old-fashioned than the horse and buggy. Much has been learned in recent years about the psychological factors in spelling—why some people have difficulty learning to spell, what are the most difficult types of error, how they can be overcome effectively. Simple common sense tells us it is wise to incorporate this new knowledge into our modern attack on spelling. Let's begin at the beginning then, and see how the child first learns about words.

The child learns. An infant's earliest efforts to talk are in fact his struggle to master the two mental processes of *recognition* and *reproduction*. His first speech is meaningless babble. He makes sounds and noises, and eventually develops the muscles that will allow him to speak. Soon he begins to understand what people say to him, but his first understandings are on a purely emotional basis; that is, he senses the tone of the voice, the manner of speaking. Then the youngster begins to imitate and to utter meaningful sounds. Little by little these sounds assume the proportions of what we call language. The child *recognizes* spoken words; he *reproduces* them. And by the time the child is old enough to attend school, he may be able to understand and speak more than ten thousand words.

In a later stage, the young one recognizes pictures, letters, and numbers, but they don't necessarily have meaning for him. At the same time he produces very crude scrawls and symbols of his own. These efforts at production, combined with his visual recognition, are soon transformed into an understanding of written words. In short, the symbols begin to take on meaning, and we say that the youngster is learning to read or to interpret written symbols. In short, the child is learning to perceive.

Perception. According to one authority, perception means a particular "form of looking." According to one dictionary, perception refers to insight, intuition, or knowledge that an individual gains by perceiving and interpreting through his senses. The perceiver may see glossy black letters or lines of various shapes on a white background. The perceiver's eyes are focused on and are impressed by a word or words. The manner in which he perceives the word form or total configuration is important in identifying the word. The child's *visual* perception of the word will be as it appears in his own handwriting.

Perception may be auditory. In this case, the child first senses that language is a tool for the conveyance of meaning. Second, he discovers that language consists of sounds that are meaningful symbols. One experimenter [1] has come up with a step-by-step analysis of auditory perception:

1. the recognition of series of sounds as meaningful information;
2. the retention of these units of related and significant information;
3. the integration of the meaningful and related symbols as language representations;
4. the comprehension of language symbols upon the completion of the three previous steps of auditory perception.

Simultaneously, the child is becoming print conscious, and he is learning to write. Although some authorities would debate the issue, it seems likely that the writing precedes the reading. In other words, the young learner writes the symbols and then begins to comprehend what they mean. After learning to read sentences and to copy them intelligently, the youngster is called upon to reproduce them from memory. He is being introduced, at the behest of proud parents and friends, of course, to the necessity for spelling. And that is where we come in.

Spelling method is physical and psychological. Our knowledge of word forms, like all other knowledge, comes to us through the senses. We learn to spell by following certain specified steps. First, we see the letters in their order or we hear the sounds. Seeing and hearing obviously are forms of "impression." Next, we write and speak the letters in the order in which they are seen and heard. Writing and speaking then are forms of expression. We repeat the word and comprehend it as a single, specific image. Hence, impression and expression form the bases for four kinds of images: (a) the sight of a word, (b) the sound of a word, (c) the way it "feels" when written, and/or (d) the way it "feels" when spoken.[2]

Imagery. Spelling is primarily a sensory-motor habit. Spellings are usually learned by repeated motor reactions to certain sensory stimuli. Most successful spellers depend upon one of their senses to tell whether the word is right or not. Most of them will tell you the word looks right. Their memory is predominantly visual. Some people receive no visual images at all or very dim ones. Some of the latter individuals remember impressions in terms of sound. They get what we call auditory images. Still others remember impressions as physical or muscular movements. In case of a word or phrase, individuals in this last group would recall the symbol or symbols in terms of lip and throat movements or the movement of the hand in writing the word.[3]

Another important research finding is that the dominant imagery may differ for an individual at different ages. For example, some experimenters have found that young children learn through auditory avenues. The older children rely upon their other powers, although this does not always hold true. It is important to understand what kind of imagery—visual, auditory, or kinesthetic—you rely on most heavily in spelling. Then concentrate on the kind of spelling tricks that capitalize on your special ability.

Intelligence and emotion. Must you have a high IQ to become a perfect speller? Certainly not. Intelligence can be important, of course, but intelligence does not explain all cases of good or of poor spelling. Generally speaking, people who score extremely low on intelligence tests have difficulty with all school studies, while those scoring high on such tests have less difficulty. This holds for spelling, reading, and other school subjects.[4] However, intelligence does not seem to be so important in spelling as in most other subjects. Tests indicate that a wide vocabulary seems more important for spelling ability than intelligence itself. Intelligence seems to affect the kind of spelling mistakes made as much as the number of them. Bright students tend to make errors with single letters, while duller students do violence to groups of letters or whole words. And physical defects, such as poor sight and poor hearing, can be much more serious obstacles than low intelligence is.

Much more important than intelligence itself is the emotional attitude of the student. Many poor spellers have never mastered the language because they got off on the wrong foot right from the start. Never having acquired satisfactory ways of learning to spell, they have encountered so many difficulties, made so many mistakes, and met with so many discouragements in spelling that unhappy emotions are always aroused in them by the spelling process. Often the poor speller is mesmerized into believing that he will never be able to spell. This belief may be reinforced by the comments of his parents, teachers, and classmates.

Deep-seated emotional attitudes, although difficult to uncondition, can be set right. What you must do is start out again and create a new cycle of success and satisfaction. After a time, a new set of attitudes will replace the old negative and anxious ones.[5] By working diligently on words that he *can* master, a person can rapidly build up his confidence. As you become convinced that you can spell a few words without mistakes, you acquire the power of positive thinking about spelling in general, and eventually you will be spelling more and more words, even the so-called hard ones.

The most important single factor in spelling success concerns one's personal feelings. Many persons have become permanently crippled spellers through indifference, carelessness, or a distaste for intellectual drudgery.[6] Consulting the psychologists, we find that impetuous children, those who are untidy or careless of detail, have trouble with spelling, whereas neat, particular youngsters do better. Nervous and hypersensitive people, who have never been accustomed to meeting rigorous requirements of any sort, also frequently rebel against working toward perfection. Spelling may be comparatively difficult for fast learners who can express their thoughts well orally, but who find written work extremely tedious, odious, or burdensome.

Now you will say, "It's nice to know that about the children. What about adults?" Several authorities have studied the spelling ability among educated adults. British educator Fred J. Schonell [7] finds that neither general intelligence nor age is significant in achieving spelling success. Failure in spelling in childhood, he considers, plays an important part in the attitudes of adults toward spelling standards. General disregard for details, a feeling of inferiority over spelling weakness, loss of confidence, apathy toward one's failure, and rationalization of spelling weakness originate in early failures. Schonell advises the correction of unhappy attitudes toward spelling early in a child's life, so that correction can be made before failure and an inferiority complex become part of the personality.

Spelling reversals. Have you ever surprised yourself by reversing letters, parts of words, or even whole words? For example, have you ever written *gril* for *girl?* This inversion tendency has a scientific name, *strephosymbolia,* deriving from two Greek words—*strephos,* "twisted," and *symbolaia,* "tokens." This inversion tendency is not limited to seeing words in reversed order, or writing letters backward or upside down. It may be observed occasionally in the very young child who has difficulty in putting his garments on the right way; who fails to remember right and left distinctions; and who loses his bearings within his own home when looking for something he knows is in a certain place. In many clinical cases the condition seems to constitute the only factor involved in being unable to read, to speak, and to write.

Practically everyone has a slight tendency to reversals, which can become a serious obstacle for some persons. Not too much is known about serious miscoordination of this kind. At one time it was believed that a strong tendency to make reversals was a symptom of partial imbecility. This theory has been abandoned, however, because many children who make reversals are intelligent in every other respect. In fact, Leonardo da Vinci, a scientific, mathematical, and artistic genius, wrote reverse script all his life. Indeed, contemporaries charged that he did so in order to conceal the heresies they pretended he composed in his unreadable handwriting! Later researchers have theorized that word reversals are caused by damage to a small part of the brain resulting from an injury, a tumor, or a hemorrhage. The most commonly accepted opinion today is the theory of cerebral dominance, which involves the interaction between the right and left hemispheres of the brain. According to Samuel T. Orton, the neurologist who proposed this theory in 1925, the condition usually corrects itself as the child grows older.[8]

The question may arise as to what should be done when the tendency exists among very-early-grade schoolchildren, or what can be done when the tendency persists. Educational experts advise that the condition will usually cure itself in time. If it persists and becomes a serious problem, remedial exercises can be investigated.

Reversal of letters can result in some very interesting sentences: "He tries to remain clam." "She takes the silver out of his finger." There are are several types of reversals: [9]

1. "static reversal," which indicates the reversal of letters showing right-left symmetry *b* and *d, p* and *g;*
2. "kinetic reversal," which is characterized by a reversal of the sequence of letters in words, for example, *was* and *saw;*
3. "transposition reversal," which involves the changing of letters of syllables (*donimant, ehre, thoery*) to a different position in the word or changing words to a different position within the sentence (*that not does make sense* for *that does not make sense*).

Kinetic reversals, static reversals, and transposition reversals occasionally are associated with facility in mirror reading. No doubt you will recall the case of mirror writing as described by Alice in *Through the Looking Glass.* She was puzzled by Jabberwocky in reverse, until she discovered its secret: "Why, it's a Looking-glass book, of course! And, if I hold it up to a glass the words will all go the right way again."

Another term used for strephosymbolia is dyslexia. Like strephosymbolia, dyslexia has Greek roots, *dys,* meaning "difficulty," and *lexis,* "word" or "phrase." We would be remiss if we didn't mention an important article entitled "The Enduring Mystery of Dyslexia" (*Reader's Digest,* February, 1976). The author, Warren R. Young, formerly science and medicine editor of *Life,* reveals that one child in every seven has strephosymbolia or dyslexia to some degree. What's more, boys so afflicted outnumber girls three to one. Research studies show that the affliction may be a potent factor in juvenile delinquency.

Many people of great achievement and in high position reverse letters, numbers, and words. Leonardo da Vinci has been mentioned. Among the possible dyslexics are Thomas Edison, General George S. Patton, President Woodrow Wilson, Hans Christian Andersen, Albert Einstein, and Nelson A. Rockefeller.

Author Warren R. Young offers some helpful advice for people who see symbols in reverse order. The advice concerns mastering a process we shall discuss in some detail in chapters that follow—the skill of encoding, and the reverse, the skill of decoding. The step-by-step process is this:

1. look at a letter;
2. say the letter aloud;
3. trace the shape of the letter in the air and on the blackboard;
4. feel a 3-D cutout of the letter.

Finally, encouraging prognosis is offered in a documented study by Margaret Byrd Rawson, who conducted research on twenty boys who were afflicted with moderate to severe reversal problems and who were trained by this multisensory method. Statistics were gathered on what the boys did when they grew up. All the boys except one went to college and eventually entered the professions of medicine, law, education, business, and the theater.

Everyone has a slight tendency to make letter reversals. What is particularly inconvenient is the fact that they are not always detected easily by the proofreader. For practice in developing your awareness of reversals, we have listed below some words in which letters are reversed or can be reversed to form new words. If the letters can be used to form another word, write the companion reversal below each word. If the reversal does not make a word, simply correct the reversal by writing the word as it should be written. Check your answers on page 221 in the Appendix.

For example:

1. liar   3. diary   5. quiet

   lair   _____   _____

2. angel   4. felt   6. sacred

_____   _____   _____

7. tried   14. was   21. rate

_____   _____   _____

8. trial   15. tiers   22. great

_____   _____   _____

9. compelte   16. nail   23. compiled

_____   _____   _____

10. flies   17. gas   24. girt

_____   _____   _____

11. appiled   18. apt   25. race

_____   _____   _____

12. note   19. break

_____   _____

13. vile   20. alter

_____   _____

OTHER EXERCISES: REITERATION

Now let's put into practice more of what you've learned about the psychology of spelling. Some people, when they do not have access to a dictionary, write a word several ways. Then, after studying the several spellings, they select the one their mind's eye tells them is correct. This is a very natural and common practice. Very likely the person has seen the word written correctly a number of times. All he needs is a reminder to help him recognize the correct spelling. When you feel quite certain that a word is correct, you may say that you have "recognized" it in your mind. Of course you can't be totally sure, but developing a keen eye for recognition is a big step toward better spelling.

Exercise 1. Glance at the following spellings. Then select the correct spelling from each group and place the letter before it in the space at the left. Check your answers on page 221 in the Appendix.

_____ 1. (a) acomodate, (b) accomodate, (c) acommodate, (d) accommodate

_____ 2. (a) across, (b) accross, (c) acroos, (d) accros

_____ 3. (a) comite, (b) commitee, (c) comittee, (d) committee

_____ 4. (a) benefeted, (b) benifited, (c) benafitted, (d) benefited

_____ 5. (a) recomendation, (b) reccommendation, (c) recommendation, (d) recamendation

_____ 6. (a) embarasment, (b) embarrasment, (c) embarassment, (d) embarrassment

_____ 7. (a) necessery, (b) necessary, (c) necesery, (d) necesaery

_____ 8. (a) ocasionaly, (b) occasionaly, (c) ocassionaly (d) occasionally

_____ 9. (a) predujice, (b) predjudice, (c) prejudice, (d) prejidice

_____10. (a) fascinate, (b) facinate, (c) fasenate, (d) fasinate

Exercise 2. After you have checked your answers for Exercise 1, see whether you can do better here. Check your answers with page 221 in the Appendix.

_____ 1. (a) alcohol, (b) achohol, (c) akohol, (d) alchohol

_____ 2. (a) desease, (b) diese, (c) deasees, (d) disease

_____ 3. (a) familiar, (b) fumilier, (c) familier, (d) familar

_____ 4. (a) cilender, (b) cylindar, (c) cilinder, (d) cylinder

_____ 5. (a) finaly, (b) finally, (c) finly, (d) finnaly

_____ 6. (a) excess, (b) exces, (c) eccess, (d) exess

_____ 7. (a) labratory, (b) labretory, (c) labritory, (d) laboratory

_____ 8. (a) speciman, (b) spesman, (c) specimen, (d) speceman

_____ 9. (a) whether, (b) wheather, (c) wether, (d) wehther

_____10. (a) sinsitive, (b) senstive, (c) sensitive, (d) sensative

Exercise 3. Follow the same instructions as for Exercise 1.

_____ 1. (a) Britan, (b) Britain, (c) Britian, (d) Brittan

_____ 2. (a) allotted, (b) alotted, (c) alloted, (d) aloted

_____ 3. (a) bacalaureate, (b) baccalaureate, (c) baccalarate, (d) bacallarate

_____ 4. (a) appropriate, (b) apropriate, (c) appropiate (d) aproprate

_____ 5. (a) anihilate, (b) annihelate, (c) annihilate, (d) anihelate

_____ 6. (a) conoisseur, (b) connoiseur, (c) connoisure, (d) connoisseur

_____ 7. (a) pyorrhia, (b) pyrhoea, (c) pyrrhorea, (d) pyorrhea

_____ 8. (a) parlimentary, (b) parliamentery, (c) parliamentary, (d) parlimentery

_____ 9. (a) hinderance, (b) hindrence, (c) hindrance, (d) hindernce

_____10. (a) dissapointment, (b) disapointment, (c) dissappointment, (d) disappointment

Spelling by reproduction. The exercises on reversal errors and on spelling by recognition have sharpened your understanding of the psychology of spelling. Now let's expand this knowledge in a study of a psychologically sound method of learning. We'll call it the seven-step method. There are many methods for learning how to spell; we'll study a number of them before we're through, in order to make a complete attack on the spelling problem. The seven-step method is a psychological and scientific one that follows a logical sequence. If you will take care to follow each step, you will find greater security and satisfaction because the results are likely to be permanent. This system is a streamlined approach to spelling success.

Seven-step method. Following are the steps that you should follow in learning the words that you have not recognized correctly in the exercise on recognition.

Step 1. Listen carefully to the word being pronounced. Many people whose hearing shows no organic defect rate low in good listening comprehension tests. Some whose hearing shows organic defects are good listeners. The difference is concentration.

Step 2. Check to see whether you have a correct aural image of the word. That is, check to see that each syllable tallies with what you really hear.

One may wrongly hear	when one ought to hear
famly	family
finely	finally
wither	whither
eathworm	earthworm
dimond	diamond
scurity	security
wear	where
guvment	government

labratory	laboratory
athaletics	athletics
umberella	umbrella
liquod	liquid
modren	modern
vigah	vigor
quite	quiet
pitcher	picture

Step 3. Look at the word and try to take a mental picture of it. Note the letters and then pronounce each syllable.

Step 4. Close your eyes and recall the picture of the word. If you cannot recall the letters or the sequence of the letters, take a second or even a third look at the word.

Step 5. Pronounce the word and write it as you do so.

Step 6. Look at the word again to reinforce your memory of the image. Write the word in a phrase or sentence.

Step 7. The following day pronounce the word. Write it as someone pronounces it to you. Then check your spelling.

REPRODUCTION PRACTICE

Exercise 1. Try the seven steps on each of the following words.

1. accommodate
2. larynx
3. across
4. temporary
5. committee
6. benefited
7. recommendation
8. embarrassment
9. necessary
10. occasionally
11. prejudice
12. fascinate
13. alcohol
14. disease
15. familiar
16. cylinder
17. finally
18. access
19. laboratory
20. whether
21. sensitive
22. specimen

RECOGNITION AND REPRODUCTION PRACTICE

Glance at the following words. Then select in each group the word that is spelled correctly and place the letter in the space provided. Check your answer on page 221 in the Appendix. Next reproduce the word by writing the correct form in Column D.

Column A	Column B	Column C	Column D
___ 1. (a) penicillin	(b) penicilin	(c) pennicillin	_____
___ 2. (a) irrelevant	(b) irrevelant	(c) irrelevent	_____
___ 3. (a) intolerence	(b) intollerance	(c) intolerance	_____
___ 4. (a) cancelation	(b) cancellation	(c) cancillation	_____
___ 5. (a) appologies	(b) apologies	(c) apolagies	_____
___ 6. (a) ambasador	(b) ambassader	(c) ambassador	_____
___ 7. (a) aquitted	(b) acquitted	(c) acquited	_____
___ 8. (a) accademy	(b) acadamy	(c) academy	_____
___ 9. (a) rheumatism	(b) rhuematism	(c) rheumetism	_____
___10. (a) asphyxiate	(b) asphyxate	(c) asphixate	_____

If you have finished the last exercises carefully, you have mastered one of the most successful methods for learning to spell. You are well on the road to good spelling. Let's take a breather in the next chapter and concentrate on another important aspect of the spelling problem— the spelling teacher.

CHAPTER IV

Do Teachers Really Teach?

To complain of the age we live in,
to murmur at the present possessors of power,
to lament the past,
to conceive extravagant hopes of the future,
are the common dispositions
of the greatest part of mankind.

EDMUND BURKE

Several writers remind us of a widespread feeling that teachers don't teach the way they used to. Teachers are told that they have forgotten the fundamentals and now "spend too much time on frills." The reasoning behind this fear is easily unriddled. A general revolution has swept through the educational world in the last few decades, mainly prompted by the followers of John Dewey. In some ways the revolution has been an extraordinary success; in others, the issue is in doubt. Before John Dewey things were different. First of all you walked to school, or if you were lucky enough to live in the country, you rode a horse. You learned to rise when answering a question. You spoke only when you were spoken to. But, most important, you studied the three R's.

In educational circles, the abbreviation A.D. can mean After Dewey —John Dewey, that is. After Dewey's day the pendulum swung away from the two D's of discipline and decorum in education to a third D—democracy—meaning, of course, greater freedom of movement, expression, and action. At the same time, however, the school population was exploding. Classroom rosters were rising faster than the bricks and mortar, and our school buildings were becoming obsolete, run-down, and overcrowded.

Between the confusion of working out the new educational methods and the urgent problems created by the overcrowding of the schools, we tended to ignore many of our teaching problems until Russian science gave us a serious scare in October 1957. "Before Sputnik," says educator B. Frank Brown, "we thought that the Russians were just peasants in baggy trousers who couldn't make a decent refrigerator. Then we woke up one morning and found that, baggy pants or not, it was the Russians who put up the first satellite. Naturally, everyone wondered what we did wrong and they began asking whether the schools were to blame." [1]

Have students had spelling? This self-searching applies to instruction in spelling even as it applies to the other problems of the curriculum. Educators all along the line, from the elementary school level through college, bemoan the poor spelling of their students. They are troubled by the fact that better reading methods have not also produced better spelling. And the evidence shows that, from the elementary school through the college level, there is a general regression in the spelling habits of our population.

Let's look then at the evidence on spelling defection and delinquency. William H. Fox and Merrill T. Eaton [2] made a spelling survey of over eighty thousand pupils in grades 2 to 8 inclusive in the city schools of Indiana; they found that 27 percent of the pupils were spelling normally, 25 percent were accelerated, and 48 percent retarded, the average retardation being one and a half grades below the expected norm. In a similar study of the spelling success of over one hundred thousand pupils in the same grades in township schools of Indiana, Fox found conditions almost identical with those discovered in the city schools. [3]

The situation is not much better in the high schools. Fred Ayer [4] reported a survey of spelling achievement of forty thousand high school students in forty-eight states. He found a great variation in spelling proficiency within the same classes and from school to school. In the overall picture, there is what Ayer calls a "deplorable falling off" in current high-school spelling.

Evidence on suburban high-school students may be cited. Officials of Jefferson County Public Schools (Colorado) proudly report that "Jefferson County can be mentioned as an exception to the national trend" of declining student achievement scores in reading, mathematics, and language arts. In the tenth grade though, "percentages of students above the national norms have remained flat or actually declined a bit in the last three years in language arts." The percentages have slid in language mechanics and spelling. "Spelling," the Jeffco officials agreed, "is a 'weak point' on which more stress must be laid." [5]

Comparisons are being made between what the so-called hippie generation knew and what the present generation of students knows. Compared with the classes of the 1960s, students for two decades have been scoring steadily worse on the Scholastic Aptitude Test (SAT), particularly in vocabulary and spelling.

It has been asked whether college freshmen of today are better or poorer in spelling than their parents. To find out, the English department of Oregon State College gave a 1927 English placement examination to its eighteen hundred freshmen in the fall of 1955. In a fifty-word spelling section, the students of 1927 did considerably better than the 1955 freshmen. [6]

It is lamentable that our entering college freshmen are so poorly prepared in English that approximately one fourth of them must be placed in noncredit remedial courses to do work on the seventh- or eighth-grade level. It is even more lamentable that if all poor spellers were placed in remedial sections, the figure would run as high as 50 percent. Researchers note that in nine cases out of ten the most glaring handicap or deficiency of entering college freshmen is in spelling.

Since 1969, the National Assessment of Educational Progress has been testing and evaluating the writing skills of Americans between the ages of nine and thirty-five. The first appraisal of writing skills in 1969 revealed that nine-year-olds showed almost no mastery of basic writing mechanics, that seventeen-year-olds demonstrated deficiencies not only in vocabulary and sentence structure but also in spelling. What's even more shocking is that participants over eighteen were reluctant to write at all. [7]

In November, 1975, the National Assessment of Educational Progress announced that writing skills of children have slipped lower and lower and that students' spelling competency too has declined. A sample of writing by a thirteen-year-old junior-high student is this selection about a *bridge:*

> The old brige was a swing brige and it was a real
> old brige. The bords was roten in the brige and
> you could see right through the brige and some

places the bord was missing.

One might expect spelling competence, like wine, to improve with age. Such apparently is not the case, as is revealed in this sentence written by a seventeen-year-old high-school student, which appeared as part of a *Newsweek* (December 8, 1975) article entitled "Why Johnny Can't Write." Granted, the sentence can be understood, but if true literacy and quality communication are the goals of education, the spelling leaves something to be desired: [8]

> John F. Kenedy if he had not buen shat he would be
> presdent now, and in World War II he was a hero in
> the war, and he had a lat of naney and a nice fanily,
> and his wife was very nice, and when I die I would
> like to b buruid in a plac like that.

There are two schools of thought on the deterioration of students' language skills. One group takes the view that standard English is a "prestige" dialect and that efforts to perpetuate it amount to an act of repression by the white middle class. Traditionalists argue that our disinclination to teach children standard English—the language of law, politics, and medicine—is in itself a fatal form of oppression. Whichever way you slice it, communication competence is repression or oppression! Of one fact we are certain, man can't live by incompetence.

The spelling situation obviously isn't good. The general decline in spelling ability has often been, and still is, a subject of public comment. Today some language experts are saying that "structural linguistics" is the villain; some are claiming that time spent watching TV is the time that might be better spent in reading, which of course is closely related to spelling.

What teachers are up against. When the teacher sets out to try to do a conscientious job of teaching his whole curriculum, including spelling, he is likely to encounter an obstinate set of stumbling blocks. First there is public enemy number one, the popular attitude toward teachers. It is a curious paradox that Americans, who in general have universal respect for education, often have little or no respect for professional educators. Furthermore, they have wanted education to be modern, foresighted, and up to date, but they haven't wanted it to be progressive. The adjective *progressive* is a compliment in the business and professional world. But it is anathema in education.

Americans want fancier and faster cars. They welcome automation in factories and offices. But they want to go slow in education. About spelling, some say, "Return drill and sanity to the classroom." Others wail, "Forget progressive education and life adjustment. Let 'em learn spelling the way I hadta." What some of the demagogues and debunkers have not told the American public is that thousands upon thousands of our schools are still back in the pre-Dewey age. Some schools have a long way to travel before they even reach the pre-Sputnik era.

Those parents who maintain that the old ways are the best ways might not care to hear some uncheerful facts about parents themselves. Though we are hearing more and more from teachers, college executives, and businessmen about "the younger generation that can't spell," the older generation should not be absolved, for in many cases they spell no better than the youngsters, if they spell as well. More truth than poetry was expressed by Tom Talman when he wrote in the *Saturday Evening Post:*

> His mind is so keen
>   That we spell what we mean,
>   As parents who talk on the sly do:
> And what makes it bad
> Is I fear that the lad
>   Will lern how to spell before I do."

Unfortunately, parents' fears may be warranted. The 1989 Gallup International Spelling Survey, conducted for the Franklin Computer Corporation, tested over 4,000 men and women in the United States, Canada, England, and Australia on ten commonly used words. The words were *magazine, sandwich, deceive, kerosene, calamity, acceleration, parallel, picnicking, cauliflower,* and *penitentiary.* The Australians were the best spellers while the Americans were the worst.

The de-emphasis of drill. In the early American schools, drill was the key to spelling, and spelling was taught as a separate subject. Drill was even used to teach reading. In fact, it was difficult to understand how a person who could read could not also spell. Drill in repeating letters in their proper order was the important thing. In 1897 Dr. J.M. Rice attacked what he saw as the futility of the spelling grind. Did drill pay? Dr. Rice decided it did not, and he managed to convince others that the time and effort spent on spelling instruction was wasted, taking away from more important subjects. But here we may well ask, Was drill per se the culprit, or was it the inefficient, old-fashioned manner of conducting drill?

Spelling is a stepchild. Another reason for the decline of spelling is purely a matter of the amount of time we have in the school day. To be successful in spelling, you have to be exact; you must drill and drill, and therefore spend more time than you do in any other skill. And in the attempt to cover all the interests considered essential to modern education, our teachers have to reckon with the time element. Also, to gain the most benefit from the many-splendored curriculum, the student has to be expert in reading rather than in spelling. Reading is the skill that has held the center of the educational scene, and spelling has tagged along as a stepchild in the curriculum.

Conflict of spelling and reading methods. Another explanation for the poor showing in spelling today is that our methods of teaching spelling conflict with those of teaching reading. Reading methods today are based on focusing young eyes on the whole word, on reading for context and comprehension. Young readers pay little attention to the syllables that make up the words or the letters that make up the syllables. The reading experts claim that letters and syllables only delay reading, for the pupil sees a whole word and its configuration, not its letters. Conceivably the cancer of configuration explains why a student writes *iol* for *oil* and *aminal* for *animal*.

Phonetics and present-day reading methods emphasize the sound and concept of the word rather than the spelling. In fact, to become a fast and efficient reader, you must break down any tendency to give attention to every single part of a word. Spelling employs a method almost opposite to current reading methods and techniques, and it is considered a separate and independent skill.

Rudolf Flesch, in his controversial book *Why Johnny Can't Read*, suggests that "reading and spelling are two sides of the same [coin], and the trouble starts as soon as you try to separate the two. The only way to teach reading is by teaching spelling *at the same time.*" [10]

What has now happened in American education? Spelling and reading were formerly taught together. Spelling was used as the foundation method for inducting children into the mysteries of reading. Children spent many weary hours naming the letters in syllables and words before they read sentences in context. The spelling and the reading book were one and the same.

According to statements of historians, the failure to make the psychological distinction between reading and spelling was responsible for an enormous expenditure of poorly directed human energy and for deplorable results in both subjects. The great subject of Horace Mann's Second Report (1838) was methods of teaching spelling, reading, and composition. Mann and his co-workers were committed to the thought that no thorough reform could be expected in the elementary schools unless the alphabet method of teaching reading was abolished. This was the old ABC method, and Mann condemned it. He and his colleagues recommended what was then called the "new" method, now called the "word" method.

Eventually methods were formulated for the teaching of reading, and these methods were quite different from those used in teaching spelling. Thus what was formerly reading came to occupy a separate place in the curriculum. One subject was called reading, and the other was called spelling. And, according to some writers, there was a vast improvement in the teaching of both reading and spelling. This may be so, yet the fact remains that our spelling proficiency has lagged behind reading. And no doubt part of the problem is our dangerous separation of reading and spelling in the schools. Whether reading and spelling should get together again, and if so, how, is a question that still faces our educational theorists.

The battle of the ABC's. Today there is a cold war going on in education, and the weapon is an old one, the alphabet. The reading experts, of course, maintain that the child does not *need* to know the alphabet—and many college students *don't* know their *ABC's*. This educational practice has been responsible for the dilemma in which students find themselves when they can't spell a word because they can't find it in the dictionary; and they can't find a word in the dictionary because they don't know the alphabet.

Supporters of alphabet instruction in school maintain that contour or configurational teaching is harmful, and that it is largely responsible for the virtual disappearance of good handwriting and spelling. Such corrupt spellings as *ners* for *nurse* are evidence that the speller does not see his words correctly, that he has blurred images of familiar words. Naturally, he omits, adds, or transposes letters. What is worse, he even substitutes one word for another! For the purpose of spelling, if for no other, it can be useful to know the alphabet.

Who is responsible for spelling instruction? Another serious problem is the question "Who should really teach spelling and when should it be done? Is the elementary teacher primarily responsible? The high-school teacher? The college teacher? The parent? In many high schools, spelling errors are pointed out to students, but little instruction is given. There is no reason for this default except that, traditionally, we have considered the subject of spelling a purely elementary one, to be ended in grammar-school days and to be recognized with a penmanship certificate. Certain words we have expected to learn as we went along; we have dealt out words from grade to grade, and expected them to be mastered forever then and there. But in view of the fact that young people of this epoch are called upon to spell more words than were their grandmothers and grandfathers, it seems altogether reasonable to expect every teacher—not only elementary but also secondary and college—to expend more time and energy in aiding all students to become more effective spellers. The dictum "Every teacher is a teacher of reading" might be paraphrased "Every teacher is a teacher of spelling, too."

Placing the blame for failure to teach spelling, or any subject, for that matter, follows this pattern within the framework of the school system. The college teacher blames the high-school teacher; the high-school teacher blames the elementary teacher; the elementary teacher blames the mother, and the mother says, "He's just like his father—spelling must be hereditary." And somewhere along the line the teacher who teaches the teachers comes in for a verbal beating. Fixing the blame, however, is not so important as considering how to correct the situation. For if no one assumes the responsibility, the student will have to teach himself or become a statistic in the national illiteracy score.

Teachers' attitudes. Granted, the lack of student interest in spelling may be exaggerated. Also, there is little doubt that spelling is not a popular subject among students. However, spelling authority Ernest Horn asserts that this lack of student interest could be the result of teachers' attitudes toward spelling. From his data Horn reports that spelling is one of the subjects teachers most dislike to teach.[11]

Teachers' attitudes toward spelling obviously are in desperate need of overhauling. And still we can't place the blame entirely on the teachers. Many of our teachers, elementary, secondary, and college, have been exposed to so many spelling howlers that they often take spelling delinquency for granted. In fact, the humor necessary to get one through the daily classroom routine often is furnished by the student papers. What would you do if you read such specimens as this contributed by an eighteen-year-old: "Once I had a date and had to brake it." And there is the case of the nursing student who wrote about "romantic fever." One teacher gleefully told of a student who declared he was "taking a partition to the principal." And his classmate wrote about "climbing a petition." The days are behind us when the teacher's nerves became jumpy or his blood pressure went up on encountering a spelling howler. Perhaps part of our problem is simply to make teachers care again about spelling.

Students' attitudes. Indifference and carelessness in the student are serious obstacles too, especially among poor spellers with good IQ's. The student doesn't seem to be totally to blame, however. In spite of the impressive terminology in the textbooks, many talented young people admit that the school curriculum offers them no challenge. Serious demoralization crops up among these students. The danger becomes acute when schools substitute cooperation for competition, de-emphasize the honor roll, overemphasize athletic prowess, and subsidize Saturday afternoon football extravaganzas. Spoon-fed on pabulum, the product of a social institution more than an educational one, the high-school graduate goes to college or into business unaccustomed to work, with a desire to "get by," sneering at the academic drudges, and hoping to get to the top in the easiest way possible—by the Peter Principle.

Spelliphobia. In the past decade we have heard of mathemaphobia, a fear and dislike of mathematics, which has been offered as a cause of so many failures in mathematics. We hear about those who are afraid of science, and we might call this scientiphobia. Another of the academic phobias is linguaphobia, which is a fear and dislike of language study. To the ever-lengthening list of academic phobias then we might add spelliphobia, a fear and dislike of spelling, which accounts for a few of the spelling failures.

What is the cure of spelliphobia? To ask the question is to answer it. For one thing, we may rest assured that just as a man who walks down a familiar road is not afraid, so a student who has been exposed to good instruction in spelling, who has a respect for good spelling, and who has won respect for spelling well will seldom become a victim of spelliphobia.

Spelling has fallen from grace. At the turn of this century, several investigators noted that spelling was declining in prestige, and they predicted further decline. In their opinion, this was a result of the decrease in letter writing which, in turn, is the result of various social changes. Among the conditions that have produced this loss of prestige may be mentioned, first, the plethora of newspapers, magazines, and books. While people are reading more, they are writing less. Second, vast improvement and greater freedom in communication make a telephone call or a telegram more satisfactory than a letter. The social leader and the business executive no longer are judged on their own spelling but on the spelling of their secretaries. As a social accomplishment and business requirement, good spelling made an exit when the secretary and the telephone made an entrance.

Conceivably, the widespread criticism of the spelling situation is an indication that spelling ability is regaining in prestige value. To be sure, it is a positive indication of a rebirth of interest in the importance of spelling and in spelling efficiency.

The lag in the application of spelling research. Research in reading is extensive. Research in spelling, though, is probably greater in scope and intensity. Important clues to the efficient study of spelling are contained in the tremendous treasury of research findings, a large proportion of which are found in readable form in the professional journals. Although there is no lag in research in spelling, there is a lag in the application of the research findings by the teacher in the classroom. Much of the information remains in the hands of the experts and is applied by a relatively tiny segment of our classroom teachers. For this failure there are several reasons, which we shall examine presently.

Though gains have been made in remedial reading, remedial spelling has lagged far behind in the development of remedial education. Some educators have assumed that remedial reading would automatically take care of the spelling problem. Such an assumption has been false, or we would not be faced with the incontrovertible evidence that the poor speller is far more frequent than the poor reader at all levels of instruction.

What can we do about spelling instruction? An analysis of contemporary educational literature then reveals that we have at our disposal scientific knowledge not known to our predecessors and that we have theoretical and practical know-how to do a better job of spelling. The evidence seems to indicate that certain factors are responsible for the situation in spelling. They are de-emphasis of drill in our schools, decreased prestige value of spelling, the stepchild status of spelling, the conflict between spelling and reading methods, spelliphobia, uncertainty about responsibility for spelling instruction, teachers' attitudes, students' attitudes, the lag in application of spelling research, and the lag in establishment of remedial spelling programs. Our chief concern is to improve the overall instructional program so that our children and grandchildren will be saved the chagrin and embarrassment that many of us have experienced. It is with this in mind that I make the following recommendations:

If instruction doesn't take. One of the depressed areas in modern education is that of remediation—what to do when the instruction doesn't take? The remedial problem is a real one in spelling education. In this age of miracle drugs, teachers would do well to employ some of the techniques of good medical practice. The good physician begins with diagnosis and proceeds to therapy. Likewise in spelling, it is not sufficient just to be aware of learning difficulties. This information, important as it is, is of value only in giving direction to instruction and practice in spelling. What we need for remediation and therapy in spelling is a plan of procedure consisting of the following steps: (a) identification of the weak spellers; (b) diagnosis of the learning difficulties of the weak spellers; and (c) provision of instruction and practice to meet the particular spelling need of individual spellers. Thoughtful remedial work can be one of the greatest rewards of teaching.

Teaching teachers to teach: To get maximum value from our schools, we are going to have to upgrade teacher qualifications. Most elementary schoolteachers, and a few high-school teachers, pursue a course in the teaching of reading. Few, if any, however, take a course in the teaching of spelling. Apparently we have not felt it necessary to stress instructional methods in this subject. It is little wonder that there is a failure in the teaching of phonics, phonemics, and spelling.

We've posed the question: "Do teachers really teach spelling?"—a question we haven't yet answered. One circumstance reported in a national magazine leads us to ask another question: "Are teachers qualified to teach spelling?" Once when the teachers' association in one of our states was supporting a bill for a flat across-the-board increase for all teachers, it urged its members to bombard the legislators with letters backing the measure. And bombard the teachers did, sending letters replete with garbled syntax, mangled grammar, and fractured spellings like *apprecate, eleminate, particlar, equatable, proposial,* and *purposal.*

One legislator, chagrined by the display of semiliteracy, said, "I feel that a teacher, like any professional person, could consult a dictionary." Another legislator said that the misspellings point up the necessity of attracting higher-quality people for quality education.[12]

Interestingly enough, surveys indicate that college presidents, chairmen of college English departments, superintendents or principals, and most noticeably teachers themselves believe that methods of teaching spelling need more emphasis in a program for preparation of English teachers. Apparently most teachers, instructors of English in particular, are teaching spelling by "doing what comes naturally." It seems reasonable then to ask that our professional educators make more adequate provision in preservice training for the teaching of spelling. It is reasonable also to ask that professional educators help teachers and school administrators set up spelling clinics where and when they are necessary.

There is a wisp of hope for the improvement of teacher education in that real scholarship is slowly replacing method magic among teachers of teachers. There is a trend toward requiring the study of linguistics in general, and the study of phonetics, phonemics, and graphemes in particular, as a part of a teacher's preparation. This is especially true for teachers of spelling and reading. Herein lies considerable hope for reducing the often criticized jargon in teacher education, for increasing teachers' linguistic scholarship, and for promoting quality education for today and for tomorrow.

Teachers should be taught about the difference between English spelling and the sound-to-letter relationships found in some languages such as Swedish and Spanish. They should be trained in a variety of approaches to the teaching of spelling, so that they are flexible in their methods and can select the approach or combination that seems best for the individual child: [13]

1. Teachers should encourage "audiles," children who employ a predominantly aural-oral analysis and who write a syllable as they hear it.

2. Teachers should urge the visual learners to recall the visual image of the word.

3. Teachers should suggest that hand (haptical) spellers practice a word by copying, by tracing, and by repetitive writing.

4. Teachers should detect the "motiles," those who rely on kinesthetic recall, the sensation of position or the muscular movements of the tongue, throat, hand, or eye. Motiles think the sound, sense hand movements in making letters, trace the word in large letters with pencil or crayon.

5. Teachers should employ *thinking* of the application of structural language principles; the speller, by association, by linguistic intuition,

or by knowledge figures out the spelling of the word. This logical approach, according to most authorities, is the most important and the most successful.

In the future there may well be a reversal of contemporary practice in the teaching of spelling. According to the Futurists, such a switch in spelling instruction might carry us

FROM	TO
self-effacement	self-image
past-oriented role image	future-focused role image
rote memorization of lists	phonemic analysis
knowledge of words for possession	knowledge of words for use
decision-made processes	decision-making processes
high priority on word drill	high priority on linguistic intuition

Teachers should be experimenters, innovators, and discoverers. After all, a concept is a concept, and no matter how it is demonstrated, teachers should find the abstraction usable. In that respect we are reminded of Jerome S. Bruner's statement in his thought-provoking book The Process of Education, which deals not only with the "structure of the subject" but with the processes of growth in children: "The foundations of any subject," Bruner says, "may be taught to anybody at any age in some form."

How many words must one learn? The question arises, "How many words and what words does one need to write and to spell correctly?" A conservative estimate is that the average person requires 10,000 words for his writing. Twenty-five hundred of these words and their derivatives are fairly well known, but not the remaining 7,500 words. Some people require 20,000 or 30,000 words for their livelihood. Beyond this core of very useful words (3,000 or 4,000) are 14,000 less common nontechnical words that serve general writing needs. Examples are arrange, application, purpose. Beyond the pale of words serving general writing purposes are the 600,000 words and proper names in the English language—scientific, legal, technical, artistic, and philosophical terms that make English the richest and most expressive tongue in the world.

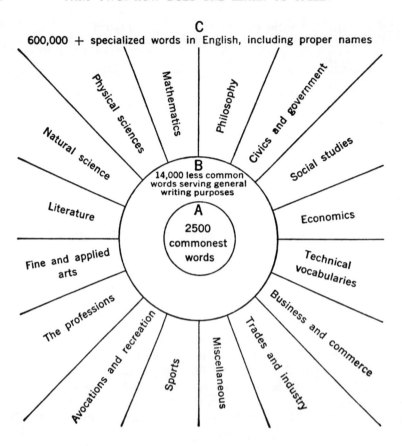

C

600,000 + specialized words in English, including proper names

Physical sciences

Mathematics

Philosophy

Civics and government

Natural science

Social studies

B
14,000 less common words serving general writing purposes

Literature

Economics

A
2500 commonest words

Fine and applied arts

Technical vocabularies

The professions

Business and commerce

Avocations and recreation

Sports

Miscellaneous

Trades and industry

A pictorial representation of these four- to six-digit numbers on word usage, reprinted from Gertrude Hildreth's *Teaching Spelling,* is more illuminating than the written representation.[14]

In conclusion. The evidence seems to indicate that people have failed in spelling in the past and that they are failing in the present. On the other hand, the evidence indicates that teachers, because of indifference, lack of preparation, or failure to apply research in spelling, are failing our youth in the teaching of this skill, which has long been, and still is, highly prized in our society. Teachers who are communication-conscious, and in particular spelling-conscious, will agree that there isn't anything so wrong with the present generation of poor spellers that a good teacher and a good dose of teaching at all levels—elementary, secondary, and college—can't cure.

In referring to a teacher who teaches at Oxford, Chaucer writes in the Prologue to the *Canterbury Tales,* "And gladly wolde he lerne and gladly teche."

CHAPTER V

The Problem for Parents

Children begin by loving their parents; as they grow older they judge them; sometimes they forgive them.

OSCAR WILDE

Let's give a moment now to the person who can be the most influential of all in the youngster's spelling success—the parent. Many parents have become increasingly anxious to understand the educational problems of their children and, if possible, to assist them in mastering their schoolwork. If you've been concerned about your child's difficulties in spelling, this chapter is designed to show you how you can best cooperate with his teachers to help him.

The parent is a VIP. For several decades educators have assumed a curious teacher-knows-what's-best attitude in dealing with parents. Speaking a mellifluous gobbledygook which is dignified by the term *pedaguese,* they have given parents the impression that the machinery of the educational process is too intricate for them to understand. Many parents were led to believe that their comments were biased and unreliable. But that day is past. A French diplomat once said, "War is much too serious a thing to be left to military men." Today we are saying, "Education in general and spelling in particular are too important to be left entirely to educators."

Parents are people. They need to be understood, and they need to understand the school program. By the very nature of things, parents are *very important people.* They are the major guides in the upbringing and the education of their children. They exert a powerful influence on their children's attitudes toward the school and teachers. Both the teacher and the parent have an enormous effect on the child's educa-

70

tional development, since what happens to the child at home or school will affect his personality permanently. In grandfather's day parents and teachers met on the days when the child entered school and when he graduated or was expelled, whichever came first. Between times all communication was on the report card or by the grapevine. But today the story is different. The school door is open to the parents.

Naturally, parents who want to tell teachers how to teach are about as welcome in most schoolrooms as they would be in the operating room of a hospital if they set about to direct the surgeon. The parent shouldn't have to do what the teacher is hired to do—that is, teach. Parents, on the other hand, generally know what they want for their children, and they should be heard and served.

You do have a place in the school environment of your child. And in your way you are one of the experts who can contribute to your child's education. Nowadays schools are considered a part of the community, and the teacher looks at the parent as the first enrichment source of information about the child—his background, his travel experiences, occupational ambitions, interests, and other information that the child brings into the classroom. Rapidly on the way to oblivion is the type of teacher that Professor Willard Abraham of Arizona State University calls the two-by-four teacher—the one who restricts the children to the two covers of a single textbook and the four walls of the classroom.

What kind of parent are you? The parents to whom our spelling information is beamed include people of many moods and emotions. First, there is the parent who is simply confused. For some years, parents have become increasingly aware of the spelling and reading needs of their children. They have read articles in periodicals and books concerning the teaching of reading and spelling—written, of course, by responsible researchers in education. They have also read books and articles by uninformed and irresponsible journalists, by self-styled experts. They have been given antidotes and cure-alls that seem simple but are based on few, if any, facts. And they have been given sensible overall views based on scientific evidence. No wonder many parents and patrons are confused. This book, I hope, will create a sounder basis for understanding.

There are also those parents who may be somewhat insecure and less knowledgeable. The teacher may find it as hopeless to reach these parents as to reach TV watchers with a radio broadcast. Even if the teacher reaches them, he may only spark an explosion damaging to both child and school. Insecurity, as experience has shown us, is often associated with gullibility.

Some parents accept every word their children tell them about school as gospel truth. Every year on the first day of school, one second-grade teacher, who understands imaginative children and gullible parents, pins the following note to her students' jackets:

Dear Parents:

If you'll promise not to believe everything your child tells you that happens at school, I'll promise not to believe everything I hear about what happens at home.

Children may not mean to lie at all, and their distortions of the truth may be entirely innocent. But their statements should be accepted with a certain reserve nonetheless. Don't be the gullible parent.

Some parents distrust the school program, and have little knowledge of the educational program. They come to school angry and ready to blame the teachers for their child's difficulty.

Closely related to the angry parents are the fearful parents, who come to an environment they consider threatening. Perhaps they relive old and unpleasant experiences that they themselves had in school. And now they are actually afraid of teachers. They dread the thought of coming to school for a conference, because they expect the teachers to blame them for their child's problem. Such parents are often upset by the teacher. In return, the teacher is occasionally upset by them. Understanding and mutual concern can open up these closed doors between parents and teachers.

Fortunately for the teacher and the child, the problem parents are a minority. Most parents are ready and able to absorb what teachers have to say. They are well adjusted, well educated, and understanding. They have prepared their children to accept the precepts of the school and have provided them with reinforcement of the values of the school. A report of the child's status in spelling may enhance their understanding of what the child can do and of what the school has been doing for him. A conference with the teacher may well lead to constructive gains for the child.

How parents may be heard. In many communities parents are invited to visit school and to observe their child. When parents visit their child's classroom, they understand more clearly what teachers are trying to do, what instructional procedures are being followed, how their child responds to learning situations, and how he gets along with his peers. Later, teachers and parents can discuss the implications and ramifications of the instruction and the conduct observed.

The parent-teacher conference is becoming more and more an important part of school reporting procedures. The conference is not intended merely as a session of reporting or lecturing by the teachers. The conference represents an attempt to discuss the progress of the student in accomplishing the mutual goal—a quality education. The conference gives the parents the chance to learn what the school is attempting to accomplish and teachers a chance to learn how the parents feel about the education their child is receiving.

School psychologist Joseph P. Rice suggests the following topics for discussion in a parent-teacher conference: (a) exploration of the causes for discipline problems; (b) the reasons why a child is not working up to his potential; (c) various adjustment problems that the child is encountering with the teacher in question; (d) recent deterioration in work habits on the part of the child; (e) an interpretation and search for any lack of ability a student may have.[1]

To Mr. Rice's suggestions we would add a step-by-step plan that parents may follow for a conference with the teacher:

1. Decide in advance what you want to ask the teacher.

2. Be prepared to furnish information that the teacher may need to know.

3. Ask teachers why certain patterns of instruction are followed.

4. Remember the important topics discussed in your conference. Continue with the plan that you and the teacher have mutually agreed upon for your child.

In many communities parents are taking positive, constructive steps to study the school situation through citizens' committees. They are studying methods and materials, and, best of all, they are studying children—their growth and development. The reports reveal that these committees have made progress. As regards spelling, more parents see the spelling problem in complex relationship to the problem of education in general. Parents, as partners of teachers, are beginning to see that times have changed, that children are expected to learn more, that automation has been and is being introduced into education, and that progress, though slow, has been made in the classroom. Nevertheless, it is not true that 75 percent of our problems can be solved by passing a law, painting a sign, or appointing a committee.

How teachers can help parents. Teachers need to look for ways to help parents upgrade their knowledge and skills in the newer methods and materials in this future-oriented world. In recent decades, child psychologists have stressed the importance of the self-image that the child develops. This is his view or opinion of himself as created by what his experiences tell him he is or what he is becoming. An innocent and insensitive parent (or teacher), for instance, may persuade a youngster that he is stupid or bright, a "problem" or a promising person, a reader or nonreader, a speller or nonspeller. And the child often becomes, in a form of self-fulfilling prophecy, what he is induced to believe that he will become.[2]

We may mention several other nuggets of common sense that every parent should possess. They are really common learnings about the difference between spelling and reading.

First, learning to read and spell are closely related, and it is a question as to how much growth in either can be hurried up through the pressure of school lessons and assignments alone. The failure of writing and spelling to keep pace with reading can in fact be a source of difficulty, retardation, and even of frustration in the case of reading exercises that demand writing.

Second, the spelling process is the direct reverse of the reading process. In spelling we proceed from sound and meaning to letter. We *encode* the written symbol representing that word. In reading we proceed from the letter and meaning to the sound. We *decode* written words and their meaning. In either case it is necessary to understand the way in which letters function to form a word or linguistic symbol.

In conclusion, a teacher can get valuable assistance from a parent by accepting the parent as he is, listening carefully to what he has to say, showing that he understands the parent's feelings about education, encouraging him to think about his child's behavior, interests, and aspirations, and explaining basic facts about the learning processes involved in language learning in general and in spelling in particular.

How parents can help children. Generally speaking, there is hope for the child whose parents have learned to spell and practice what they preach. They obviously have powers of observation, and those powers are the first essential for the good spellers. These parents think there is no substitute for good spellers, and their attitude backs up what the child learns in school.

In some homes the three R's receive lip service but are not practiced. Reading, writing, and arithmetic receive attention merely as a conversation piece. The father even snickers that the boss misspells "ninety" but still gets a promotion to the chairmanship of the board. The mother, after listening to the televised presentation of the National Spelling Bee, remarks that an easy word like *sluiced* tripped the contestant. And one or both parents may make a spelling lesson seem a bête noire and the spelling teacher an ogre by asking a simple question: "Have you *memorized* your spelling words for your teacher?"

Do you realize that the home where education is truly valued is a powerful reinforcing agent for the child's education? Do you attach distinction to adults who are good spellers? Some parents do. And they attach a stigma to poor spellers. Others, however, think it's cute and charming to be unable to spell. So when the going becomes rough in the spelling class, the youngster stops trying. Not only does he rationalize his own weakness but he uses it as an attention-getting device to establish his status on the adult level.

Parents are responsible for furnishing an environment in which a child finds spelling important and the practice of good spelling a reality. You may not realize it, but environmental influences are often the root of a spelling problem. If the child has a faulty pronunciation, he may find spelling difficult. It is one thing if the child has a speech impediment such as stuttering or stammering. But it is quite another if the child has faulty pronunciation because he has heard only a foreign language in his home, or because he has grown accustomed to slovenly enunciation encountered in his home environment. There have even been cases of children who acquired a lisping habit by imitating other children who lisped. Parents can be of real service to the child and his teacher by setting a good example themselves. Furthermore, parents are doing their child a favor when they refrain from unnecessary baby talk, once the child is old enough to start learning to speak. After all, a child has about all he can cope with in mastering the reading and spelling symbols, and he only becomes confused by baby talk. Parents can help in another way, and their child will be quite amenable to this idea. Encourage the boy or girl to listen to the TV commentators who are known for their excellence of diction, enunciation, and pronunciation. By the power of positive suggestion you are instilling your child with a consciousness of speech, syllabication, and spelling.

Perhaps the teacher will suggest you go further and assist your child with simple remedial exercises at home. If so, there is a simple four-step method, suggested in *Parents' Magazine* [3], which you can use for working in brief sessions on words that are particular handicaps. Success with just a few especially hard spellings will spur your child on to greater efforts in the schoolroom:

1. Write the word your youngster is to learn as large as you can on a blackboard or a sheet of paper. Use the form of writing your child is using at school. Then say the word and have your child look at it and pronounce it.

2. Have your child trace this large model of the word with a forefinger, while he slowly says the word, not the individual letters within the word. Take care that the youngster does not distort the sound of the word as he pronounces it.

3. Have the youngster continue to trace the word while saying it slowly. This will help the child get the feel of the word in his muscles along with the sound of it, as well as help him form a visual image. He should do this until he thinks he can write the word on his own.

4. Let the child cover the model and try to write the word independently. Next have him compare his word with the large one. If he has written correctly, have him cover the model and rewrite the word. He should do this until he has written the word independently several times. If he writes the word incorrectly, start over again.

These four steps appeal to the muscles, to the kinesthetic images. They may be all your child needs. On the other hand, your child may have a spelling problem because of eye or ear defects. He may be farsighted, or he may be nearsighted. Some children have a visual defect known as strabismus, which is the technical name for cross eyes, being derived from the Greek word for squinting. Sometimes a child's eye movements are so irregular that he fails to get a visual image of the word. Other children have astigmatism, a defect responsible for the imperfect formation of distinct images. On the other hand, the child may have an area deafness. Maybe he does not hear certain sounds, or he is unable to tell the difference between certain sounds. You can help your child and his teacher by having your child's eyes examined or by arranging for a hearing test.

Psychological conditions that you have not even suspected may be preventing your child from achieving in the spelling class. A boy or girl can be experiencing emotional maladjustments resulting from frustration, insecurity, excessive timidity, a fear of failure, a lack of confidence, tension in his home or school, his parents' indifference to his work—even from frustration because his writing vocabulary lags behind his speaking and reading ability. Occasionally a child is the victim of what the psychologists call sibling rivalry—excessive fear of being unable to compete with a brother or sister. A parent then should be careful about comparing a child's spelling with that of other children or other members of the family. In fact, the less you discuss his spelling problems—except with his teacher—the better it is for him.

The spelling problem may be attributed to such conditions as mental immaturity, inability to follow directions or to do abstract thinking, even to a lack of curiosity about words, their meanings, and their use. Since children in this group often see no reason for writing, they have no burning desire to express themselves in writing. At least you can make a start in helping your child by buying him a picture dictionary. Also you can suggest that he write the names of those nearest and dearest to him—his pets, his friends, or his relatives.

Since we've mentioned a picture dictionary, we may call your attention to a suggestion made by Gertrude A. Boyd, a well-known authority on teaching language to the young. The child may construct his own picture dictionary and thus be better prepared to use commercial dictionaries and regular dictionaries. The youngster may collect words and pictures having to do with his and his friends' interests—animals, cars, and actions. In this way, he is learning that words are associated and do fall into categories. Eventually these words and pictures will help him in his initial writing activity.

After the child recognizes the categories, he is ready to arrange words in alphabetical order. His next step is to place appropriate pictures with the words.

If we have been heavy on generalities, we may avoid being soft on specifics and outline the role for a parent in the learning-to-spell process. Sometimes a child has spelling trouble because he hasn't practiced writing. Possibly your child hasn't practiced because you, like impatient parents, write for him because you can do it better and faster. At the same time, the youngster might be saying, "Please, Mother, I'd rather spell it myself." Your top job is to help your child with *starting* to spell. He will take care of *stopping*.

Let your child scribble with a soft pencil or crayon. Four- and five-year-olds can copy letters and numbers from the calendar, labels on breakfast-food boxes, newspaper headlines, book and magazine titles, names of TV programs, names of characters in the comic strips, names of actors and actresses in TV programs. Children of any age learn some numbers, letters of the alphabet, and words from toys, advertisements, word games, pictures, anagrams, and crossword puzzles. You might even keep your child's writings as you keep his baby pictures.

What else can a parent do? Well, what about taking the time to show your child how to write his name? Encourage your child to keep a scrapbook, to take messages for members of the family, to enclose notes to relatives and friends, to copy a laundry or grocery list or a recipe, to write a list of things to be purchased at the pharmacy. In short, make spelling a family affair.

Well-meaning parents can pretest words the child is learning to spell and then retest after he has studied them. The parent can render a splendid service in discouraging guessing and in encouraging reasonable hypothesizing about doubtful or tricky words. Work with your youngsters until their spelling level is up to par with their classmates. And while we're on the subject of helping the young generation, what harm would there be in helping your child look up words in the dictionary?

The question arises, "What should you do with the boy or girl who does not respond to the regular classroom instruction and the simple home remedial exercises?" This is where the specialist takes over. In medicine, the general practitioner often feels the need to refer cases to the specialist. At last educators are beginning to adopt this practice of referral. For several years now, we have used the practice of referral in reading, and we are extending remedial practice to spelling. If serious problems persist in your child's spelling, it's best for you to consult the school about professional remedial work.

The remarks and information about parents, teachers, children, and spelling have been serious stuff. The purpose has been to show that spelling is really serious business. At the risk of being accused of capriciousness, I'm going to quote what Pedagogue Pete writes in a teachers' journal about a Johnny who can't read and who can't spell either:

> According to sponsors,
> School parties are a mess.
> According to seniors,
> They are a 'hug' success.

Canadian wit and author Stephen Leacock expressed more truth than fiction when he wrote, "People look on spelling as one of the troubles of childhood, like measles and Sunday School and having to obey Father." Clearly, Leacock's view is more down-to-earth than author Garrison Keillor's: in Lake Wobegon "all the women are strong, all the men are good-looking, and all the children are above average."

CHAPTER VI

Two Basic Methods

We drove the Indians out of the land,
But a dire revenge those redmen planned,
For they fastened a name to every nook,
And every boy with a spelling book,
Will have to toil till his hair turns grey,
Before he can spell them the proper way.

EVA MARCH TAPPAN

We've taken time out from our practical work to consider two personalities who are basic to the spelling problem—the teacher and the parent. Let's return now to the practical business of learning to spell. In this chapter we'll discuss the fundamentals of two important methods—the sight-sound method, which involves phonics and syllabification, and the mnemonic method, whereby you learn to devise amusing memory tricks to fix a word in your mind. We'll discuss other learning methods in the following chapters.

Spelling by sight. The current debates and discussions on phonics in spelling call attention to two processes by which a person learns to spell—by sound and by sight. The scholars who say we learn to spell by *sight* present rather convincing evidence on the predominant role of the eye and on the actual hindrance of the ear. In the 1860's a German named Bormann produced evidence that deaf and dumb people write only from their visual memory. With the deaf the memory of the word forms is not confused by the auditory memory of sounds.

79

The first really scientific study of spelling uniquely by sight was done by A. I. Gates of Columbia University. Gates and a co-worker found that, with reading ability equal, deaf children greatly excel normal children in spelling ability. According to the statistics compiled, the spelling ability of the deaf is about twice that of the normal child. It is altogether likely that this superiority is a result of the deaf child's more careful visual study of words. The superiority of the deaf, when reading ability is rendered constant, increases perceptibly with longer school experience. And the deaf child's ability to distinguish between correct and incorrect spelling increases with extraordinary rapidity, in comparison with normal children, as their reading experience is extended.

Why is this possible? Some experts say that the deaf owe their remarkable spelling primarily to a particularly effective way of perceiving words. Normal children, despite wider opportunities in reading and writing, do not develop this preciseness and accuracy of word observation. The reason: they rely mainly on the easier, perhaps more natural ear methods. Normal children, enjoying auditory experience, learn to depend primarily upon a phonetic translation of the sounds into letters which represent them.

Spelling by sound. The facts about deaf children and their spelling reveal the importance of the eye in spelling. However, the evidence does seem to indicate that, except for the deaf, mastery of speech sounds is related to spelling ability at all levels—from elementary school through high school and college. To use our knowledge of the sounds of words to best advantage in learning to spell, we must make a brief investigation of phonics and phonetics.

If you're a theatergoer, you will recall *My Fair Lady,* the Broadway musical in which Professor Henry Higgins breathes phonetic life into Miss Eliza Doolittle, the erstwhile "flahr" girl. Few people know that behind George Bernard Shaw's satirical thrust at the vanity of the upper classes lay a genuine interest in the science of phonetics. It was G.B.S. who ridiculed our "orthographic monstrosity" by popularizing his special spelling for *fish: ghoti.* The *gh* represents the *f* sound in *laugh,* the *o* represents the *o* in *women,* and the *ti* digraph comes from the *sh* sound in *nation.* It all adds up to a pretty poor kettle of ghoti.

"Phonetics," the dictionary says, "is the science of dealing with speech sounds." It is a technical subject, involving the study of special phonetic alphabets, diacritical marks, syllabication, and pronunciation. Phonics is a simplified version of phonetic knowledge which is used

for teaching reading and writing in schools. Some of the conclusions
of phonetic studies have been very useful for students of spelling.

Spelling phonetically is just the reverse of reading phonetically.
Instead of going from the printed word to the spoken word, as you
do when you learn to read, in spelling phonetically you go from the
spoken word to the written. If you are sure you know the proper
pronunciation of the word you want to spell, and if you know a little
bit about the phonetic rules that govern the different spellings of
spoken sounds, you will find it much easier to guess the correct spelling. Let's consider some of the findings of phonetic scholars concerning
the sounds of the English language and the letters that are used
to represent them.

English spelling, as we've already said, is highly irregular in comparison with the spelling of other languages. But it's helpful to know
that irregularities occur in English words much less often than we
imagine. Phonetic researchers [1] tell us, for example, that out of a
sampling of 3,000 basic words 85 percent are spelled with complete
regularity—that is, each sound is spelled with the same letters in every
word every time it occurs. In the unphonetic words, it is rare that
more than one letter is irregular. The secret then for the spelling student
is to learn what sounds are always spelled the same way, what sounds
are spelled irregularly, and what the particular problems behind those
irregular sounds are likely to be. Take the ordinary consonants, for
example. The b, d, hard g, h, l, m, n, p, r, and t sounds are spelled
regularly about nine tenths of the time. Thus, whenever you are uncertain about the spelling of those particular sounds, you can make a
good guess that they are spelled regularly. Sometimes they are doubled,
of course (bb, dd, mm,), but statistically this happens less than 1 percent
of the time. Thus, if you're uncertain whether or not one of these
consonants is doubled, you can make an intelligent guess that it is
not. About 82 percent of the consonant blends (bl, gl, gr, cl, etc.) are
spelled regularly. Thus you can be fairly certain that a consonant blend
is spelled the regular way.

One well-known researcher has classified spelling-to-sound relationships according to frequency and low frequency, as regular or
irregular, as variant or invariant. The consonant f is interesting in that
it is regularly f. In other words, it is considered high frequency and
invariant. Of 20,000 very common English words containing f, only
the two-letter word of is pronounced irregularly (that is, like a v instead
of like an f).[2]

One of the most regular, invariant, and least troublesome sounds
is v, as in vital and ever. Curiously enough, the letter v never ends

have
halve

a word. When the sound v ends a word, as is often the case, the symbol representing the sound, otherwise known as a phonogram, is ve. The e is cosmetic, added for the sake of appearance, because English-speaking people have not been and are not accustomed to seeing English words end in v. When the suffix -ing is added, the e is dropped: loving, roving, diving.

The variant relationships are those that are regular except that they relate the same spelling to two or more pronunciations depending upon letters, phonology, or history of the language. The letter c is pronounced as s before e, i, y, plus a consonant or consonant combination (cycle, cinder, center). The letter k corresponds to k, except in initial positions before n (knew, knowledge, knave). Thus some spelling is determined by the letter-sound concept.[3]

Historically speaking, we find that the k may have been introduced originally to alleviate some of the confusion caused by having c represent both k and c. However, the innovation did not always succeed, as the modern words shirt and skirt indicate. The word skirt is derived from the Old Norse word skyrta, "shirt," and the word shirt is derived from the Old English scyrte, "skirt"—another kind of reversal.

Vowels are more complicated, but a look at the ordinary spellings of the vowel sounds is helpful too. You learned in school the five long vowels, which are spelled and pronounced regularly as they appear in mate, mete, mite, mote, and mute. And the five short vowels whose regular spelling is illustrated in bag, beg, big, bog, and bug. You can often count on these basic sounds being spelled the regular way. With the long vowels there are some alternate possibilities, however. The long a is sometimes spelled ai or ay, as in paid and pay. The long e can be spelled several alternate ways: ee as in need, ea as in each, and ie as in relief. The long o can be spelled oa, as in boat, and ow as in bow. The long u can be spelled ue, as in hue, or ew, as in few. The advantage in being aware of the alternate possibilities is that, when you are doubtful that a long vowel sound is spelled in the regular way, you can make a good guess that one of the alternates is correct.

Now let's take a look at a few vowel sounds that are spelled irregularly most of the time. With these it's not possible to guess the probabilities, and the particular words must usually be learned by heart. The advantage in examining them is to learn which sounds they are and what the alternate spellings will probably be.

First, there is the neuter, all-purpose vowel which can be spelled

a (as in alone), e (as in reveal), i (as in docile), o (as in stupor), or u (as in *circus*). Usually the spellings of this sound vary according to the sounds that surround it, but it is best to learn them by heart.

(2) Second, remember that both the long and short u sounds may be spelled u or oo, as in *push* and *book* for the short sound and *rude* and *food* for the long sound.

(3) Third, you have several vowel + r combinations. For example, study the alternate possibilities in the sentence, "The first stern words are heard on our journey to see Myrtle."

(4) Fourth, there are two diphthongs (a diphthong consists of two vowels fused into one); each diphthong has two spellings: *ou* as in *house* can also be spelled *ow* as in *how;* and *oi* as in *oil* can also be spelled *oy* as in *toy*. These spellings must be learned separately with each word.

The first step in the sight-sound method involves the phonetic study of spelling—that is, the connections of spoken sounds with the letters that are used to spell them. The second step involves the study of syllabication—that is, the ways that spellings are traditionally divided into syllables. We'll discuss syllabication after the following practice exercise.

PRACTICE EXERCISE: PHONETICS

Pronounce each word correctly. Remember what you have learned about phonics. Then write the correct spelling of each word in the appropriate space. Compare the corrected spelling with the incorrect. Check your dictionary for the correct spellings.

1. metter	11. fastinate	21. foolhearty
2. critize	12. groul	22. finnancial
3. apothacary	13. delapidated	23. ridiclous
4. shinny	14. delerious	24. explaination
5. deverrsion	15. devistation	25. fernish
6. breakfuss	16. displaid	26. profficient
7. excorting	17. dispiccable	27. persue
8. tangable	18. dispized	28. repremanded
9. choosen	19. elegible	
10. croquettish	20. exerrsion	

If you were successful in correcting most of the misspellings in the exercise, you are ready for further study in phonetics. Your next step is to do some syllabicating.

A syllable is that part of a word which is uttered with a single impulse of the voice. The infant babbling *ma-ma* is uttering two syllables. The syllable then is the real unit of pronunciation. The word *syllable* has three units, whereas the word *syl-lab-i-cate* has four. By the use of a thin space, dots, or dashes, the dictionary tells at just what point the syllable begins and ends.

Suppose a person is asked to spell antidisestablishmentarianism, a polysyllabic word containing too many separate letters to be taken in by a single glance of the eye. Psychologists tell us that the perception span is from three to five distinct objects. But if the individual knows how to break the word into syllables, he is saving himself the trouble of memorizing the order of all the letters. Instead of learning some twenty letters, he learns eleven syllables, and then combines these into a single word.

Someone looking for a little practice in pronunciation and in syllabication will find a challenge in this limerick about a tiger.[4]

> A tiger by taste anthropophagous
> Felt a yearning within his esophagus.
> He spied a fat Brahmin
> And said, "What's the harm in
> A peripatetic sarcophagus?"

Let's use the limerick as a basis for an exercise in syllabication.

PRACTICE EXERCISE: SYLLABICATION
Consulting your dictionary, divide the following words into syllables. Write the syllabicated word in Column B. Count the number of syllables in each word, and place the number in Column C. See answers on page 221 in the Appendix.

COLUMN A	COLUMN B	COLUMN C
1. anthropophagous	_____	_____
2. esophagus	_____	_____
3. Brahmin	_____	_____
4. peripatetic	_____	_____
5. said	_____	_____
6. sarcophagus	_____	_____

It's time-consuming to consult the dictionary for the syllabication of every word that you wish to divide at the end of a line of writing or typing. If you are sure of the proper pronunciation of a word you want to spell, and if you know some principles that govern syllabication, you can save time and energy by figuring out your own syllabication. Eventually you will find yourself taking a lot of the guesswork out of spelling. In fact, the various investigations show that mature students, adults, and superior spellers do tend to study words by syllables.

Before going any further, though, let's set up some guideposts for syllabicating a word. It's not the vowel sounds but the intervening consonants that cause difficulties in division. The question is, Do the consonants remain with the preceding vowel; or do they go with the following vowel? In deciding where the consonants go, you may find the following rules useful:

SYLLABICATION CHART [5]

I. If one consonant comes between two vowels
either

the consonant goes with the preceding vowel if the preceding vowel is short and unaccented: *sol-i-tude, ten-or.*

or

the consonant goes with the following vowel if

a. the preceding vowel is long: *so-ber, fla-vor.*
b. the second vowel is accented: *di-vine.*
c. both the preceding and following vowels are unaccented: *re cipro-cal, insti-tute.*

II. If two or more consonants come between vowels
either

terminal blends (*nd, rd, ft,* etc.) are divided: *bor-der*

or

initial blends (*st, sl, sp,* etc.) are divided if the preceding vowel is short: *mis-take, dis-trict.*

a. Initial blends go with a following vowel if the latter vowel is accented: *ne-glect, re-flect, com-plex.*
b. Initial blends go with a following vowel if the preceding vowel is long and accented: *mi-grate, ni-trate, vi-brate.*

   c. Initial blends go with a following vowel if both the preceding and the following vowels are unaccented: *in-te-gral, des-e-crate, dia-gram.*

or

if an initial blend (*tr, sp,* etc.) and a final blend (*nt, nd,* etc.) come between two vowels, the initial blend goes with the following syllable: *pan-try, per-spire.* The blend, *sh, sk, sp,* and *st* are both initial and final blends: *ship, ash; skip, ask; spin, asp; stir, dust.*

III. When final consonants are doubled before a prefix, as *shop, shopping,* the added consonant goes with the suffix. But when the word ends with a double consonant, the division comes before the suffix: *bluff, bluff-ing.*

PRACTICE EXERCISE: SYLLABICATION

Consulting the syllabication chart, syllabicate the words below. Then check your syllabication with that of the dictionary. Answers appear on page 221 in the Appendix.

1. accommodate	8. datum	15. stimulus
2. appendix	9. etiquette	16. tedious
3. awry	10. focus	17. terrify
4. basis	11. index	18. valley
5. charade	12. irreparable	19. vertebrate
6. cherub	13. nucleus	20. valet
7. curriculum	14. preface	

ANOTHER PRACTICE EXERCISE: SYLLABICATION

The following misspellings are quite common ones, and could have been avoided had the speller kept in mind some principles of syllabication. Write the correct spelling in the appropriate space. Check your dictionary for the correct spelling, and write the syllabified form of each word.

1. continous   3. candlelight

_____   _____

2. corection   4. defficient

_____   _____

5. initate   14. studing

_____   _____

6. embroidry   15. mocassin

_____   _____

7. parsite   16. mumified

_____   _____

8. vetran   17. whiprwills

_____   _____

9. insidently   18. sincerly

_____   _____

10. neglence   19. adiction

_____   _____

11. Massechussets   20. ommited

                          _____

12. orgin   21. colect

_____

13. ruffan

_____

Sight-sound method. Spelling researchers have come up with some interesting evidence about some people and the way they learn to spell, through the eye and through the ear. As people grow older or as they are exposed to more education, they rely more on the visual image of a word, and less upon the auditory image. Apparently people start out with a predominantly auditory image and have to change to the visual. Otherwise they find themselves falling by the wayside in our educational system, which has been and still is predominantly visual. In these days, though, we have more and more audio-visual education, and that is a good sign for spelling education.

A speller has to rely on phonics and syllabication in learning to spell. He has to rely also on a correct visual image of the word or expression. That is, he observes closely the spelling, noting the length of the word, the letters on the line (m, n, o, etc.), those having parts above the line (*l, t*, etc.), and those having parts below the line (*g, q*). He makes a mental picture of the configuration of the word. At the same time the observer associates the word with a related one. *Slept*, for instance, would be associated with *sleep*. If the word is of foreign origin, the speller should find out the translation of the expression such as *laissez-faire* and *au revoir*. Thus he is taking a multicapsule of learning: observing a word or phrase, pronouncing it, getting a visual image of it, and associating the word with another one.

PRACTICE EXERCISE: SOUND-SIGHT METHOD

The following is a list of phonetic spellings that could be avoided by making a correct picture of the words. Look at each misspelled word in Column A. Then pronounce the word correctly. Next write the correct spelling in the appropriate space. Consult your dictionary to check on yourself; and, as you do so, note the syllabicated word and write the syllables in Column B.

COLUMN A   COLUMN B

1. apaul   ap-pall

   _____   _____

2. carrage

   _____   _____

3. comittie

   _____   _____

4. compatable

   _____   _____

5. connoissure

   _____   _____

6. debree

   _____   _____

7. grosely

   _____   _____

COLUMN A   COLUMN B

8. paralel

_____   _____

9. nausious

_____   _____

10. drempt

_____   _____

11. colonade

_____   _____

12. Pennsylvanion

_____   _____

13. morsal

_____   _____

14. inheirited

_____   _____

15. parliment

_____   _____

16. essencial

_____   _____

17. courtious

_____   _____

18. extreemly

_____   _____

19. intricut

_____   _____

20. syrum

_____   _____

The mnemonic method. A second spelling help you may find useful is the memory device which has the rather impressive name of *mnemonics*. A mnemonic is any artificial device for memorizing that depends on arbitrary associations, such as "vbgyor" for the colors of the spectrum or "Thirty days hath September . . ." for the number of days in each month. The word, pronounced *nee-mon-iks,* is derived from a Greek word meaning "mindful." From the same stem comes the name Mnemosyne, Memory, mother of the nine Muses.

It is important that you know whether you rely upon your eye, upon your ear, upon your hand, or upon a combination of the senses, when you are spelling a word. Or you may learn to spell by learning rules. Oftentimes merely taking time to analyze yourself is all that is necessary.

For most individuals there is a well of words the spelling of which is always troublesome and which defies scientific knowledge and rules. These demon words fit no pattern, they follow no rule, and their spelling makes little or no sense. Learning to spell them is a matter of sheer memory, mouthing the letters of the words repeatedly, or writing the words x number of times. For such words, an association of ideas may be a solution.

The mnemonic principle is based upon association of ideas. You invent a motto from an event or from an association with a person: an indispens*able sable* caused the *current* occurrence. You may use a clue about the etymology or origin of a word; for example, mnemonics is related to Mnemosyne. You may form an association by exaggerated pronunciation. Occasionally you may break the word into parts (*to* +*get* +*her*) or you may use a play on words: "*I* like a compliment." These devices often help you develop necessary memory connections after all other means have failed.

There is scientific evidence supporting mnemonics, another name for which is *group labeling.* Researchers have found that "a learner can increase the span of apprehension to a limited extent and to an impressive extent by group labeling." In this technique, memory-span tasks involving random succession of letters, in which the longest is 7, can be increased by being grouped into words. Then the sequence under observation can include as many as 20 or more letters.[6]

It is only fair to warn you that special schemes such as these should not be overdone lest they turn out to be a hindrance rather than a help. A few mental supports, such as associating *w(here)* with *here,* may tide you over a tough spot, but too many of these spelling tricks are a burden on your memory and are not a substitute for a good method of learning. Furthermore, any mnemonic is a crutch, something you can use until you automatically spell the word without thinking, without consulting the dictionary, or without asking someone. But if a rule is a crutch, so is the dictionary. In due time you throw away any crutch.

The best mnemonic devices are probably those that you think up for yourself and that help you to see the word as it should be spelled. Someone else may think your private memory trick silly, but if it works for you, it will help to make you a better speller. After you have devised the trick that clicks for you, don't hesitate to use it.

Found here and there in professional journals and books are mnemonic suggestions made by outstanding teachers. A few specific examples of those memory aids may help you to make up your own:

accidentally
The clerk accidentally omitted John's last tally.

accommodate
This is best remembered together with the word recommend, another demon.

achievement
Do you see EVE in achievement?

acknowledge
There is an edge in acknowledge.

advice-advise
When pupils confuse the pronunciation and the spelling of advice and advise, use this sentence: I shall remember your advice about ice.

all right
Would alwrong look all right?
A misspelled word is not all right; it's all wrong.

altar
Many a bachelor became stuck for life when he marched to the altar.

amateur
Remember ate in amateur.

among
The little word on is found in among.

angle-angel
Angel is soft as in gelatine.
Angle is hard as gleaming steel.

announcement
The word announcement ends in cement.

arctic
Always pronounce the *arc* in arctic.

argument
He lost an *e* in the *argument*.

arrangement
There is a *gem* in arrangement.

attendance
At ten (we will) dance.
We need your atten*dance* at the *dance*.

auxiliary
Look for a *liar* in auxi*liar*y.

balloon
Most balloons look like a *ball*.

bargain
It is not a barg*ain* unless you really *gain*.

believe
Do you beli*eve* in *Eve*?

calendar-calender
The calend*ar* hanging on the wall tells us the *day*.
The mills calender paper.
Calend*ars* keep *dates* straight.

capital-capitol
The capitol building is surmounted by a *dome*, the base of which
is shaped like an *o*.

cemetery
We get there with e's.
Three e's are buried in cemetery.

choose
Choose rhymes with *ooze, booze*, and *snooze*.

chose
Chose rhymes with *rose, hose*, and *nose*.
Compare: Some people once *chose* a *rose*;
            some now *choose booze*.

college
College is a privilege.

competition-repetition
Two pet words, competition and repetition.

complement-completes
The *complement completes* something.
compliment

A compliment is what *I* like to get.

currant-current
It's natural to find an *ant* in this food.
You wouldn't find an insect near an electric *current*.

definite
Despite the sounds that you *recite*,
Your end is fixed by what you *write*.

dependable
A dependable worker is *able*.

descendant
A descendant has an *ancestor*.

desert-dessert
Everyone prolongs *dessert*, even in spelling, but hurries through a *desert*.

dilemma
In a *dilemma* was *Emma*.

does
Connect it up in some fantastic way with deer, with a *doe*, with a whole herd of *does*.

embarrass
Two pairs of twins to cause double trouble, *rr*, *ss*.
When you say the alphabet, one r goes with one s; therefore, it would be logical to have two r's go with two s's.

fallacy
A fallacy in an argument leads to a *fall*.

February
February makes one say "Br!"

fundamental
Fundamental contains two words, *fun* and *dame*.
A song entitled "There Is Nothing Like a Dame" is about *fun* and a *dame*.

grammar
Anyone can spell the first half; copy the second part from the first in reverse order.
There's a *mar* in gram*mar*.

grateful
We're grateful to *Kate*.

hear
Listen: you *hear* with your *ear*.

independent

We made quite a *dent* in England in 1776.

indispensable
Able people are indispens*able*.

innocent
In no cent is there much buying power.

Jones'-James'
Do those who write it *Jone's* and *Jame's* know that they have to change a person's name to Mr. Jone or Mr. Jame?

juice
We like ju*ice ice* cold.

laboratory
This is easy to spell if one puts *labor* into it.

loose-lose
The opposite of tight is *loose*.
This is the word that rhymes with *noose*.
Whenever you use
One *o*, you lose.

misspell
Girls, no little *miss* should misspell this word.

nickel
The fare one used to pay on an *el*evated train.

noticeable
The wrong way would put a *cable* in the word, making it almost unpronounceable.

outrageous
The outr*ageous* idea makes people *rage*.

parallel
If you're up to *par* you can give *all*.
The two *l*'s in par*all*el are parallel to each other.

picnicking
At a picnic the ant is *king*—picnicking.
There's a *nick* in picni*ck*ing.

piece
Slice the first p*iece* thin.

potatoes
Pota*toes* have eyes and *toes*.

practical
She's a practic*al gal*.

principal-principle

He should be your *pal*; if he isn't, you can wish it at least.

My princi*pal* gave me the princi*ple*.

My *pal* gave me the ru*le*.

Associate princi*ple* with ru*le*.

Learn the princi*ples* (rules) of golf.

privilege

Protect your school privileges. Keep your *i*'s on your privileges.

pronunciation

The *nun* knows pro*nun*ciation.

receive

This little jingle illustrates except after *c* with the word that causes the most trouble.

r-e

c-e

v-e

is

very

easy.

repetition

Repetition is a *pet* word with com*pet*ition.

resistance

Increase resis*tan*ce with *tan*.

seize

Seize him by the *ear* (*e* before *i*).

separate

Pa rates 100 percent on this.

There is a *rat* in sepa*rat*e.

significant

Sign if I cant (can't).

sincerely

There is a *rely* in since*rely*.

stationery

A station*er* sells station*ery*.

Stationery is paper for letters.

tenant

As crowded as an *ant* in an *ant*'s nest.

there

Easy to find, just *here* and *there*.

together

The objective of many young men *to get her*. When the objective is won, they are to*get her*.

tragedy
Every *age* has its tr*age*dy.

tranquillity
Associate with *quill* (pens used in olden days).

vaccines
Va*cc*ines and va*cc*inations are administered in doses measured in *cc*'s.

village
Very logical to find a *vill*age built around a *villa*.

villain
To eliminate the spelling *villian* for *villain*, picture a vill*ain* standing in the *rain* with water dripping from his mustache.
In books, this cur has often *lain* in wait beside her *villa*.

weather
We *eat* in all kinds of w*eat*her.

weird
You can hear *we* in *we*ird; make us see it.

whether
I wonder whe*ther* they're toge*ther*.

whose
Who possesses the *hose?*

witch
The old w*itch* cursed the girls with an *itch*.

EXERCISE ON MNEMONIC DEVICES

Now that you've had an opportunity to look over a number of the mnemonic schemes which have helped other students, go back to the previous exercises and pick out a group of words that gave you particular trouble. In the space below, compose your own mnemonic devices. Then we'll go on to one of the most useful tools a spelling student can use—the English dictionary.

CHAPTER VII

The Dictionary: Anatomy of an Ally

What speech esteem you most? The king's, said I.
But the best words? O, Sir, the dictionary.

ALEXANDER POPE

Your use of the dictionary as an aid to spelling is important. However, it is one thing to be a passive dictionary user. It is quite another to be an active user. Being an active user means being word conscious, discovering trouble spots in words, becoming alert to them and becoming suspicious about your spelling of any words containing troublesome spots. Even the best of spellers have these suspicions and, as a result, rely upon their dictionaries, not only when they come to strange words such as *xylophagous,* but also when they deal with common but tricky words such as *accommodate.* There is ample evidence to show how students in doubt have been able and are able, within a very short time, to eliminate most misspellings from their written work by an increased use of the dictionary.

We may be reminded of the college dean, who in berating a student for poor spelling, offered the advice, "You should consult a dictionary whenever you are in doubt. It's as simple as that."

"But, sir," the student wailed, "the trouble is that I'm never in doubt."

A dramatic message about the library and the dictionary user appeared one time in *Newsweek,* which periodically devotes a full page

97

to its "Responsibility Series." The message was a public service in support of National Library Week and centered around the poor spelling of college graduates. The title, "Whatever happened to the liberry?" attracted national attention and elicited many letters to the education editor of *Newsweek*. The thought-provoking message follows:

what ever happend to the liberry?

This message is from... **Newsweek**

There are eighteen misspelled words on this page. They were not *writen* by *parints*, *kindegarten puples*, *enimy sergaents* nor *amature authers*. They were taken from the examination papers of young men and women who have just had the *benifit* of one of the best things in American life... a college education. Proper spelling is a sign of a well *disaplined* mind. In our *oppinion* a graduate who can't write a *defnite*, precise *analisis* may turn out to be a type with a *tendencie* to split atoms that will *assend* us all through the *cieling*. In the spirit of progress a student should be encouraged to "throw the book out the window" once in a while — but never the dictionary!

Misspelled words are from a list of "335 Real Spelling Demons for College Students," compiled by Edna L. Furness, Professor of English Education at the University of Wyoming, and Gertrude Boyd, Professor of Education at Arizona State University. Used with permission of *Newsweek*.

A writer's most valuable tool is the dictionary. There and only there does the speller find complete and reliable information about words. Between the covers of the dictionary lie the facts about a word and many aids in understanding it: the accepted spelling, the accent, pronunciation, definition, the present standing of the word, and other information.

Among the numerous endorsements of the dictionary perhaps none is more revealing than that of Ralph Waldo Emerson. "Neither is a dictionary a bad book to read," he wrote. "There is no cant in it, no excess of explanation, and it is full of suggestion—the raw materials of possible poems and histories." Anatole France expressed his admiration when he wrote: "A dictionary is merely the universe arranged in alphabetical order." Ambrose Bierce, an American author, took a dimmer view. "A dictionary," he said, "is a malevolent literary device for cramping the growth of a language and making it hard and inelastic." As we will see, there is truth in the several points of view.

Development of the dictionary. The history of the dictionary, like the history of spelling, is a fascinating one. The first word books were really Latin-English glossaries, of which many appeared in the Middle Ages and the Renaissance. They were called by various novel names, of which *hortus* (garden) and *thesaurus* (hoard) were especially popular. There was one glossary called *The Storehouse of Little Ones* and another called the *Garden of Words*, each containing about ten thousand English words with their Latin equivalents.[1]

On one hand, the forces leading to the development of the dictionary were intellectual. The Renaissance created a race of pedantic English writers who gloried in using Latin-Greek polysyllables in a Latin-English syntax. The hapless English reader had to puzzle out the unfamiliar new words as best he could. The dictionary of hard words, the real predecessor of the modern dictionary, was developed to furnish such explanations. The first English word book labeled dictionary, Cockeram's *The English Dictionary* (1623), is subtitled, "A New Interpreter of Hard English Words." It is proposed to assist "the more speedy attaining of an Elegant Perfection of the English Tongue" by "Ladies and Gentlewomen, young Schollers, Clarkes, Merchantes, as also Strangers of any Nation."

But there were also social reasons for the growing popularity of dictionaries. As more and more people were rising in the world, they sought some way of assuring themselves that their language was "right." Thus the word books began to be replaced by dictionaries giving attention to literary usage, etymology, syllabication, and pronunciation, not to mention meanings. And the "hard word" dictionaries took on the character that to many minds they still possess: that of being the final arbiter of speech. The belief was that, with rare exceptions, there can be but one and only one correct spelling for each word. And priority was given to "right writing" as an indication of an individual's education and culture. This belief and this priority were both firmly established by the end of the eighteenth century. Spelling was no longer considered a proper field for individual initiative or experimentation. This attitude toward the dictionary as the final authority on language remains with us today.

Dr. Samuel Johnson's true claim to fame lies in lexicography. He was the one who, in one of those moments of whimsy and self-deprecation which made the Great Bear a personable fellow, defined a lexicographer as a "writer of dictionaries, a harmless drudge, that busies himself in tracing the original and detailing the significance of words." He, in his work long referred to as "the dictionary," was the first to base his definitions on the usage of the best writers of his own and earlier times. He established the principle that a language belongs to those who use it, namely, the people. The successors of Dr. Johnson have followed his precept and example in compiling dictionaries. Probably the most ambitious project is the Oxford English Dictionary (OED), begun in 1860 and completed in 1989. This monumental work of twenty volumes, a true ark of the English tongue, lists and defines all English words, from the twelfth through the twentieth century, enters all uses of a word, and includes dated quotations in which the word appears.

The Oxford English Dictionary, Merriam-Webster, Random House, and Funk & Wagnalls are unabridged dictionaries, which are the giant-sized ones—the Paul Bunyans of the general group. About 500,000 entries appear in each of the unabridged books. Another thing, the giant-sized volumes contain many technical and scientific words and terms.

The story of Noah Webster, our great American lexicographer, is a fascinating one. A Connecticut Yankee, Webster, like other youngsters in the colonies, read and studied books written by Englishmen and published in England. Since it was difficult to get books from England during the Revolutionary War, Webster spent time and energy writing his made-in-America dictionary, which was first published in 1806. Almost immediately he set to work on a more comprehensive dictionary, which was published in 1828 as An American Dictionary of the English Language.

The last word in Webster's 1828 dictionary was *zygomatic*. The last word in Webster's *Third New International Dictionary* is *zyzzogeton*, a genus of South American leafhoppers. *Webster's Third New International* has more than 450,000 words, six times as many as the 70,000 in the first American dictionary.

The abridged dictionaries are the portable ones. They range from desk dictionaries for office and home use to those published for schools. Four excellent single-volume dictionaries in common use today are *The Random House College Dictionary, Webster's New World Dictionary, Webster's Ninth New Collegiate Dictionary*, and *The American Heritage Dictionary*. In addition, there is *The World Book Dictionary*, which contains more than 225,000 entries and is intended for family use. It is "the first dictionary designed to be used with an encyclopedia."

Edward L. Thorndike of Teachers College at Columbia University was especially interested in children. He spent many years researching how children learn to spell, pronounce, and use words. Eventually, he came out with a dictionary written just for children. When Thorndike died in 1949, Clarence L. Barnhart continued the project, which was known as *The Thorndike-Barnhart Dictionary*. Still published today, it is known as *The Scott-Foresman Dictionary*.

Besides the unabridged and the one-volume dictionaries, there are the multivolume dictionaries. The English have published *The Awful Spellers' Dictionary*.[2] The British school system, like the American, has its own spelling problems. This dictionary is a boon to the frustrated speller trying to look up the correct spelling when he hasn't the foggiest idea how the word is spelled in the first place. Say that he wants to spell *philately* or *phantasmagoria*, and he can't find the words in the standard dictionaries. But in *The Awful Spellers' Dictionary*, these *ph* words are entered under *f* with the correct spelling following.

As a waggish editor of the Kearney (Nebraska) *Daily Hub* commented: "Like we sed, this is a grate advanse in lexycografy, even if we don't hapen to nead it ourselves."

Words, words, words. Statistics show that 50 percent of our writing consists of only 100 words used in various combinations; further, that 3,000 words make up 98 percent of vocabulary commonly used. All in all, we use very few of the hundreds of thousands of words in the dictionary.

So much for how many dictionary words we use in our writing.

The words found in the dictionary may be roughly divided into three groups. The first group includes hard words that are determined by extraordinary circumstances: "The pharmacist filled a prescription for synthesized *cortisone*." "*Transcendentalism* is a subjective philosophy."

The second group includes words frequently seen, usually easily understood, but suddenly charged for the individual—*synthesize* and *subjective* in the preceding sentences. The third group includes common, familiar words that unexpectedly have to be differentiated, such as *cure* versus *treat* and *home* versus *house*, or clarified, such as *parable, stir, lanai*. As a rule, people aren't called upon to clarify these common words when special circumstances arise. In fact, the common words often are more difficult to define than the hard words.[3]

A dictionary is an indispensable reference book for the speller, the writer, the reader, and the speaker. A modern dictionary that has been carefully researched and edited answers most questions about many words—how they are spelled, how they are pronounced, where they came from, and how they are used. There is, however, a word of caution about the limitation of a dictionary as authority for language.

In the *Education of Henry Adams*, the author says that the greatest challenge man has is coping with change. So with changes in language. Since language is constantly changing, a dictionary is never altogether complete. For example, sometimes a common term like *rock music*, which is relatively new, is not listed. Older dictionaries don't list words like *nylon* or *nucleation*, and a 1960 dictionary didn't include *cosmonaut, AIDS, free base, junk food, reggae*, and *yuppie*.

Changes in sound and spelling occurred in the past. Let's look at several homographs, words that have different origins, meanings, and pronunciations. For example, "The physician *wound* a bandage around the *wound*." Now, the Middle English verb *wind*(en) had a long u (spelled ou) in the past tense. In Modern English this *ou* in *wound* developed the pronunciation as we find it in bound, found, and ground. On the other hand, an Old English noun *wund* (meaning a wound) eventually was written with the Norman French digraph *ou* (pronounced as the *ou* in you). Possibly, the pronunciation of the verb *wound* (as in bound) was an influence in preserving the former or contrasting pronunciation of the noun *wound*.

Then there is the noun *wind*, and the verb *wind*. Obviously, the long i sound prevails in verbs like wind, find, and grind. The normal pronunciation of the noun *wind* would be as in mind and kind, and that was the pronunciation in the eighteenth century. Presumably, the short i found in the noun *wind* is due to the influence of the derivatives, windmill, windy, in which the short *i* is normal. Thus spelling loses touch with the actual sounds, and words become homographs.

A *new* dictionary substantiates the basic fact of language—that language is always *new*, always changing. A dictionary is therefore an authority in only a relative sense. The day the dictionary is printed, it has become dated and is not wholly authoritative for *tomorrow.*[4]

The future dilemma of the dictionary. In this day and age, outer space is an area of uncertainty. Will *space probe, space diseases, space platform, space flight, space suit,* and *space age* be written as two words or as one word? What other words will be introduced when people travel in new kinds of airplanes? [5]

Writing changes, the meanings of words change, through usage or misusage. We grant poets special permission, called poetic license. In one of his poems about spring, e. e. cummings invents the compounds *mud-luscious* and *puddle-wonderful.*[6] Lewis Carroll, in a poem called "Jabberwocky," invents nouns like *rath,* a sort of green pig, and *toves,* or something like badgers. He makes his own portmanteau adjective, *slithy,* which means lithe and slimy. And he invents verbs such as to *gyre,* to go round and round like a gyroscope, and to *gimble,* to make holes like a gimlet.

Using the dictionary. A good dictionary is a speller's best friend. Secretaries and professional writers consider a dictionary as essential as a typewriter, a desk, or a chair. In everyday reading, writing, and speaking there are many occasions when one must consult a dictionary. No one person is expected to master in his lifetime the spelling of all the words in the English language, not to mention the variant spellings for several thousand of them.

Successful guessing. How can you find a word in the dictionary if you don't know how the word begins? The real problem is how to spell the first part. The experts employ seven tricks, quoted from Dell Publishing's *How to Spell It Right,** when "guesswork fails to flush out a word you want." Use these tricks when you're at a loss, and you will soon be a more self-confident dictionary user:

- If a word sounds as if it begins with "s" but doesn't, look for it under "ps" (*psalm, psychology*) or "c" (*cyst, cellar*).

---

*Used with permission of Dell Publishing Company.

- If a word sounds as if it begins with "f" but doesn't, turn to "ph" (phase, phobia).
- If a word sounds as if it begins with "r" but doesn't, try "wr" (wrench, wrath).
- If a word sounds as if it begins with "n" but doesn't, look for it under "gn" (gnarl, gnaw), or "kn" (knoll, knack), or "pn" (pneumonia), or "en" (enema, energy).
- If a word sounds as if it begins with "k" but doesn't, turn to "c" (chasm, colic).
- If a word sounds as if it begins with "j" but doesn't, try "g" (gelatin, genial).
- If a word sounds as if it begins with "o" but doesn't, go to "en" (encore, entrée).

The person who is engaged in a spelling-improvement plan will find the dictionary a fascinating book because of the wealth of information contained between its covers. By consulting it, you can quickly check the spelling, syllabication, pronunciation, accentuation, derivation, and etymology of words. You can find information concerning mythological characters, scientific and philosophical theories, place names, and important people, living and dead. If you understand its various features, you can make the dictionary one of your most useful tools. Let's look it over more closely.

Guide words. The guide words in the dictionary are the single words in heavy type that appear at the top of each column. The guide word in the left-hand column is the same as the first word on the page. The guide word at the head of the second column is the same as the last word on the page. Use the guide words and save yourself the trouble of looking up and down each page to find the location of a word. If, for example, the guide word at the top left is speed, and the guide word at top right is sperm, this means that the word spelling, and all other words alphabetized and listed on the page, will fall between speed and sperm.

Entry words. The entry word is the word you would be looking up. It is printed in boldface (like the heading of this paragraph) to give it more prominence. Let us look carefully at several dictionary entries in order to see what information they contain. We shall begin by observing closely the entries in the Second College Edition of the New World Dictionary of the American Language. This dictionary serves our purpose well, because it contains a modern and complete record of words and phrases, full etymologies, and very discriminative synonyms. We may take for observation purposes the entry word *syllable:* [7]

syl · la · ble (sil'əb'l) n. [ME. *sillable*<*Ofr. sillabe*<**L.** *syllaba* <Gr. *syllabe*, a syllable, lit., that which holds together <*syllambanein*, to join<*syn-*, together + *lambanein*, to hold: for IE. base see LATCH 1. a word or part of a word pronounced with a single, uninterrupted sounding of the voice; unit of pronunciation, consisting of a single sound of great sonority (usually a vowel) and generally one or more sounds of lesser sonority (usually consonants) 2. any of the parts into which a written word is divided in approximate representation of its spoken syllables to show where the word can be broken at the end of a line: in this dictionary, the syllables of entry words are separated by centered dots 3. the least bit of expression; slightest detail, as of something said - *vt., vi.*-bled, -bling to pronounce in or as in syllables

Correct syllabication is indicated in the entry word. We have already discussed the rules for syllabication in Chapter VI. They are useful to know in spelling, because a word should always be hyphenated at the end of a syllable. If and when you aren't sure of the correct syllabication of a particular word, check the entry word in the dictionary.

Diacritical marks and the pronunciation key. A diacritical mark is a symbol printed above a letter or group of letters in a word. The mark indicates the correct pronunciation. Take the word *diacritical.* With diacritical marks the word looks like this:

$$\text{dī ə krit' i- k'l}$$

Examples of complete and partial words to guide you in the correct pronunciation of the diacritical marks are found at the bottom of each page in this dictionary. This is the pronunciation key. If the letter *a* contains no diacritical mark above, for example, it is pronounced as the *a* in the word fat. If it is written with a dash above it (ā), it is pronounced as the *a* in mate.

After the entry word comes the pronunciation transcription, enclosed in parentheses and expressed in phonetic symbols. We may add, because the dialects are varied and because dictionaries vary in their methods of syllabicating words, these pronunciations may seem to be at variance with the way in which you usually pronounce the word.

The dictionary's pronunciation, however, at least indicates how many people pronounce the word, and most assuredly may be relied upon as an acceptable pronunciation.

*Below are the common diacritical marks used to indicate English speech sounds.

PRONUNCIATION KEY

SYMBOL	KEY WORDS	SYMBOL	KEY WORDS
a	asp, fat, parrot	b	bed, fable, dub
ā	ape, date, play	d	dip, beadle, had
ä	ah, car, father	f	fall, after, off
e	elf, ten, berry	g	get, haggle, dog
ē	even, meet, money	h	he, ahead, hotel
i	is, hit, mirror	j	joy, agile, badge
ī	ice, bite, high	k	kill, tackle, bake
ō	open, tone, go	l	let, yellow, ball
ô	all, horn, law	m	met, camel, trim
o͞o	ooze, tool, crew	n	not, flannel, ton
oo	look, pull, moor	p	put, apple, tap
yo͞o	use, cute, few	r	red, port, dear
yoo	united, cure, globule	s	sell, castle, pass
oi	oil, point, toy	t	top, cattle, hat
ou	out, crowd, plow	v	vat, hovel, have
u	up, cut, color	w	will, always, swear
ur	urn, fur, deter	y	yet, onion, yard
ə	a in ago	z	zebra, dazzle, haze
	e in agent	ch	chin, catcher, arch
	i in sanity	sh	she, cushion, dash
	o in comply	th	thin, nothing, truth
		th	then, father, lathe
		zh	azure, leisure
		ŋ	ring, anger, drink
		'	

*Reprinted from the Frontispiece of the New World Dictionary of the American Language, Second College Edition. Cleveland, Ohio: World Publishing Co., Inc., 1974. Used with permission of the publisher.

> **u** in focus
> (this indistinct vowel
> sound is called *schwa*)

ə r   perhaps, murder

FOREIGN SOUNDS

à   This symbol, representing the *a* in French *bal* (bäl) can best be described as intermediate between (a) and (ä).

ë   This symbol represents the sound of the vowel cluster in French *coeur* (kër) and can be approximated by rounding the lips as for (ô) and pronouncing (e).

ö   This symbol variously represents the sound of *eu* in French *feu* (fö) or of *ö* (or *oe*) in German *Göthe* (or *Goethe*) (gö'tə) and can be approximated by rounding the lips as for (ō) and pronouncing (ā).

ǒ   This symbol represents a range of sounds varying from (ō) to (ô) and heard with such varying quality in French *coq* (kǒk), German *doch* (dǒkh), Italian *poco* (pǒ'kǒ), Spanish *torero* (tǒ re'rǒ), etc.

ü   This symbol variously represents the sound of *u* in French *due* (dük) and in German *grün* (grün) and can be approximated by rounding the lips as for (ōō) and pronouncing (ē).

kh   This symbol represents the voiceless velar or uvular fricative as in German *doch* (dǒkh). It can be approximated by arranging the speech organs as for (k) but allowing the breath to escape in a stream, as in pronouncing (h).

H   This symbol represents a sound similar to the preceding but formed by friction against the forward part of the palate, as in German *ich* (iH). It is sometimes misheard, and hence pronounced, by English speakers as (sh).

n   This symbol indicates that the vowel sound immediately preceding it is nasalized; that is, the nasal passage is left open so that the breath passes through both the mouth and nose in voicing the vowel, as in French *mon* (mōn).

r   This symbol represents any of various sounds used in languages other than English for the consonant r. It may represent the tongue-point trill or uvular trill of the r in French *reste* (rest) or *sur* (sür). German *Reuter* (roi'tər), Italian *ricotta* (rē kǒt'tä), Russian *gorod* (gǒ'rǒd), etc.

'   The apostrophe is used after final *l* and *r*, in certain French

pronunciations, to indicate that they are voiceless after an unvoiced consonant, as in *lettre* (let'r'). In Russian words the "soft
sign" in the Cyrillic spelling is indicated by (y'). The sound can
be approximated by pronouncing an unvoiced (y) directly after
the consonant involved, as in *Sevastopol* (se'väs-tô'pəly').

PRACTICE EXERCISE: THE PRONUNCIATION KEY

Examine the word *pronounce*. According to the pronunciation key,
the word is spelled prə nouns. Now in comparing this with the spelling
form, you will notice that the word ends in a silent letter. The pronunciation key helps you discover the trouble spot in this word, the silent
e.

Using the pronunciation key, find the pronunciation of the following
words. Next, observe that the pronunciation key helps you master
the trouble spots in the words.

1. mortgage	6. establishment
2. preliminary	7. answer
3. mutable	8. bologna
4. formulate	9. stubbornness
5. format	10. diphtheria

PRACTICE EXERCISE: PHONETIC SPELLING

Consult your dictionary for the phonetic spelling and the diacritical
marking of the words below. Then pronounce these frequently mispro-
nounced words.

1. acumen	12. exquisite
2. adult	13. February
3. advertisement	14. forehead
4. amateur	15. government
5. appropriate (verb)	16. grievous
6. arctic	17. mischievous
7. athletics	18. often
8. coupon	19. perspire
9. data	20. similar
10. decadent	21. status
11. despicable	

Accentuation. In general, English is a rather strongly stressed or accented language. The force of the stress varies considerably among

individual speakers and among social groups. A word of three or more syllables is likely to have a principal and a secondary stress. Take, for example, the word *secondary*, which is syllabicated and accentuated as follows:

sek′ ən der′ ē

A heavy accent mark immediately follows the syllable *sek*, which is spoken the most strongly. A lighter mark indicates the syllable getting minor stress *(der)*. A syllable receiving no stress, here *en*, is followed by a hyphen.

PRACTICE EXERCISE: ACCENTUATION

In Column A, syllabicate each of the following words. In Column B, write the syllable on which the primary accent falls. Use the dictionary if necessary.

	COLUMN A	COLUMN B
1. incidentally		
2. admiral		
3. aspirant		
4. decorous		
5. inquiry		
6. harass		
7. lament		
8. superfluous		
9. precedent		
10. gondola		
11. admirable		
12. disastrous		
13. condolence		
14. clandestine		
15. inquirer		
16. hospitable		

	COLUMN A	COLUMN B
17. lamentable	_____	_____
18. secretive	_____	_____
19. precedence	_____	_____
20. obligatory	_____	_____

Parts of speech. Following the pronunciation transcription in the dictionary entry comes an indication of the word's part of speech. It is abbreviated in italic type. When a word may be used as more than one part of speech, the entry will be divided into sections for each one.

PRACTICE EXERCISE: PARTS OF SPEECH
Consulting your dictionary, find the part of speech of the words which follow:

1. alack
2. alas
3. diligent
4. decidedly
5. beginning
6. dominion
7. egotistical
8. funny
9. go
10. intention
11. deliberate
12. recalcitrant
13. obstreperous
14. improvise
15. whom
16. visit
17. progressive
18. convince
19. blow
20. power

Morphology. Next comes, in some dictionaries, mention of irregularities, if any, in the different grammatical formations of the word, including unusual formation of the plurals of nouns, the participles, and the past tenses of verbs, or the comparative and superlative forms of adjectives. If these inflectional formations are perfectly normal, the entry continues directly with the derivation of the word.

PRACTICE EXERCISE: MORPHOLOGY
The words listed below are nouns, verbs, and adjectives. Consult your dictionary for the plurals of nouns. Write the plural form in the space provided. Write the principal parts of the verbs in the appropriate

spaces. Note if the comparative or superlative forms of the adjectives are irregular. If so, write those forms.

1. focus	8. be	15. write
2. addendum	9. bad	16. parenthesis
3. erratum	10. synopsis	17. dynamo
4. analysis	11. criterion	18. Negro
5. axis	12. phenomenon	19. tomato
6. good	13. château	20. potato
7. drink	14. do	

Derivations. It has been said that every word in our language is a frozen metaphor, a frozen picture. Perhaps you are interested in the romance that lies within each word. If you wish to know from which language a word comes, and what it originally meant in that language, you can find this information in the dictionary. The study of words, which is called etymology, comes from the Greek word *etymon,* meaning true, and the Greek ending *logia,* meaning the study. Obviously "etymology" means the study of true origins. This sort of incidental information about the origin and history of a word can help you with your spelling for the simple reason that you will understand more fully why the word is spelled the way it is. If you can remember that a word is of Greek origin, that is, is either derived from Greek roots or borrowed directly from a Greek word, you may be relatively certain that *f* will usually be spelled *ph.* This is the case, for example, in *philosopher, philanthropist,* and *physiology.*

One who pays attention to etymologies uncovers surprising and fascinating information about words. For example, *nausea* is a classical word in modern dress. It is derived from another Greek word, *naus,* meaning a ship. The seafaring Greeks knew about the miseries of seasickness, but in thinking of this discomfort they associated it with the ship rather than with the sea. Take the word *window.* In Middle English, the English spoken from approximately 1100 until 1400, we have the word *windoge.* But this has its origin in the Teutonic word *wint* (wind) and the Latin word *oculus* (eye). Window, then, means "wind-eye"—that is, an opening for the air to enter.

The history of every word begins with its root. Yet, the root cannot always be ascertained. Furthermore, we must not expect the root to contain all the significance that successive civilizations have attached to the words that have grown out of it. There is Sophocles, which means "the wise one," and the derivative *sophomore*. Consulting a book entitled *Horsefeathers and Other Curious Words*, by Charles E. Funk and Charles E. Funk, Jr., we find that an older spelling was *sophimore*. The general belief is that this form resulted from *sophism* plus the suffix *-or*, which may be defined as the "one who practiced sophism," otherwise known as argumentation, especially on a fallacious premise. The present spelling is based on the theory that a second-year high-school student, having been exposed to erudition, exploits this modicum of knowledge to a degree far beyond its true value. In such behavior he is wise (Greek *sophos*), but he is wise to the point of folly (Greek *mōria*). In other words, he is a wise fool, which in its Anglicized form is *sophomore*.

Most people enjoy knowing the origin of their names and their original meaning. Elizabeth is pleased to know that her name is from Hebrew and means consecrated to God. Leo may be surprised to know that he is a lion; Leona may not be aware that her name means lioness. Roy no doubt will be proud that he is a king. Rufus, be he blond or brunet, may wonder at life's ironies when he looks in the dictionary to find that his name originally meant red-haired. Greek and Roman mythologies gave us many names and words, as do other mythologies. Ancient names have real significance: *Jove* is the source of *jovial*, and Plato furnishes the root for *platonic*. Derivatives from Mercury appear in *mercurial* and *mercurochrome*.

DICTIONARY EXERCISE: ETYMOLOGY

Consulting the dictionary, find out the language from which each of the following words is derived. Then note the language of origin and the original word in the spaces provided. Look for clues to the modern spelling.

ENGLISH WORD	LANGUAGE OF ORIGIN	ORIGINAL WORD
Example:		
dock	Anglo-Saxon	docce
1. supercilious	_____	_____
2. profane	_____	_____
3. chauffeur	_____	_____
4. television	_____	_____

ENGLISH WORD	LANGUAGE OF ORIGIN	ORIGINAL WORD
5. psychosomatic	_____	_____
6. alcohol	_____	_____
7. candle	_____	_____
8. bedlam	_____	_____
9. candidate	_____	_____
10. vulcanize	_____	_____
11. cereal	_____	_____
12. tantalize	_____	_____
13. hoosegow	_____	_____
14. morphine	_____	_____
15. algebra	_____	_____
16. herculean	_____	_____
17. curfew	_____	_____
18. bonfire	_____	_____
19. alcove	_____	_____
20. assassin	_____	_____

Definitions. Next in order are the definitions, the recordings of various meanings that the word has had in its existence. It's often said that you really haven't added a new word to your vocabulary until you can spell it. It's also true that you really haven't learned to spell a word until you can use it correctly. The definitions begin with lower-case letters and are numbered with arabic numerals. The number serves as a convenience in consulting the entry.

The arrangement of meanings is difficult, no matter what plan is used. Unknowing students sometimes suppose that the first meaning given for the word is the most common one, but that is not always the case. Sometimes the meanings are arranged in the order in which they appeared in the language, progressing from the oldest meaning to the most recent one. Some of our American dictionaries follow this practice. Some dictionaries put first the meaning in most common usage today. And some, like the New World Dictionary of the American Language, place the most general meaning first and the most specific last. The best advice that can be given is to consult the introductory part of the dictionary to see which plan has been followed.

Consulting the word *spell* in the *New World Dictionary*, observe that the most specific meaning is given last.

> **spell:** 1. to name, write, or signal the letters which make up (a word, syllable, etc.), esp. the right letters in the right order; 2. to make up, or form (a word, etc.): said of specified letters; 3. to signify; mean [hard work *spelled* success].

Synonyms. At the end of many entries, you may find synonyms for different levels of usage—popular, literary, and learned. Albert C. Baugh offers three examples of these synonyms: *holy, sacred, consecrated; time, age, epoch; rise, mount, ascend.* The first word in each series is English, the second is derived from French, and the third word is derived from Latin.

Variant spellings. Andrew Jackson said, "It is a damned poor mind that can think of only one way to spell a word." If, as you wonder whether to write *check* or *cheque, theater* or *theatre,* you agree with President Jackson, you will be pleased to learn that many of our English words have a secondary spelling, often the British form. Alternate spellings are listed in the dictionary in preferential order. *Theater* is entered first, for example, and hence is the preferred form. Secondary spellings, or the British forms, are not wrong, but American forms are preferred.

PRACTICE EXERCISE: PREFERRED SPELLING
Write in Column C the preferred spelling of the following words. Consult the dictionary if necessary.

A. British Spelling	B. American Spelling	C. Preferred Spelling
1. honour	honor	_____
2. colour	color	_____
3. labour	labor	_____
4. centre	center	_____
5. metre	meter	_____
6. travelling	traveling	_____
7. theatre	theater	_____
8. chaperone	chaperon	_____

A. *British Spelling*	B. *American Spelling*	C. *Preferred Spelling*
9. advisor	adviser	_____
10. develope	develop	_____
11. nitre	niter	_____

Capitalization. To capitalize or not to capitalize: That is the question. There are many rules for using capital letters. You should be familiar with the important rules. You capitalize:

1. the first word of a sentence.
   Example: You are learning to spell.
2. the first word of a direct quotation.
   Example: She said, "That was your last chance."
3. the first word and important words in titles of books or themes.
   Example: The Old Man and the Sea.
4. the first word of a line of poetry.
   Example: "Be not the first by whom the new are tried."
5. the words I and O at all times.
   Example: O Captain!, my Captain!"
6. proper nouns and abbreviations of proper names.
   This rule concerns persons (titles of courtesy, initials of a name, family relationships, organizations, and salutations), places, and prevailing practices (holidays, events, languages, races, etc.), as follows:

PERSONS	EXAMPLES
Titles of courtesy:	His Honor
First word of a salutation of a letter:	Dear Mr. Jones
Initials of a name:	J. D. Smith
Family relationships:	Aunt Mary, Father (but: *my* father)
Names of organizations, clubs, corporations, churches, political parties:	Rotarians General Motors Methodist Church Democrats

PLACES	EXAMPLES
Definite place names	Cincinnati
	the North

OTHER USAGE	EXAMPLES
Deity and words associated with Deity:	God, the Trinity
Countries, nationalities, geographic names, languages:	France, French, Pacific Ocean, Arabic
Holidays	Fourth of July Christmas Day
Names of days and months:	Monday, January

You do *not* capitalize:

1. Points of the compass;
   Example: four miles south
2. the names of the seasons;
   Example: spring, summer
3. studies (languages excepted);
   Example: botany
4. conjunctions, articles, prepositions in a title (exceptions: opening articles and prepositions with five or more letters).
   Examples: The Prince and the Pauper, Golf Without Tears.

Abbreviations. An abbreviation is a shortened way of spelling a word. Not all words can be abbreviated. Those that have a shortened form belong most appropriately to manuals, books of reference, business and legal documents, and scholarly footnotes. "When in doubt, spell it out" is the golden rule to be followed if you are tempted to use short forms that are not clear in themselves. Here are some exercises that will help you in learning some of the more common and useful abbreviations.

PRACTICE EXERCISE: COMMONLY USED ABBREVIATIONS
Consult your dictionary and set down in the right-hand column the abbreviations for the following:

KINDS OF WORDS THAT MAY BE ABBREVIATED	COMPLETE SPELLING	ABBREVIATION
Months of the year	January	_____
	February	_____
	March	_____
	April	_____
	August	_____
	September	_____
	October	_____
	November	_____
	December	_____
Expressions of time, weight, area, length, and quantity	amperes	_____
	foot	_____
	hour	_____
	inch	_____
	pound	_____
	ounce	_____
	year	_____
	gallon	_____
	island	_____
	carat	_____
	mile	_____
	minute	_____
	miscellaneous	_____
	measurement	_____
	population	_____
	pair	_____

pint   _____

quart   _____

square   _____

temperature   _____

weight   _____

yard   _____

Business and professional terms		
attorney	_____	
company	_____	
department	_____	
magazine	_____	
market	_____	
assistant manager	_____	
paid	_____	
proprietor	_____	
superintendent	_____	

Titles of honor, respect, and rank		
Master of Arts	_____	
colonel	_____	
esquire	_____	
governor general	_____	
junior	_____	
lieutenant commander	_____	
a married woman	_____	
mademoiselle	_____	
recording secretary	_____	
senator	_____	
reverend	_____	

Words or expressions	anno domini	_____
that may be reduced	ante meridiem	_____
to initial letters or	before Christ	_____
initial sounds	care of	_____
	District of Columbia	_____
	free on board	_____
	House of Representatives	_____
	I owe you	_____
	intelligence quotient	_____
	Mountain Standard Time	_____
	Old Testament	_____
	miles per hour	_____
	postscript	_____
	Philippine Islands	_____
	registered nurse	_____
	Reply, if you please	_____
	(Fr. répondez s'il vous	
	plaît.)	_____

Perhaps these exercises have given you a clearer idea of the makeup and resources of your dictionary. If you are aware of all the dictionary's many special features, you will find it perpetually useful. Let's turn now to a new method of spelling—the structuring method.

CHAPTER VIII

Structuring:
Another Method

A well-educated gentleman may not know many languages, may have read very few books, But whatever language he knows, he knows precisely; whatever word he pronounces, he pronounces rightly; above all, he is learned in the peerage of words; knows the words of true descent and ancient blood at a glance from words of modern canaille; remembers all their ancestry, their intermarriage, their distant relationships.

JOHN RUSKIN

There are several characteristic methods by which words have been formulated in the English language. One is the imitative method, which results in what are called onomatopoeic words—words that sound like what they stand for. Words like *whizz, hiss, fizz, twitter,* and *titter* are echoes of the physical sound being imitated. *Cuckoo* is an imitation of the cry made by the bird, and hence the name of the bird itself. Sometimes imitation takes a repetitive form. In one type, the base word is duplicated, and the result is words like *tweet-tweet* and *mama.* In a second type, there is an alteration of the second element, as in *bow-wow, zig-zag,* and *tick-tock.* There is a third type, in which both parts have separate meanings, such as *tip-top, walkie-talkie, peepie-creepie,* and *jeepers-creepers.* Other iterative words that have achieved status among educated people are *sing-song, hoity-toity,* and *killer-diller.*

Compounding. A common device for word creation is that of compounding, which consists of joining two or more words to form a new word. The structuring method of spelling involves a knowledge of the different ways words have been compounded in the English language. For a start, let's look at the various combinations of words that can be compounded. Compound words can consist of

1. nouns compounded with nouns: for example, *railroad, weekday,* and *treetop.*
2. nouns compounded with adjectives: for example, *airtight* and *seasick.*
3. adjectives compounded with nouns: for example, *greenhouse* and *blackboard.*
4. adverbs compounded with nouns: for example, *underage* and *underground.*
5. verbs with adverbs: for example, *strike-out* and *sit-down.*
6. nouns with verbs: for example, *hand-picked.*
7. verbs with nouns: for example, *playboy.*
8. adjectives with verbs: for example, *shortstop* and *whitewash.*
9. nouns with adverbs: for example, *handout.*
10. adverbs with verbs: for example, *overpass.*
11. adverbs with adjectives: for example, *evergreen.*
12. Sometimes three words may be compounded: for example, *hand-to-mouth, mother-in-law,* and *hand-me-down.*
13. And sometimes compound words can consist of complete clauses: for example, *good-bye* and *albeit.*

Hyphenation. With compound words it is often difficult for the speller to know whether or not the compounding words are hyphenated. Among the words that are never hyphenated are these:

anything	nowadays
foreground	outlaw
forehead	outlet
forever	overthrow
heretofore	somewhere
moreover	throughout
newspaper	whoever
nonetheless	yourself

Among the words that are always hyphenated are these:

son-in-law
follow-up
forget-me-not

It is impossible to set down a rule making clear which compounds should be written as separate words, which should contain hyphens, and which should be written as one word. Your only safe guide is the dictionary, and sometimes the compilers of the dictionaries disagree. There is a trend away from hyphenation at present, but there are several compounds in which hyphens are regularly used. Here are a few rules to guide you in hyphenating compound words:

Compound nouns. Compound nouns are hyphenated *when*

two distinct functions are united in one person or thing;
Example: secretary-treasurer.

a noun is followed by another part of speech;
Example: hanger-on.

a verb is followed by another part of speech.
Example: do-nothing.

For practice, insert the hyphen where it belongs in the following words. Check your answers on page 221 in the Appendix.

1. Attorney General
2. Knight Templar
3. Executive Director
4. jack o' lantern
5. fly by night
6. will o' the wisp
7. a know it all
8. a take off
9. a go between
10. jack of all trades

Compound adjectives. Compound adjectives are hyphenated *when*

a noun or adjective is followed by a participle;
Example: green-eyed monster.

a noun is followed by an adjective;
Example: freckle-faced.

two nouns are used as an adjective;
Example: father-son event.

they are adjectives of nationality;
Example: Anglo-Saxon.
a number is followed by a noun;
Example: eight-cylinder motor.
they are numbers such as *twenty-one, twenty-two, etc.*
a verb is followed by other words;
Example: pay-as-you-go policy.

For practice, write each word in the space provided as it should be, combined or hyphenated. Leave the space blank if the word or words are correct. Check your answers on page 221 in the Appendix.

1. a thirty day expert   _____

2. forty nine   _____

3. one hundred   _____

4. a silver plated bracelet   _____

5. Deadeye Dick   _____

6. per cent   _____

7. child like   _____

8. micro biology   _____

9. one eyed giant   _____

10. six cylinder car   _____

Special compounds. Certain compounds follow special rules. Compounds beginning with *self* are usually hyphenated. Compounds of prefixes such as *anti, ex, re, pro, vice* are hyphenated only when followed by certain words.

Example: self-esteem, ex-husband, and vice-president

The prefix *re* is sometimes hyphenated when it means again.
Example: re-form (like a line, but: reform movement, etc.)

The prefix is hyphenated before a word beginning with a capital letter.
Example: pro-European and anti-Semitism.

For practice, insert the hyphen where and if it belongs in the following words. Check your answers on page 221 in the Appendix.

1. self help

2. re cover (cover again)

3. anti Communist

4. ex wife

5. pro British

6. re release

7. re collect (remember)

COMPOUNDING BY AFFIXING

Perhaps the most common process of word-creation is that of compounding a single full word with a prefix or suffix. Take the basic word *fact*, for example. By adding prefixes, we have derived from it the words *infect* and *disinfect*. Using other prefixes and suffixes, we have derived the words *affection* and *affectionate*.

Here is a familiar word composed of three parts: *satis-fact-ion*. If you know the meaning of the prefix *satis*, the meaning of the root *fact*, and of the suffix *ion*, you can arrive at the meaning and spelling of the word. *Satis* means enough, *fac* means do, and *ion* refers to the process of something. If you put the three meanings together, you can guess that the word *satisfaction* means the process or act of doing enough.

The recent decline in general spelling ability is due in part to the fact that fewer and fewer students are taking Latin, the language from which so many of our compound words are derived. While it isn't necessary to read and write Latin fluently in order to spell well, anyone wishing to succeed at spelling should keep a weather eye out for Greek and Latin component parts and for their various combinations in everyday words.

The successful speller will find it worth his while to study the list of common Latin roots below.[1] Study the meaning of each root. Then note the examples of English words containing a Latin root. See whether you can think of other words containing the root:

LATIN ROOT	MEANING	EXAMPLE
ag, act	do, act	agent, action

LATIN ROOT	MEANING	EXAMPLE
aqua	water	aquatic
audio	hear	audience
bene	well	benediction
ceive, cept	take	concept, conceive
cor, cordis	heart	cordial
corpus, corporis	body	corporal, corpse
cursus	run	concourse
credo	believe	credit
deus	God	deity
dict, dic	say	dictate
dominus	lord	dominate
duct	lead	conductor
ego	I, myself	egotist
fac, factus	make, do	fact
fer	carry	reference
frater	brother	fraternal
jungo, junctum	join	junction, conjugal
lat	carry, bear	relate
mitt, miss	send	remit, mission
mors	death	mortal
pater	father	paternal
pes, pedis	foot	centipede
port	carry	transport
scribe, scriptum	write	scripture, scribble
spec	look	spectator
solus	alone	solo
sta	stand	stable
tang	touch	tangent
tract	draw	subtract
utili	useful	utility
vent	come	convention
verto, versus	turn	invert
video, visum	see	visible
voc, voke	call	provocation, revoke

For practice, insert in the appropriate space in each word below the

Latin root which is equivalent to the word between parentheses. Then write the entire word in the space at the right. Check your answers on page 221 in the Appendix.

1. _____ rium (water)   _____

2. _____ torium (hear)   _____

3. _____ fit (well)   _____

4. _____ ration (body)   _____

5. _____ ity (death)   _____

6. tran _____ (write)   _____

7. at _____ (draw)   _____

8. tele _____ (see)   _____

9. _____ itude (alone)   _____

10. re _____ ion (lead)   _____

Latin prefixes are as important in compounding as Latin roots. Prefixes have their greatest value in the exact meaning they convey to words. Thus, when a person learns that re means *back*, and *remit* means *send back*, he will deduce that *reduce* means *lead back*, if he is told that *ducere* means *to lead*. Every good speller becomes familiar with the principal prefixes, their meaning, and examples. Study the list of Latin prefixes below:

PREFIX	MEANING	EXAMPLE
ab	away, from	absent
ante	before	anteroom
anti	against	antibiotics
circum	around	circumference
de	down	descend
dis	apart	discriminate
e, ex	out	export, exit
in	not	inaccurate
inter	among	interchange
mis	wrong, bad	misconduct
non	not	nonconformity
per	through	perfect

PREFIX	MEANING	EXAMPLE
post	after	postponement
pre	before	prewar
pro	forward	pronoun
re	back	rebuild
se	apart	separate
semi	half	semicolon
sub	under	subway
super	above	superintendent
trans	across	transcontinental
ultra	beyond, excessive	ultramarine

PRACTICE EXERCISE FOR THE PREFIX MIS

Insert mis in the following list. Then write the whole word in the space provided at the right. Check your answers with those on page 221 in the Appendix.

1. ____shape _____
2. ____speak _____
3. ____spell _____
4. ____spend _____
5. ____state _____
6. ____step _____
7. ____take _____
8. ____hap _____
9. ____demeanors_____
10. ____construe_____

11. ____chief _____
12. ____fire _____
13. ____name_____
14. ____use_____
15. ____understand _____
16. ____print _____
17. ____trust _____
18. ____fortune_____
19. ____behave _____
20. ____pronounce_____

PRACTICE EXERCISE FOR THE PREFIX DIS

Given the following words, supply the prefix dis. Then write the whole word in the space provided at the right. The answers are on page 221 in the Appendix.

1. ____appear _____
2. ____appoint_____

3. ____satisfy_____
4. ____similar _____

5. ____sect _____ 13. ____sever _____

6. ____service _____ 14. ____sension _____

7. ____semble _____ 15. ____sipate _____

8. ____credit _____ 16. ____regard _____

9. ____pel _____ 17. ____sociate _____

10. ____sertation _____ 18. ____pose _____

11. ____entangle _____ 19. ____soluble _____

12. ____suade _____ 20. ____turb _____

PRACTICE EXERCISE FOR THE PREFIX *IN*

In is a flexible prefix. It becomes *il* before *l,* as in *illiterate.* Insert *il* in the following list of words. Then write the word in the space provided at the right.

1. ____legal _____ 8. ____liberality _____

2. ____legality _____ 9. ____lustrate _____

3. ____legible _____ 10. ____literacy _____

4. ____legibility _____ 11. ____luminate _____

5. ____legitimate _____ 12. ____lumination _____

6. ____legitimacy _____ 13. ____lusionment _____

7. ____logical _____ 14. ____lusive _____

Also, *in* becomes *im* before *m,* as in *immortal.* Insert *im* in the following list of words. Then write the word in the space provided at the right.

1. ____material _____ 6. ____minent _____

2. ____mature _____ 7. ____modest _____

3. ____mediate _____ 8. ____moral _____

4. ____memorial _____ 9. ____mune _____

5. ____migrant _____ 10. ____mutable _____

Next to Latin, Greek is the richest source of prefixes in compound English words. Greek prefixes have been used increasingly since the early nineteenth century for scientific words.[2] Below is a table of Greek prefixes in order of their importance in English:

PREFIX	MEANING	EXAMPLE
syn	with, together	synthesis
para	beside, beyond	parallel
epi	upon	epitaph
a, an	not	agnostic
apo	away from, off	apostasy
anti	against	antidote
dia	through	diagram
ana	on, up, backward	anatomy
cata	down, against	catalogue
en	in	energy
pro	before	prophet
peri	around	perimeter
ec, ex	out of	eccentric
mono	one, alone	monotone
poly	many	polygamy

For practice, insert in the space in front of the words below the appropriate Greek prefix which is the equivalent for the word or words in parentheses. Then write the word in the space provided at the right. Check with the words on page 222 in the Appendix.

1. _____chronize (together) _____

2. _____scope (around) _____

3. _____gram (before) _____

4. _____meter (through) _____

5. _____gamy (one) _____

6. _____phet (before) _____

7. _____tax (together) _____

8. _____tony (one) _____

9. _____toxin (against) _____

10. _____logue (away from, off) _____

SUFFIXES

Like the prefixes, suffixes frequently have definite meanings; *cle, icle, cule, et, ette, kin, ling,* and *let,* for example, all mean smaller or lesser. Study the noun suffixes which follow.[3] Note the suffix proper and then the whole word.

NOUN SUFFIX	EXAMPLE
ac	maniac, hypochondriac
ace	populace, menace, furnace
acy	fallacy, privacy, aristocracy
ade	promenade, serenade, barricade
age	baggage, plumage, salvage
aire	millionaire, legionnaire
al	arrival, festival, trial
an	artisan, Republican, American
ance	abundance, luxuriance, entrance
ancy	constancy, pregnancy, flippancy
ant	confidant, applicant, covenant
ar	liar, vicar, calendar, commissar
ard	laggard, drunkard, standard
ary	granary, dispensary, dictionary
asm	enthusiasm, pleonasm, iconoclasm
ate	acetate, mandate, candidate
cy	normalcy, democracy, aristocracy
dom	kingdom, dukedom, freedom
e	naïveté, fiancé, finale
eau	portmanteau, château
ee	pongee, filigree, refugee
eer	volunteer, privateer, engineer
en	kitten, mitten, heathen, citizen
ence	confidence, independence
ency	emergency, despondency
end	dividend, minuend, legend
ent	correspondent, rodent, assent
er	customer, farmer, meter
ery	artillery, finery, stationery
ese	Portuguese, Genoese, Chinese
ess	goddess, abbess, huntress
et	cadet, blanket, bassinet
ette	cigarette, lorgnette, vignette
ety	propriety, piety, society
eur	chauffeur, amateur, connoisseur
hood	manhood, priesthood, likelihood

NOUN SUFFIX	EXAMPLE
ial	credential, official
ian	physician, mortician, barbarian
ice	prejudice, armistice, avarice
ics	aesthetics, dietetics, statistics
ide	cyanide, bromide
ier	premier, chiffonier, cashier
ine	machine, heroine, gasoline
ion	million, possession, confession
is	basis, emphasis, thesis, crisis
ism	rationalism, capitalism, idealism
ist	socialist, dentist, scientist
ite	socialite, bauxite, granite
itis	arthritis, appendicitis, neuritis
ity	creativity, ability, integrity
ive	motive, detective, directive
kin	bodkin, lambkin, manikin
le	girdle, thimble
let	starlet, gauntlet, eyelet
ling	stripling, gosling, duckling
ment	allotment, government
ness	goodness, ugliness, kindness
ock	bullock, hassock, hillock
oir	reservoir, abattoir, choir
on	silicon, electron
ory	conservatory, category
or	supervisor, motor, splendor
os	pathos, ethos, cosmos
ry	husbandry, cavalry, foundry
ship	kinship, lordship, friendship
sion	erosion, compulsion, expansion
ster	youngster, roadster, huckster
t	complaint, weight, height
tain	captain, chieftain, fountain
th	width, length, growth
tion	mention, formation, composition
trix	executrix, aviatrix
try	deviltry, casuistry
tude	attitude, fortitude, certitude
ty	novelty, specialty, certainty
ule	capsule, globule, molecule
um	curriculum, chromium, linoleum

Noun suffix	Example
ure	agriculture, furniture, failure
us	chorus, alumnus, sinus
y	dolly, laundry, facility

The suffixes which characteristically go with verbs are fewer in number, perhaps, than the noun suffixes. Notice the following verb suffixes and the examples:

Verb Suffix	Example
ate	contemplate, fascinate, syncopate
en	listen, fasten, open, glisten
esce	acquiesce, coalesce, effervesce
ify	ratify, falsify, glorify, fortify
ize	rationalize, specialize, nationalize

Some endings, such as *ly* and *ward*, are, generally speaking, adverb suffixes.[4] Study the following suffixes, note the examples. Find likenesses and differences between them.

Adverb Suffix	Example
ly	slowly, rapidly, speedily
time	anytime, sometime, everytime
ward	homeward, forward, backward
ways	sideways
where	anywhere, somewhere, nowhere
wise	timewise, crosswise
way	anyway
day	someday
long	headlong
meal	piecemeal
place	anyplace
side	beside

In addition to the noun, verb, and adverb suffixes, there are adjective suffixes.[5] Study the following adjective suffixes. Note the likenesses and differences among adverb, noun, verb, and adjective suffixes.

Adjective Suffix	Example
able	sociable, amenable, navigable
ac	ammoniac

Adjective Suffix	Example
al	congenital, heretical
an	urban, German
ant	abundant, important, reluctant
ar	similar, consular
ary	arbitrary, exemplary, primary
ate	separate, graduate
ed	contented
en	golden, craven
ent	competent, diligent, impatient
eous	advantageous
ese	Chinese
esque	grotesque
ful	grateful
ial	special
ian	Italian, Grecian
ible	horrible, visible, audible
ic	fantastic
ical	philosophical
id	humid
ile	fragile
ing	seeing
ine	bovine, equine, canine
ious	pretentious, religious
ish	mannish, stylish
ite	infinite
ive	relative
less	sinless
like	homelike
ly	divinely
ory	sensory
ose	verbose
ous	continuous
some	handsome
th	ninth
y	heavy

Below is an exercise in adding noun, verb, adjective, or adverb suffixes. In the example that has been worked out, you are given orig____. To this you add *in* for the noun. You add *ate* for the verb. You add *al* for an adjective. To the adjective form you add *ly* for the adverb. Fill in the verb, adjective, and adverb suffix forms for each word. Check with page 222 in the Appendix.

Noun	Verb	Adjective	Adverb
1. origin	originate	original	originally
2. inclusion			
3. continuation			
4. abomination			
5. stupidity			
6. laborer			
7. glory			
8. decision			
9. contention			
10. dramatization			
11. conclusion			
12. critic			

Words ending in ABLE and IBLE. The addition of suffixes is quite scientific, as you have seen. The process of affixing follows established linguistic principles, which are helpful to the successful speller. Now that you are conscious of word formation, you are ready to go on to the complicated problems of *able* and *ible*.

Words ending in *able* and *ible* illustrate the point that the pronunciation of a word may deceive and mislead you in spelling it. In fact, the last syllables of the two words *detestable* and *conbustible* are identical in pronunciation, yet one we write with *able,* the other with *ible.* The answer for this spelling pecularity often lies in the Latin derivation of the words. Only a scholar of Latin would be able to unlock the secret, and then only for Latin scholars. Fortunately, there are circumstances which favor an ambitious speller even if he has never studied Latin. The encouraging fact is that, with some exceptions, most *able* and *ible* words fall into patterns you can learn. And if you become familiar with the several revealing characteristics of the *able* and *ible* words, you have a chance for success in handling these two troublesome suffixes: [6]

Words ending in ABLE

The following tests will be helpful in determining which words are spelled *able.*

1. The *whole word* test. First, note the following words:

adapt able	favor able
agree able	impression able
avail able	lament able
break able	perish able
change able	predict able
correct able	prefer able
credit able	read able
depend able	suit able
detect able	work able

Now see what happens when you take away the *able.* You will observe in each case that you have a complete word. You have then a test for an *able* word. Drop the *able* in each case and a full word is left.

2. The *whole word minus e* test. Note the following words: *final -e rule*

adorable	movable
blamable	presumable
curable	probable
deplorable	receivable
endurable	valuable

Now drop the *able,* and you have a full word that lacks only a final e. Thus you have the second test for the *able* words. Forms usually are spelled with an *able* if the root needs only a final e to be a full word.

3. The *y or i* test. Note the following words:

appreciable	justifiable
compliable	pitiable
deniable	reliable
fortifiable	sociable

Now remove the *able,* and note that the root ends in *i* or that the original ends in *y.*

4. *The long a test.* The root appears in other words formed on the long *a* sound. Note the following words:

calculable	mutable
demonstrable	navigable
estimable	tolerable
inflammable	reparable
irritable	vegetable

5. *The hard c or g test.* The root ends in hard *c* (as in *cold*) or hard *g* (as in *gold*). Observe the following words:

applicable	impracticable	irrigable
despicable	indefatigable	
impeccable	revocable	

6. *Exceptions.* You know that if a word meets the whole word test, the *y* or *i* test, the long *a* test, or the hard *c* or *g* test, it will add able. The following words are exceptions, however. Visualize each word. Study each word and then write it in the blank provided.

1. affable _____	11. ineffable _____
2. amenable _____	12. inevitable _____
3. arable _____	13. inexorable _____
4. capable _____	14. inscrutable _____
5. controllable _____	15. inseparable _____
6. culpable _____	16. insuperable _____
7. equitable _____	17. irrevocable _____
8. formidable _____	18. malleable _____
9. hospitable _____	19. memorable _____
10. indomitable _____	

Words ending in IBLE. With *ible* words you may apply similar tests:

1. *The incomplete word test.* The ending is usually *ible* if the root is not a full word. This rule is true about 98 percent of the time.

admissible	indivisible
credible	infallible
compatible	permissible
comprehensible	plausible
edible	possible
feasible	reversible
terrible	susceptible
horrible	visible
impossible	

2. *The ion test.* The ending is usually *ible* if *ion* may be added directly to the end of the word.

access	accession	accessible
collect	collection	collectible
corrupt	corruption	corruptible
deduct	deduction	deductible
instruct	instruction	instructible
digest	digestion	digestible
exhaust	exhaustion	exhaustible
impress	impression	impressible
percept	perception	perceptible
perfect	perfection	perfectible

Exceptions to this rule are *correctable, detectable,* and *predictable.*

3. *The ns root test.* If the root ends in *ns or ss,* the ending will likely be *ible.*

admissible	permissible
comprehensible	repressible
defensible	responsible
irreprehensible	sensible

4. *The soft c or g test.* If the base, root, or stem ends in soft *c* (as in *cent*) or soft *g* (as in *gem*), the suffix will more than likely be *ible.*

coercible	enforcible	negligible
convincible	incorrigible	reducible
crucible	intelligible	seducible
deducible	invincible	tangible
eligible	legible	

Words ending in ANCE, ENCE, ANT, and ENT. Two of the most troublesome groups of words in English spelling are those ending in *ance* and *ant* and *ence* and *ent*. Most of them are nouns and adjectives derived from verbs of different Latin conjugations, whose vowel signs are generally represented in these endings. The predominating vowel of the first conjugation in Latin was *a*. The other conjugation vowel which has survived is *e*. Our pronunciation will not help distinguish between the two endings, since both get the neutral vowel *schwa*, as in *defendent*. There is a slight tendency to level the two in the direction of the ending with *e*, but for the present about all we can do is (a) learn the individual forms by memory, (b) consult the dictionary frequently, or (c) take a chance on several tests of the letters.

Words ending in ENCE. *1. Vowel + r verb test.* Look to see whether the word is a verb ending in an *r* preceded by a vowel and is accented on the last syllable. If it fulfills these conditions, it forms its noun with *ence*. For example, *confér, cónference*. The accent shifts to a preceding syllable, and the *r* remains single before *-ence*. But in *occúr, occúrrence*, the accent is retained as in the original word, and the *r* is doubled before *-ence*.

PRACTICE EXERCISE

Underline the words in which the accented syllable of the original word is retained. Consult page 222 in the Appendix for the answers.

1. abhorrence
2. concurrence
3. conference
4. deference
5. deterrence
6. incurrence
7. inference
8. preference
9. recurrence
10. reference

2. The sist or xist test. If the word ends in *sist* or *xist*, the ending will likely be *ence*. For example, *subsistence*. *Resistance* is an exception to this rule.

PRACTICE EXERCISE

Underline the roots ending in *sist* or *xist*.

existence   persistence   consistence
insistence   subsistence

3. The ci test. If the root ends in a *ci* which has a *sh* sound or an *i* which has an *e* sound, the suffix will be *ence*.

PRACTICE EXERCISE

In the following words, underline the *ci* having a *sh* sound, or the *i* having an *e* sound.

efficiency	insufficiency	obedience
conscience	sufficiency	experience
	proficiency	

Words ending in -TION, -ATION. The suffixes *-ion, -tion,* and *-ation* cause students considerable trouble. The following tests may be helpful.

1. *The whole word test.* First, note the following words.

adoption	distortion	perception
assertion	election	refraction
collection	exemption	production
conviction	exhaustion	suggestion
corruption	extraction	
digestion	instruction	

Now see what happens when you take away *-ion.* You will observe in each case that you have a complete word.

PRACTICE EXERCISE

For each of the following complete words, supply the ending *-ation.*

accredit _____	consider_____
adapt_____	lament _____
argument _____	reform _____
confront _____	

2. *The whole word minus e test.* Note the following words and observe that *-tion* always follows a long vowel.

acceleration	concentration	irritation
appreciation	education	navigation
calculation	elimination	perforation
certification	imitation	toleration

collation	implication	vegetation
communication	indication	violation
complication	irrigation	

Drop the -ion, and you have a full word that lacks only the final e. Thus you have a second test for -ion words.

PRACTICE EXERCISE

Some forms are spelled with an -ation if the root needs only a final e to be a full word. For each of the following words lacking the final e, supply the ending -ation.

ador_____	memoriz _____
convers_____	naturaliz _____
determin_____	observ _____
imagin_____	prepar _____

Words ending in -SION. If you are forced to choose between -tion and -sion, take a chance on -sion, which is the most common spelling. The following tests will be helpful with the suffix -sion.

1. *The whole word test.* The suffix -ion may be added directly to words ending in ss, which follows a short vowel.

accession	impression
digression	obsession
discussion	procession
expression	profession

2. *Root tests*

   a. Note the *de* in the following words:

collide—collision	explode—explosion
conclude—conclusion	persuade—persuasion
divide—division	pervade—pervasion
evade—evasion	

   b. Observe the *nd* and the *ns*.

comprehend—comprehension	reprehend—reprehension
extend—extension	tend—tension
pretend—pretension	

c. Give attention to the root ending in rt.

convert—conversion
divert—diversion
adverse—aversion
Exceptions: *desert, desertion; insert, insertion*

d. Note whether the root ends in se.

immerse—immersion
revise—revision
tense—tension

Words ending in ANCE.

1. *The hard c or g test.* If the root ends in a hard c or g, the suffix will be *ance.* Examples are *significance* and *extravagance.*

2. *The long a test.* Consider whether the root has a long *a* in a related word. For example, *ambulance* is related to *ambulatory.* In such words the suffix will be *ance.*

PRACTICE EXERCISE
For each of the following words write the related word having a long *a* sound. Consult page 222 in the Appendix for the answers.

1. acceptance _____   6. radiance _____

2. dominance _____   7. observance _____

3. importance _____   8. significance _____

4. substance _____   9. tolerance _____

5. jubilance _____   10. variance _____

Words Ending in ARY and ERY. The *ary-ery* problem is really quite simple. There are some three hundred words that end in *ary.* There are a few that end in *ery.* Seven of these pose no problem because they are seldom misspelled.[7] They are:

artillery	celery	flattery	refinery
bakery	finery	very	

Seven more ery words are commonly misspelled. You should study them carefully. They are:

cemetery	distillery	millinery	stationery
confectionery	dysentery	monastery	

PRACTICE EXERCISE

It helps to know that words ending in ary are adjectives and nouns indicating persons and things. For example, secondary and missionary, whereas those ending in ery are abstract nouns; for example, flattery. Complete the following words by supplying the appropriate ending:

arbitr _____   infirm _____

auxili _____   judici _____

bound_____   liter_____

centen _____   prelimin_____

contempor_____   reaction _____

diction _____   secret _____

diet _____   solit_____

element _____   tempor _____

evolution _____   tribut _____

exempl_____   vision _____

honor _____   vocabul _____

imagin _____   volunt_____

Words ending in AR, ER, and OR. The suffixes ar, er, and or mean the same thing—the agent, the one who, the person who. There is really no text or device that will help you with these words. The suffix or is the most common, however. It is important to study the ar, er, and or words you will use most frequently. They are [8]

ar

beggar	collar	peculiar	scholar
bursar	dollar	polar	similar
calendar	familiar	registrar	singular
circular	grammar	regular	vicar

er

adjuster	comptroller	laborer	purchaser
advertiser	consumer	lawyer	receiver
adviser	designer	ledger	shipper
amplifier	employer	manager	stenographer
appraiser	eraser	manufacturer	subscriber
beginner	farmer	prisoner	teacher
bookkeeper	foreigner	merger	teller
caterer	interpreter	officer	tiller
character	jeweler	passenger	treasurer
			writer

or

accelerator	counselor	governor	solicitor
actor	creditor	incinerator	spectator
administrator	debtor	indicator	sponsor
auditor	depositor	inferior	successor
author	dictator	inventor	superior
aviator	distributor	investigator	supervisor
bachelor	doctor	janitor	surveyor
calculator	duplicator	operator	survivor
collector	editor	proprietor	tabulator
commentator	educator	protector	tailor
competitor	elevator	radiator	tractor
conductor	emperor	realtor	traitor
contractor	escalator	refrigerator	vigor

Words ending in ISE, IZE, and YZE. More than four hundred words end with these three suffixes. What complicates the problem is that you can't tell any difference in the pronunciation of the three endings. Hence you cannot rely on your ear to help you. You will find it helpful to remember that with several exceptions, such as *apologize*, the *ize* verbs have nouns in *ization: dramatize, dramatization.* You can make some progress, however, through a process of elimination.[9]

1. *Testing by elimination:*

    Step 1.   First, eliminate the only two words that end in *yze: analyze* and *paralyze*.

    Step 2.   Eliminate a few words ending in *cise: incise, exercise, excise, exorcise, circumcise.*

Step 3.   Eliminate words ending in *guise*, such as *disguise*.

Step 4.   And leave out the three words ending in *mise*: *surmise, demise, compromise*.

Step 5.   You now eliminate several words ending in *prise*: *enterprise, surprise, comprise, apprise*. Exception: *prize*.

Step 6.   You eliminate a *rise* word: *sunrise*.

Step 7.   Now you eliminate several words ending in *vise*: *advise, devise, improvise, revise, supervise*.

Step 8.   Next, eliminate a few words ending in *wise*: *clockwise, likewise, lengthwise, otherwise, sidewise*.

Step 9.   Observe these last words that do not fall into any group, study them carefully:

advertise   chastise   franchise

despise   merchandise

After all this elimination, you have left approximately four hundred words ending in *ize*, and that figure represents about 90 percent of the words in this group.

PRACTICE EXERCISE

Complete the following words by writing in the *ise, ize,* or *yze.* Consult page 222 in the Appendix for the answers.

1. vulcan _____   11. patron _____

2. civil _____   12. penal _____

3. alphabet _____   13. organ _____

4. amorti _____   14. pulver _____

5. paralog _____   15. desp _____

6. general _____   16. rational _____

7. harmon _____   17. apolog _____

8. hypnot_____   18. atom _____

9. idol _____   19. author _____

10. compr _____   20. franch _____

Words ending in EFY and IFY. In learning these words you follow the same process of elimination. There are only four words that end in *efy* and they are liquefy, putrefy, rarefy, and stupefy. Learn these four exceptions and your problems with *efy* and *ify* are behind you.

Words ending in SEDE, CEDE, and CEED. This spelling problem again is easily solved by elimination.

1. Eliminate the three words ending in *ceed*: *exceed, proceed, succeed*.
2. Eliminate the one word ending in *sede*: *supersede*.
3. Note that *cede* is a word in itself. This happens to be the commonest form in words ending with this sound. And at that, there are only six of them:

accede	precede
concede	recede
intercede	secede

If you have mastered the rules in our chapter on structuring to this point, you already have a good idea of what structuring is. Structuring requires learning the methods by which words have traditionally been compounded in the English language and the practices which govern the addition of the common suffixes and prefixes to them. It is one of the most useful methods we have, and if you learn structuring thoroughly, you won't have far to go to become a superior speller.

While we're studying language rules of this kind, let's include a few more—the rules governing *ie* and *ei*, the rules for the final *e*, and the rules for doubling consonants.

EI or IE? Although there is much ado about the confusion in the use of *ie* and *ei*, there is a simple rule that takes care of all cases.

> Write *i* before *e*
> Except after *c*
> Or when sounded like *a*
> As in *neighbor* and *weigh;*
> And except *seize* and *seizure*
> And also *leisure,*
> *Weird, height,* and *either,*
> *Forfeit* and *neither.*

Test one. Observe whether the *ei* or *ie* is sounded like a long *e*, as in complete. Note the words *achieve, priest,* and *field* for the long *e* sound. Now note *ceiling* and *deceive* for the long *e* sound after *c*. You may test by the jingle:

> When sounded long *e*
> Write *i* before *e*
> Except after *c*.

Five exceptions to this part of the rule are *either, neither, leisure, seize,* and *weird.* The exceptional five words that have the long *e* sound are found in the sentence: "Either or neither financier seized a weird species of leisure."

Test two. Observe that the *ei* is sounded like *ay* as in *weigh.* The following words fit this pattern:

deign	inveigle	surveillance
eight	reign	veil
feign	reindeer	vein
freight	skein	weigh
inveigh	sleigh	weight

Note the long *a* sound in *reign.* Although the long *a* sound is not apparent in *foreign, sovereign, sovereignty,* you may associate these words in the sentence: "The *foreign sovereign reigned,* and the *sovereignty* is called a *reign.*"

Test three. Observe that the *ei* is sounded as long *i* in two words: height and sleight.

Below is a diagram summarizing the ei-ie rules.

DIAGRAM FOR TESTING **IE-EI** WORDS

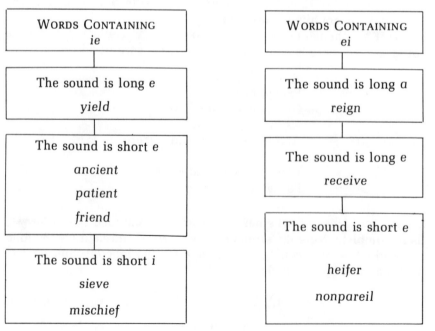

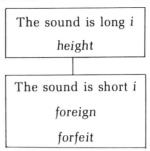

How and when to drop the final E. The rules for the final e are probably the best known of all spelling rules. Successful spellers know them because they are the most useful. The rules concern words ending in a silent or mute e, which is found at the end of a word and which is not sounded as a separate syllable. *Move, like, prove,* and *make* are examples of about nine hundred such words in the English language. Poor spellers make errors like this: *comeing, moveing, likeing.* The following tests will help you avoid such errors:

Test one. Observe the word that ends in e, such as *come, move,* or *desire.* Drop the e before you add a suffix beginning with a vowel. For example, *mover, movable, moving.*

Test two. Observe the dozen or so exceptions to the final e rule—a very small number in comparison to the number of words to which the rule applies:

1. Observe the words ending in ce or ge. Keep the e when adding a suffix beginning with a vowel because the e is needed to keep the sound of the soft g or c. For example, *noticeable* and *vengeance.*
2. If the suffix begins with i in a word ending ce or ge, drop the e because a g or c followed by i is soft. For example, *noticing* and *raging.*
3. Note whether any confusion of words arises because of adding the suffix. For example, *singing* and *singeing, dying* and *dyeing.*
4. There are four exceptions to these rules: *once, only, ninth,* and *wholly.*

PRACTICE EXERCISE

Form new words in the following examples. Then write the word in the space provided.

A

1. lose + ing _____   11. notice + ing _____

2. shine + ing _____   12. practice + ing _____

3. write + ing _____   13. relieve + ing _____

4. advise + ing _____   14. accuse + ing _____

5. care + ing _____   15. decide + ing _____

6. challenge + ing _____ 16. suppose + ing _____

7. compete + ing _____   17. dine + ing _____

8. complete + ing _____ 18. divide + ing _____

9. perceive + ing _____ 19. trace + ing _____

10. oppose + ing _____

B

1. achieve + ing _____   6. trace + able _____

2. believe + able _____ 7. service + able _____

3. achieve + ment _____ 8. taste + ful _____

4. survive + al _____   9. use + ful _____

5. pronounce + ment _____ 10. manage + ment _____

How to double the consonant.   To double or not to double the consonant when adding a suffix? This is a question that plagues many a
speller. Does *committed* have two t's? Why does *traveling* have one
l, while *compelling* has two *l*'s? The rule for doubling is sure to help
you in your dilemma.

Test for doubling. Observe whether the word is a monosyllable
ending in a single consonant preceded by a single vowel. An example
is the word *run*. If so, double the consonant before adding a suffix
beginning with a vowel. For example, *runner* and *running*.

PRACTICE EXERCISE

Look over the following list and check those words to which the rule
applies. Consult page 222 in the Appendix.

1. trim	6. differ
2. grin	7. forgive
3. look	8. help
4. scrub	9. rest
5. chip	10. nod

Before going any further see whether you have checked five words. If you have, you probably checked them correctly. If you wish to verify your answers, turn to the key on page 222.

You, like the well-educated gentleman of whom Ruskin wrote, now know more about how words are structured and how the parts of the word, the roots, the prefixes, and the suffixes, point up definite meaning. Structuring is a flexible method for creating names of new inventions, new scientific terms, and new sociological expressions. One who knows the elementary principles of compounding words can structure and spell the many words that occur in everyday life.

You have come a long way in your study of the linguistics approach to spelling mastery. You know the exact meaning of many Greek and Latin prefixes. You know the meaning of about two hundred Latin roots. And you have used the tests for adding the suffixes such as able, ible, ar, er, or, ance, ence, ary, and ery. Now, you can eliminate much of the guesswork in spelling. But since practice is important in spelling—and so is review—we may take some time for practice in and review of structuring.

Review Exercise I. Among the problem suffixes are able and ible. You have learned that an analysis of the word, related words, and pronunciation can be clues that tell whether the suffix is able or ible. To see whether you are reducing your guessing and the margin of error, supply the appropriate letter in each of the words which follow. After supplying the letters, consult page 222 in the Appendix.

1. accept_ble	9. desir_ble
2. terr_ble	10. depend_ble
3. revers_ble	11. defens_ble
4. memor_ble	12. siz_ble
5. permiss_ble	13. avail_ble
6. irrit_ble	14. admiss_ble
7. excit_ble	15. aud_ble
8. flex_ble	

Review Exercise II. If you are successful in handling the two most troublesome suffixes, *ance* and *ence,* you have some evidence of your progress in spelling. Here, too, related words and pronunciation are important clues. Given the words that follow, supply the appropriate letter and then check your answers with the Appendix, page 222.

1. exist_nce	9. accept_nce
2. guid_nce	10. acquaint_nce
3. perform_nce	11. pres_nce
4. excell_nce	12. occurr_nce
5. abund_nce	13. intellig_nce
6. audi_nce	14. experi_nce
7. consci_nce	15. mainten_nce
8. conveni_nce	

Review Exercise III. See whether you can add the appropriate suffix—*ar, er,* or *or*—to the following words. The answers appear on page 222 in the Appendix.

1. schol__	11. begg__
2. lawy__	12. debt__
3. passeng__	13. dictat__
4. vic__	14. beginn__
5. tell__	15. govern__
6. stenograph__	16. tail__
7. supervis__	17. employ__
8. educat__	18. realt__
9. interpret__	19. teach__
10. writ__	20. contract__

Review Exercise IV. Write the letter *c* after the following words that are correctly spelled. If a word is incorrect, write the correct form in the appropriate space. Check the answers on page 222 in the Appendix.

1. paralize_____
2. advertise_____
3. chastise_____
4. sunrise_____
5. otherwise_____
6. disguise_____
7. analize_____
8. prize_____
9. exercise_____
10. apprize_____

11. surmise_____
12. fertilize_____
13. civilize_____
14. legalize_____
15. sterilize_____
16. criticize_____
17. capitalise_____
18. advise_____
19. compromise_____
20. vulcanize_____

Review Exercise V. The words ending in *ary* and *ery* are easier than you think. Keeping in mind the seven troublemakers, supply the *a* or the *e* in the following words. The answers are found on page 222 in the Appendix.

1. auxili_ry
2. cemet_ry
3. bak_ry
4. cel_ry
5. infirm_ry

6. imagin_ry
7. secret_ry
8. element_ry
9. vocabul_ry
10. volunt_ry

Review Exercise VI. Let's see whether you are free from double trouble. Note the pattern *drip, dripped, dripping.* Note, too, *insult, insulted, insulting.* Now write the letter *c* after the following words that are correct. If a word is incorrect, write the correct form. The answers are on page 222 in the Appendix.

1. equiped_____
2. omitting_____
3. traveled_____
4. refered_____
5. beginning_____

6. controling_____
7. compeling_____
8. appealed_____
9. dropping_____
10. deterring_____

Review Exercise VII. Insert in the appropriate space the Latin or Greek prefix which translates the English word in parenthesis. Write the entire word in the space provided and check your answers with page 222 in the Appendix.

1. _____script (after) _____

2. _____logue (down, against) _____

3. _____phone (far) _____

4. _____phony (together)_____

5. _____navigate (around) _____

6. _____satisfaction (apart) _____

7. _____fit (well) _____

8. _____theism (many) _____

9. _____dict (before) _____

10. _____rupt (between) _____

Review Exercise VIII. After you have studied the *ie* and *ei* chart, add the missing letters in the sentences that follow. The answers are on page 222 in the Appendix.

1. N__ther w__rd for__gn counterf__ters in th__r l__sure s__zed __ther h__rs or h__fers from the h__ghts.

2. I rec__ved __ght rec__pts for the fr__ght that the n__ghbor sent.

3. The misch__vous bel__f of the cash__r y__lded a f__rce penalty.

4. The ch__f's fr__nd was rel__ved when she saw the th__f running through the f__ld.

5. My n__ce was certain that a handkerch__f would help rel__ve her gr__f.

6. The good n__ghbor held the r__ns while the children shr__ked and stood up in the sl__gh.

7. The sk__ns of yarn w__gh as much as a p__ce of cloth.

8. When the horses n__gh, they strain th__r v__ns.

9. You perc__ve that you are having a br__f rev__w.

10. The w__ght of the plaster in the c__ling is dec__ving.

Review Exercise IX. We must remember that there are many Greek roots that are recognizable in English words. The following five are among the important ones. Write in the appropriate space the Latin equivalent of the Greek root. Check your answers with page 223 in the Appendix.

GREEK ROOT	MEANING	LATIN EQUIVALENT
1. scope	see	_____
2. graph	write	_____
3. pod	foot	_____
4. the	god	_____
5. hydr	water	_____

Review Exercise X. Now try this exercise indicating English words derived from the Greek forms that follow. The answers are in the Appendix, page 223. Remember that, by its Greek derivation, the suffix *-ology* means the study or science of something.

GREEK WORD	MEANING	THE ENGLISH WORD FOR
1. bio	life	the study of life is _____
2. geo	earth	the study of the earth is _____
3. zo	animal	the study of animals is _____
4. cosm	universe	the study of the universe is _____
5. anthrop	man	the study of man is _____

We have now made a thorough review of what you have learned so far. Let's now proceed to another method of attack.

PART THREE
What Words
and
How to
Spell Them?

CHAPTER IX

Phonemes and Graphemes: A Final Approach

They spell it Vinci and pronounce it Vinchy; foreigners always spell better than they pronounce.

MARK TWAIN

Our system of writing—the alphabet—is, in relation to the whole of man's history, a comparatively modern invention. Early history was recorded in a sequence of pictures called picture writing. A picture of a house, B, meant house, A meant an ox, D meant a door, and so on. There was a symbol for every word in the language, and this meant as many as 10,000 to 20,000 symbols. The Chinese system is still based on this principle, with some modifications. Systems of this sort have certain advantages, the chief of which is that they are largely independent of pronunciation.

Eventually the Egyptians discovered that a symbol could stand for a sound. Although the Egyptians had the idea of an alphabet, they never learned to use one. During the three hundred years of their supremacy, the Phoenicians, a Semitic nation of traders who inhabited a narrow strip of land along the western coast of Palestine, borrowed the alphabet from the Egyptians. The Phoenicians improved the Egyptian phonetic system and transmitted it to the Hebrews and the Greeks. This close connection between the Greek and Hebrew alphabets shows up in our word *alphabet,* composed of the first two letters of the Greek alphabet, *alpha* and *beta,* which correspond to *aleph* and *beth* in the language of the Hebrews.

The Phoenicians introduced the alphabet to the Greeks, who improved upon this communication instrument. Whereas the Egyptian and Semitic alphabets lacked representation of the vowels, the Greeks supplied them and completed the alphabet. Hence the Greeks were the first people to form and to use a true alphabet. Our own alphabet is a product of several Mediterranean civilizations—Egyptian, Mesopotamian, Phoenician, Arabic, Greek, Hebrew, and Roman.

During the 3,500 years since the idea of the alphabet was conceived, many alphabets have come into existence, but the Greek alphabet has held first place among all the symbol systems. Language authority Margaret M. Bryant tells us that each of the forty or more Greek city-states had its own alphabet. It was the Ionian Greek alphabet, however, that the Athenians accepted in 483 B.C. It was the Ionian that became the basis of the Coptic alphabet early in the Christian era, and of the Cyrillic or Slavonic alphabet about A.D. 900. The Cyrillic, as we know, consists of the letters in which Russian is written. It was the Chalcidian, another Greek alphabet, that became the basis for the Roman borrowing.

The story of the alphabet from pictures to symbols is long, fascinating, and revealing—revealing man's longing to communicate with his fellowman, and man's penchant for streamlining and intellectualizing communication.

With the alphabet, things were easier. All you had to learn was the letter system. When you wanted to write a word, all you had to do was to determine the sounds and put the appropriate letters on paper.

Alphabets are rather readily adaptable to other languages besides those for which they were originally developed. For example, our Roman alphabet, devised for Latin, has been adopted by most of the languages of western Europe and the New World. Though it is superior to many Oriental alphabets, it leaves much to be desired in indicating sounds. For one thing, our alphabet lacks signs for many sounds—for example, the initial consonants of this and thick, and the final sound of song. Furthermore, our alphabet has only five vowel letters, while many languages have a much larger number.[1]

Glancing back into history, we learn that people depended only upon their ears in their spelling and that they recorded phonemes. Thus, writing originally was purely phonetical. In due time, however, scribes began to imitate the spelling of those whose manuscripts they copied, and the spelling of their teachers and elders. Since the spoken-word forms inevitably change, the older, extinct forms of speech were written long after they had ceased to be heard by human ears. Hence traditional spelling, which is found in every language with a literary history, has become almost almighty since the invention of the printing press.[2] Obviously modern English orthography represents a pronunciation of many eras and of many foreign words. Our spelling includes words of Old English origin (milk), words of Greek and Latin origin (cosmonaut), words of Swedish origin (smorgasbord).

Importance of the alphabet. For some people the alphabet seemed of divine origin. The name for the Sanskrit alphabet is *Devanagari*, which means "pertaining to the abode of the gods."[3]

The alphabet represents an extremely practical and sophisticated way of transcribing the sounds of a language. Credit for its invention is usually given to the Phoenicians, who around 1500 B.C. adapted twenty-two signs from the Egyptian writing system to the sounds of their own language. The signs stood only for consonants. The Greeks, who traded with the Phoenicians, borrowed these signs to form the Greek alphabet. Since the Phoenician alphabet had more consonants than the Greeks needed, the Greeks used the extra signs to stand for vowels, giving them a full alphabet. From the Greek alphabet comes the Roman alphabet used by Western people today. Chinese, which uses thousands of signs to stand for words, is the only major language that does not have an alphabetic system of writing.

The present alphabet does not have separate signs for every English sound, and some signs stand for more than one sound. As a result, there have been calls for a new alphabet from time to time, one that would accurately match sounds with signs. The likelihood that such an alphabet would be adopted is very slim. To do so, a new and more complex writing system would have to be put in place. Laws, contracts, and treaties would have to be rewritten. And whose pronunciations would this alphabet transcribe? It would seem that the present alphabet is here to stay, at least as far as anyone can tell now.[4]

Linguists and spelling. In recent years the linguists have succeeded to some extent in reducing English to a system. The linguist says to the speller, "Let's reverse the method of learning to spell. Instead of looking at the letters to be pronounced, let's look at the sounds to be spelled." So the linguist starts with a sound, for example, the phoneme *i*. Next he collects words having that sound: habit, easily, been, English, build, busy, bonnie, pulley, myth, women, chamois. He notes the different spellings for the sound and he looks for patterns in which these spellings occur.[5]

The speller who approaches spelling according to this method needs to understand the terms *phoneme* and *grapheme*. A phoneme is a unit of speech sound. H. A. Gleason, in *An Introduction to Descriptive Linguistics,* writes: "A phoneme is the minimum feature of the expression system of a spoken language." Robert A. Hall, Jr., defines a phoneme as a significant unit of speech sound. A grapheme is a unit of visual shape. A grapheme is a letter or a symbol. The twenty-six letters of our alphabet constitute our basic graphemic units. Graphemes can be either simple or compound. So can phonemes. Examples of double graphemes are *th,* and *ng,* two graphemes functioning as one. In traditional spelling terminology we called such combinations digraphs. Examples of other double graphemes are *ay, pp, sh,* and *mm.*

Our spelling has some rhyme and reason in terms of the generalizations linguists have discovered concerning the relationship between phonemes and graphemes. The generalizations follow this pattern. In the chart you see below, some English phonemes are represented by a number of graphemes. You will find it profitable to study the list of phonemes, their corresponding graphemes, and words illustrating the various sounds and spellings. You will note that the phonemes are sometimes represented by special linguistic symbols.

PHONEME AND GRAPHEME CORRELATION: VOWELS[6]

PHONEMES	GRAPHEMES	EXAMPLES
i	i, ie, e, ia, ee, o, u, y, ui, ois, ey	hit, sieve, England, marriage, been, women, busy, myth, build, chamois, honey
e	e, ea, a, ai, ay, eo, oe, ie, ei, ae	met, feather, any, said, says, leopard, foetid, friend, heifer, aesthetic
ae	a, ai, ay, au, i	hat, plaid, prayer, laughter, meringue
u	oo, u, ou, o	book, put, could, wolf, woman
a	a, o, ea, ow, au	father, rot, heart, knowledge, haul
ɔ	a, aw, o, oo, ou, au, oa, oi	all, raw, off, door, sought, fault, broad, reservoir
ə	u, o, oo, ou, oe	cup, son, flood, couple, does
iy	ea, ee, ie, i, ei, oe, eo, ae, e, ey	sea, meet, believe, machine, deceive, amoeba, people, Caesar, be, key
ey	ai, a, au, ay, ea, ei, ey	aim, late, gauge, dray, break, vein, they
ay	i, y, ie, ei, eye, aye, ai, uy, ye, igh, ui	bite, shy, tie, height, eye, aye, aisle, guy, lye, high, guide
uw	ue, ou, u, ew, ui, o, oe, eu, oo	flue, group, rule, flew, fruit, move, canoe, neuter, woo

| ow | o, oa, ow, ou, oe, ew, eau, au, oo, eo, oh | sole, road, flow, soul, doe, sew, beau, hautboy, brooch, yeoman, oh |
| aew | ou, ow, ough, au | out, now, plough, kraut |

PHONEME AND GRAPHEME CORRELATION: CONSONANTS[7]

PHONEMES	GRAPHEMES	EXAMPLES
p	p, pe, pp, gh	pen, ripe, stopper, hiccough
b	b, be, bb	bed, imbibe, bubble
t	t, te, tt, ed, ght, th, phth	ten, kite, kitten, walked, night, thyme, phthisis
d	d, de, dd, ed	den, ride, ladder, angered, raised
k	k, ke, c, ck, cc, ch, cq, qu, lk, cch, cque	keep, like, cash, back, account, character, acquaint, liquor, folk, bacchanal, sacque
g	g, gg, gu, gh, tg	give, beggar, guard, ghost, mortgage
f	f, fe, ff ph, gh, ft	feel, life, muffin, physics, rough, often
v	v, ve, vv, f	visit, five, flivver, of
θ	th	thin, myth, pathos
$\eth$	th, the	then, scythe
s	s, ss, es, c, ce, sc, sce, st, sch, ps, se	gas, class, lakes, city, office, scenic, fasten, schism, psychiatrist, effervesce, vase
z	z, sc, es, zz, ze, ss, se, s, x	zone, discern, canes, dazzle, daze, possess, rose, criticism, anxiety
$\int$	sh, ti, si, ci, su, sci, ce, se, psh, ch	ship, exertion, mission, special, sugar, conscience, ocean, nauseous, pshaw, machine
t$\int$	ch, t, tch, ti, te	church, natural, patch, question, righteous
3	si, s, zi, z, ge	vision, usual, brazier, azure, rouge
d$_3$	g, ge, dge, je, di, gg	magic, cage, edge, jesuit, soldier, exaggerate
h	h, wh	hill, who
l	l, le, ll	love, gale, lullaby
m	m, me, mm, mn, chm, gm, lm, mb	mile, mime, hammer, solemn, drachm, paradigm, calm, dumb
n	n, ne, nn, gn, kn	nice, line, dinner, gnaw, knife

ŋ	ng, n, ngue	ring, tongue
r	r, re, rr, rh	run, fire, current, rhythm
w	w, u, o	water, quick, choir
hw	wh	whit, white
y	y, gn, j, i, ny	yes, lorgnette, hallelujah, opinion, canyon

The purpose of being familiar with the regular phonemes and graphemes is simple: If you are aware of the different letters that the sounds are spelled with, you will have a better chance of guessing the correct spelling of a word that troubles you. On the following pages there appear lists of words frequently used and misspelled in different professional specialties.[8] The complete word will appear in Column A. In Column B one or more phonemes from the word appear in isolation. In Column C the appropriate grapheme for each phoneme is noted. After studying the entire word, and after noting the specific phonemes and corresponding graphemes, write the word in Column D. Then check it with Column A.

AGRICULTURE

COLUMN A (word)	COLUMN B (phoneme)	COLUMN C (grapheme)	COLUMN D (word to be written)
1. acre	k	c	_____
2. catalyst	i	y	_____
3. cultivate	ey	a	_____
4. dairy	e	ai	_____
5. furrow	r, ow	rr, ow	_____
6. fertilizer	z	z	_____
7. granary	i	y	_____
8. harrow	r	rr	_____
9. incubator	k, b	c, b	_____
10. irrigate	r, ey	rr, a	_____
11. hybrid	ay	y	_____
12. pollination	l, ʃ	ll, ti	_____
13. potato	ə, ey	o, a	_____

| 14. raspberry | z, i | s, y | _____ |
| 15. marketable | a, k | a, k | _____ |

ART

COLUMN A	COLUMN B	COLUMN C	COLUMN D
1. canvas	k, s	c, s	_____
2. cartoon	k, uw	c, oo	_____
3. ceramic	s, k	c, c	_____
4. contour	k, uw	c, ou	_____
5. design	z, n	s, gn	_____
6. easel	iy, z	ea, s	_____
7. exhibit	gz	x	_____
8. frieze	iy, z	ie, z	_____
9. graphic	f, k	ph, c	_____
10. palette	t	tt	_____
11. stencil	s	c	_____
12. wedge	dʒ	dge	_____
13. lithograph	θ, f	th, ph	_____
14. etch	tʃ	tch	_____
15. studio	uw	u	_____

BIOLOGY

COLUMN A	COLUMN B	COLUMN C	COLUMN D
1. alligator	l, ə	ll, o	_____
2. amphibian	f	ph	_____
3. chrysalis	k, i, i	ch, y, i	_____
4. hippopotamus	p, p	pp, p	_____
5. invertebrate	ə, ey	e, a	_____
6. neuron	uw, ɔ	eu, o	_____

7. parasite	ae, s, ay	a, s, i	_____
8. protoplasm	z	s	_____
9. pollen	l	ll	_____
10. rhinoceros	r, s	rh, c	_____
11. species	iy, ʃ	e, ci	_____
12. stamen	ey	a	_____
13. zoology	z, ow, ɔ	z, o, o	_____
14. microscope	k	c	_____
15. crocodile	k, ay	c, i	_____

CHEMISTRY

Column A	Column B	Column C	Column D
1. chemical	k, k	ch, c	_____
2. nucleus	uw, ə	u, u	_____
3. laboratory	b, t, i	b, t, y	_____
4. research	ər	ear	_____
5. benzine	z, iy	z, i	_____
6. naphtha	f, θ	ph, th	_____
7. paraffin	f	ff	_____
8. petroleum	ə, i	e, e	_____
9. bauxite	ɔ, ay	au, i	_____
10. uranium	ey	a	_____
11. molecule	ɔ	o	_____
12. molybdenum	i, ə	y, u	_____
13. valence	ey, s	a, ce	_____
14. synthesis	i, s	y, s	_____
15. cellular	l	ll, l	_____

DENTISTRY

Column A	Column B	Column C	Column D
1. abscess	s	sc	_____
2. brace	s	ce	_____
3. cavity	i	y	_____
4. extraction	$\int$	ti	_____
5. filling	l	ll	_____
6. inflammation	m	mm	_____
7. molar	ow, l	o, l	_____
8. porcelain	s, i	c, ai	_____
9. sensitive	e, i	e, i	_____
10. toothache	uw, k	oo, ch	_____
11. treatment	iy	ea	_____
12. drill	l	ll	_____
13. bridge	d_3	dge	_____
14. bicuspid	iy, k, i	i, c, i	_____
15. acute	t	te	_____

EDUCATION

Column A	Column B	Column C	Column D
1. absence	s, s	s, ce	_____
2. accredited	k, id	cc, ed	_____
3. baccalaureate	k, ɔ	cc, au	_____
4. curriculum	r	rr	_____
5. instruction	$\int$	ti	_____
6. lounge	aew, d_3	ou, ge	_____
7. maladjusted	ə	u	_____

8. registration	$d_3, \int$	g, ti	_____
9. syllabus	i, l	y, ll	_____
10. valedictorian	k	c	_____
11. pupil	p	p	_____
12. guidance	ay	ui	_____
13. intelligence	l, d_3	ll, g	_____
14. college	l, d_3	ll, ge	_____
15. educated	d, k	d, c	_____

ENGINEERING

COLUMN A	COLUMN B	COLUMN C	COLUMN D
1. alignment	ay, n	i, gn	_____
2. calorimeter	i, t	i, t	_____
3. conical	k, k	c, c	_____
4. cylindrical	i, k	y, c	_____
5. density	s, i	s, y	_____
6. hydraulic	ay, ɔ, k	y, au, c	_____
7. logarithmic	g, ð	g, th	_____
8. oblique	k	qu	_____
9. regenerative	d_3	g	_____
10. stress	s	ss	_____
11. tolerance	l	l	_____
12. transistor	z, i	s, i	_____
13. technology	k	ch	_____
14. metallurgy	t, l	t, ll	_____
15. coefficient	k, f, $\int$	c, ff, ci	_____

GEOLOGY

COLUMN A	COLUMN B	COLUMN C	COLUMN D
1. archipelago	k, e	ch, e	_____

2. basalt	s	s	_____
3. glacier	ʃ	ci	_____
4. oxide	ks	x	_____
5. moraine	r, ay	r, ai	_____
6. plateau	ow	eau	_____
7. prairie	e, i	ai, ie	_____
8. seismograph	ay, z, f	ei, s, ph	_____
9. stratosphere	f	ph	_____
10. terrain	r, ey	rr, ai	_____
11. torrid	r	rr	_____
12. tributary	b, e	b, a	_____
13. volcanic	k, n	c, n	_____
14. vortices	s, z	c, s	_____
15. antediluvian	d, l, v	d, l, v	_____

JOURNALISM

COLUMN A	COLUMN B	COLUMN C	COLUMN D
1. advertise	ay, z	i, s	_____
2. column	m	mn	_____
3. correspondent	r, a	rr, o	_____
4. editor	d, t	d, t	_____
5. feature	iy, t ʃ	ea, t	_____
6. financial	n	n	_____
7. illustrated	l, ey	ll, a	_____
8. issue	ʃ, uw	sue	_____
9. manuscript	n, p	n, p	_____
10. obituary	b, e	b, a	_____
11. rotogravure	t, ae, u	t, a, u	_____
12. sequel	s, kw	s, qu	_____
13. syndicated	i, k, t	y, c, t	_____

| 14. wirephoto | ay, f, t | i, ph, t | _____ |
| 15. release | iy | ea | _____ |

LAW

Several letters of each word are found in Column A. The phonemes for the missing letters are found in Column B. The corresponding graphemes are found in Column C. After studying the phonemes and graphemes, write the complete word in Column D.

COLUMN A	COLUMN B	COLUMN C	COLUMN D
1. a____l	p, iy	pp, ea	_____
2. a____rn__	t, ɔ, i	tt, o, ey	_____
3. b__l	ey	ai	_____
4. convic__on	ʃ	ti	_____
5. __ri__inal	k, m	c, m	_____
6. de__n__	f, e, s	f, e, se	_____
7. de__n__ent	l, i, kw	l, i, qu	_____
8. do__sti__	m, e, k	m, e, c	_____
9. __lt__	g, i, i	g, ui, y	_____
10. i__o__n__	n, s, e, s	nn, c, e, ce	_____
11. j____	ə, dʒ	u, dge	_____
12. pl__d	iy	ea	_____
13. ver__ict	d	d	_____
14. pa__le	r, ow	r, o	_____
15. w__ne__	i, t, s	i, t, ss	_____

LITERATURE

Given the phoneme i—that is, the short i—find the words in the following literature vocabulary that have the i sound.

1. appendix	8. fiction	15. sonnet
2. ballad	9. sentence	16. legend
3. biographer	10. index	17. lyric
4. dialect	11. librarian	18. pentameter

5. drama   12. literary   19. rhyme
6. essay   13. prologue   20. novel
7. fable   14. satire

If you have identified six words, very likely you have checked the right words. The answers are found in the Appendix, page 223.

MATHEMATICS

In addition to the phonemes we have already listed, there is one combination of phonemes which has a special graphemic representation in English spelling. The phoneme is ər. The graphemic representations are:

ear as in yearn
ir as in first
or as in worm
yr as in myrrh
ar as in liar
er as in germ

Study the following words taken from the vocabulary of the mathematician. Then write in the appropriate space the words which contain this phoneme.

1. bisector _____   11. integer _____
2. circumference _____   12. isosceles _____
3. decimal _____   13. linear _____
4. denominator _____   14. numerator _____
5. derivative _____   15. perimeter _____
6. diameter _____   16. perpendicular _____
7. equation _____   17. radius _____
8. fraction _____   18. tangent _____
9. hypotenuse _____   19. trapezoid _____
10. infinity _____   20. trigonometry _____

If you have written nine words, the chances are good that you have answered correctly. The answers are found in the Appendix, page 223.

MEDICINE

Certain letters are underlined in the words in Column A. The graphemes are written in Column C. Write in Column B the appropriate phoneme for each grapheme. Then write the complete word in Column D. Check the word you have written with the word in Column A. The proper phonemes are noted on page 223 in the Appendix.

COLUMN A	COLUMN B	COLUMN C	COLUMN D
1. ambulance	———	l, ce	———
2. antibiotics	———	i, o, c	———
3. appendicitis	———	pp, i, i	———
4. cancer	———	c, c	———
5. convalescent	———	c, sc	———
6. coronary	———	c, ə, y	———
7. cortisone	———	c, s, o	———
8. measles	———	ea, es	———
9. inoculation	———	n, c, ti	———
10. physician	———	ph, y, ci	———
11. symptom	———	y	———
12. pneumonia	———	eu	———
13. epidemic	———	i, m, c	———
14. sanitation	———	a, ti	———
15. medical	———	d, c	———

NURSING

Study the following words taken from the vocabulary of the nursing profession. Then write in the appropriate space the words that have the phoneme k.

1. anesthetic ———

2. chloroform ———

3. clinic ———

4. ether ———

5. intern———

6. medication ———

7. operation ———

8. patient———

9. recovery _____   13. bandage _____

10. stretcher _____   14. thermometer _____

11. surgeon _____   15. sterilized_____

12. conscious _____

If you have written six words, you probably have written the correct answers. The *k* words are found in the Appendix, page 223.

POLITICAL SCIENCE

Study the following words taken from the vocabulary of the political scientists. Next write the words having the phoneme ∫ in the space at the right.

1. ambassador _____   11. inauguration _____

2. bureaucracy_____   12. judicial _____

3. congressional_____   13. justice _____

4. constitution _____   14. legislation_____

5. consul _____   15. naturalize_____

6. dictatorship _____   16. oligarchy_____

7. disfranchise _____   17. patronage _____

8. emigration _____   18. reclamation _____

9. fascism _____   19. secretariat_____

10. corporation _____   20. socialism_____

If you have written eleven words, you probably have written the correct words. You may check your answers with those given in the Appendix, page 223.

Your work with phonemes and graphemes is the final step in your spelling education. You are ready now to try the demons.

CHAPTER X

Facing the Demons

My spelling is Wobbly. It's good spelling but it Wobbles, and the letters get in the wrong places. A. A. MILNE
WINNIE-THE-POOH

People sometimes ask whether spelling is taught as well today as it once was. They invariably voice the complaint that too many adults make spelling errors. Educators, on the other hand, defend their own efforts by citing several facts. First, they remind us that a much higher percentage of children graduate from high school today than did fifty years ago. Among this unselected population are some who do not have the verbal abilities that were a prerequisite for educational progress in another age. Second, they point out that today's children have larger oral vocabularies than did their grandfathers and they are more daring in the use of this extended vocabulary in writing. It is true, though, that spelling disability is much more common than it once was thought to be. But the problem of spelling does not seem insurmountable when we note one research finding: At the various levels of instruction it is a relatively small number of words that cause a great deal of trouble. The most important and most often misspelled words are known as a crucial core. They are also known as spelling demons. Several studies of these critical or crucial words have been made.

What are spelling demons? One research study is that of Thomas Pollock, of New York University, conducted between 1950 and 1964. In this study, English teachers in high schools and colleges throughout the country reported 90,000 instances of misspellings. But a large percentage of the 90,000 misspellings involved only nine words: *their* *(there), too (to), receive, believe (belief), all right, separate, coming, until,* and *character.*[1]

Maybe English spelling makes a lot more sense than we've been led to believe. Paul R. Hanna and others, in a computerized study of 17,000 words, produced evidence on sense in our spelling system. The tome is a colossal one with a colossal title to match: *Phoneme-Grapheme Correspondences as Cues to Spelling Improvement.*[2] Translated, the dignified title means that most English words sound the way they are spelled.

Hanna identified two categories of the comparatively few spelling troublemakers, the demons. The first class consists of words in which particular phonemes can in no way be analyzed or explained. The second category of spelling demons contains rarely used or unique phoneme-grapheme correspondences.

An associate of Paul R. Hanna, Richard E. Hodges, studied the second category. Hodges discovered forty English words containing unique sound-to-letter (phoneme-grapheme) correspondences. Examples of unique or difficult-to-explain vowel sounds are *shoe* and *through.* Examples of difficult-to-explain consonant sounds are *diaphragm, raspberry, schism.*[3]

In the case of these three difficult-to-explain consonants, spellers may find it helpful to remember that the English language doesn't particularly like three consonant sounds in a row. As a consequence, words long established in the language will, in many dialects, often drop one of the three consonants.

In analyzing Fitzgerald's list of 222 demons (see Appendix B), Richard E. Hodges found fifty words that would *not* be demons, if students understood the alphabet *(had, can, with),* if they knew about compounding words *(maybe, outside, snowman),* and if they knew how to add suffixes to root words *(play, played; get, getting; swim, swimming).*[4]

Why the spelling demons? Philologists, semanticists, and language scholars know that the English writing method, both historically and structurally, is phonemic. However, through the centuries, the language has evolved from a consistent sound-to-letter, from a phoneme-to-grapheme correspondence. It has become a mélange of complexities and apparent inconsistencies. The speller without a vast fund of language information has to contend with the demons the best way that he can. Here are the reasons for the demons:[5][6][7]

Reason 1: The English language employs more than two times as many sounds or phonemes as there are letters in the English alphabet.

Reason 2: Since no one-to-one relationship between letter and sound exists in English, several letters or combinations of letters may represent a sound: *tame, aim, gauge, dray, break, vein, they.*

Reason 3: A certain letter or combination of letters may stand for one sound in one word and another sound in another word: *feather, leak, break.*

Reason 4: Some words have alternate spellings, both of which are authentic: *monolog, monologue.*

Reason 5: Some words contain silent letters, which are not pronounced in the initial, medial, and final syllables: *honest, comptroller, answer.*

Reason 6: Homonyms or homophones are words pronounced in the same way but they differ in spellings: *bread, bred; read, red; flower, flour; lute, loot; due, do.*

Only 8 words use *ea* to represent long *a*. All except *yea* have homonyms: *break, brake; bear, bare; great, grate; pear, pair; steak, stake; tear, tare; wear, ware.*

Homonyms account for a third of the most commonly misspelled words.

Reason 7: Some two hundred structure or function words (*the, have, are, too, two, quite,* etc.) are usually the most irregular in their spellings. Yet they make up about two thirds of the words used in the writing of the English language.

There are certain words that have "trouble spots" or "hard spots." The question arises then, what does the speller do about the hard spot? To be sure, researchers do not agree on the policy of marking hard spots in words. One school argues that all people do not find the same parts difficult. Another group argues that particular errors in some words follow a definite pattern and warrant instruction in the error tendency. However, research studies show that good spellers tend to discover and concentrate upon the difficult parts of words far more frequently than poor spellers do. Hence the information indicating the trouble spots of a word may be valuable in helping you concentrate your attention where it is most needed.

The 605 spelling demons. A list of 605 words follows. These 605 are among the most frequently misspelled words in the English language. As you will note, the hard spot or the hard spots in each of the hard words is underlined.[8] Look well at the spelling demon as it is listed in Column A. After you think you have a good image of the word, look at the letter or letters in Column B. These are the spots that have tricked many spellers. Now you should have a good image of the whole word and some knowledge of the trouble spots. Try yourself by supplying the letters missing in the words in Column C. (Words minus hard spots.) Now take the fourth step. See whether you can write the word in Column D with 100 percent accuracy. Last, check yourself by comparing the word you have written with the word as it appears in Column A. If a word offers stubborn resistance to your efforts, check back to the previous chapter or chapters noted in Column E for the principle that applies to it.

A. Easy Words	B. Hard Spots	C. Words Minus Hard Spots		D. Chapter to Check
abeyance	ey	ab__ance	___	IX
abscess	sc	ab__ess	___	IX
absence	ce	absen__	___	IX
absolutely	e	absolut_ly	___	IX
absurd	urd	abs___	___	IX
abundant	u, ant	ab_nd___	___	VII, VIII
acceptance	cc	a__eptance	___	VIII, IX
accessible	cc, ible	a__ess____	___	VIII, IX
accidentally	cc, a	a__ident_lly	___	VIII
accommodate	cc, mm	a__o__odate	___	VI
accumulate	cc	a__umulate	___	IX
accurate	cc, ate	a__ur___	___	IX
accustomed	cc, o	a__ust_med	___	IX
achieved	ie	ach__ved	___	VIII
acknowledge	c, d	a_knowle_ge	___	IX
acknowledgment	c, dgm	a_knowle___ent	___	IX
acquaintance	c, a	a_quaint_nce	___	VIII, IX
acquainted	c	a_quainted	___	IX
across	ross	ac____	___	VI
addressed	dd	a__ressed	___	IX
adequate	e	ad_quate	___	VII
advice	ce	advi__	___	IX
adviser	se	advi__r	___	IX
adhesive	hes	ad___ive	___	IX

A. Easy Words	B. Hard Spots	C. Words Minus Hard Spots		D. Chapter to Check
advisable	sa	advi__ble	___	VIII
aerial	ae, ia	__r__l	___	IX
affectionately	f, ate	af_ection___ly	___	IX
affects	a	_ffects	___	VII
aggravate	gg, a	a__r_vate	___	IX
aisle	is	a__le	___	II
alcohol	coho	al____l	___	VII
allotted	ll, tt	a__o__ed	___	IX
all right	ll, r	a__, _ight	___	VI
already	l	a_ready	___	VI
altar	ar	alt--	___	IX
alter	er	alt--	___	IX
altogether	l	a_together	___	VI
always	l	a_ways	___	VI
amateur	a, eur	am_t___	___	VII, IX
amethyst	e, y	am_th_st	___	VII, IX
among	o	am_ng	___	IX
analysis	y, is	anal_s__	___	VII, IX
analyze	yze	anal___	___	VIII
angle	le	ang__	___	VI
anniversary	n, a	an_ivers_ry	___	VII, VIII
annual	nua	an___l	___	VI
anonymous	y, ous	anon_m___	___	IX
answered	w	ans_ered	___	II
anxiety	ie	anx__ty	___	VII
anxious	iou	anx___s	___	VIII
apartment	part	a____ment	___	IX
apologize	p, o, z	a_ol_gi_e	___	VIII
apology	p, o	a_ol_gy	___	VII, IX
apparatus	pp	a__aratus	___	IX
apparently	pp, e	a__ar_ntly	___	VIII

A. EASY WORDS	B. HARD SPOTS	C. WORDS MINUS HARD SPOTS		D. CHAPTER TO CHECK
appearance	ea, a	app__r_nce	___	VIII
appetite	pe, e	ap__tit_	___	IX
appreciate	pp, ia	a__rec__te	___	VIII
appropriate	ri	approp__ate	___	VII
appropriation	ri	approp__ation	___	VI
approval	pp	a__roval	___	IX
arctic	c	ar_tic	___	VII
argument	u	arg_ment	___	IX
arithmetic	e	arithm_tic	___	VII
arrangement	e	arrang_ment	___	VIII
arrival	r, al	ar_iv__	___	VIII, IX
articles	les	artic___	___	IX
ascend	c	as_end	___	IX
ascertain	sc	a__ertain	___	IX
association	s, cia	as_o___tion	___	IX
assassinate	ss, ss	a__a__inate	___	VII, IX
athletics	thl	a___etics	___	VII
attaching	tt	a__aching	___	IX
attacked	tt, ck	a__a__ed	___	IX
audience	u, ie	a_d__nce	___	VIII, IX
authority	u, o, ity	a_th_r___	___	VIII, IX
auxiliary	u, li	a_xi__ary	___	VI
awful	w	a_ful	___	II, IX
awkward	w	a_kward	___	IX
bachelor	e	bach_lor	___	VIII
bacillus	ll	baci__us	___	IX
banana	n	ba_ana	___	VII
barbarous	a, ous	barb_r___	___	VI
bargain	ai	barg__n	___	IX
baseball	e	bas_ball	___	VIII

A. Easy Words	B. Hard Spots	C. Words Minus Hard Spots		D. Chapter to Check
battalion	tt, li	ba__a__on	___	VI
bearing	ea	b__ring	___	IX
beautifully	ly	beautiful__	___	VIII
becoming	m	beco_ing	___	VIII
before	e	befor_	___	VIII
beggar	a	begg_r	___	VIII
beginning	nn	begi__ing	___	VIII
belief	ief	bel___	___	VIII
believe	ie	bel__ve	___	VIII
believing	ie	bel__ving	___	VIII
benefited	e, t	ben_fi_ed	___	VII
bicycle	i	b_cycle	___	VIII
biscuit	c	bis_uit	___	II
bookkeeper	k	book_eeper	___	VIII
boundaries	a	bound_ries	___	VI
breathe	e	breath_	___	IX
brilliant	lia	bril___nt	___	VII
Britain	ai	Brit__n	___	IX
bulletin	e	bull_tin	___	VII
bureau	ureau	b_____	___	VI
business	usi	b___ness	___	IX
busy	us	b__y	___	IX
cafeteria	e	caf_teria	___	VII
calendar	e, a	cal_nd_r	___	VIII
campaign	aign	camp_____	___	II, IX
cancel	cel	can___	___	IX
candidate	did	can___ate	___	VII
can't	n't	ca___	___	VII
canvass	vass	can_____	___	VI
capacity	c	capa_ity	___	IX

A. Easy Words	B. Hard Spots	C. Words Minus Hard Spots		D. Chapter to Check
capital	al	capit__	___	VI
captain	tain	cap____	___	IX
career	aree	c____r	___	IX
catastrophe	phe	catastro___	___	IX
cemetery	e, e, e	c_m_t_ry	___	VIII
certain	ai	cert__n	___	IX
certificate	er	c__tificate	___	IX
changeable	eable	chang_____	___	VIII
changing	gi	chan__ng	___	VIII
characteristic	c	chara_teristic	___	VII
chauffeur	u, eu	ch_ff__r	___	II
children	ld	chi__ren	___	VII
chocolate	o	choc_late	___	VII
choose	oo	ch__se	___	IX
chosen	o	ch_sen	___	VI
circumstances	i, ces	c_rcumstan___	___	IX
clothes	thes	clo____	___	VII
coarse	oa	c__rse	___	IX
college	e	coll_ge	___	VIII
colonel	olo, e	c___n_l	___	VI
colossal	l, ss	co_o__al	___	VI
column	umn	col___	___	II
comfortable	able	comfort____	___	VIII
coming	m	co_ing	___	VIII
commission	mm, ss	co__i__ion	___	VIII
committee	mmittee	co_____	___	VI
community	mm	co__unity	___	VIII
comparative	a	comp_rative	___	VIII
compelled	ll	compe__ed	___	VIII
competent	e, e	comp_t_nt	___	VIII
competition	e, i	comp_t_tion	___	VIII

A. EASY WORDS	B. HARD SPOTS	C. WORDS MINUS HARD SPOTS		D. CHAPTER TO CHECK
complacence	cence	compla_____	___	VIII
completely	ete	compl___ly	___	VIII
compulsory	sory	compul____	___	VIII
complexion	xion	comple____	___	VII
concession	ess	conc___ion	___	VIII
conceivable	ei, a	conc__v_ble	___	VIII
conferred	rr	confe__ed	___	VIII
connection	n	con_ection	___	VIII
conqueror	ue, or	conq__r__	___	VIII
conscience	sc	con__ience	___	VIII
conscientious	sc, tious	con__ien_____	___	VIII
consciousness	sc	con__iousness	___	VIII
consistent	e	consist_nt	___	VIII
continuous	u	contin_ous	___	VII
control	rol	cont___	___	VIII
controlled	l	control_ed	___	VIII
convenience	e, ie	conv_n__nce	___	VIII
coolly	ll	coo__y	___	VII
cooperate	oo, e	c__p_rate	___	VII
cordially	di	cor__ally	___	VII
correspondence	re	cor__spondence	___	VIII
corridor	rri	co___dor	___	VI
courageous	ou	c__rageous	___	IX
course	ourse	c_____	___	VI
courteous	ou, eous	c__rt____	___	VI
courtesy	ou, es	c__rt__y	___	VI
criticized	c, z	criti_i_ed	___	VIII
cruelty	elty	cru____	___	VII
crystal	ys, al	cr__t__	___	IX
curiosity	io	cur__sity	___	VII
customer	u, o	c_st_mer	___	VII

A. Easy Words	B. Hard Spots	C. Words Minus Hard Spots		D. Chapter to Check
cylinder	y, i	c_l_nder	——	IX
cynical	cy, cal	__ni___	——	IX
deceitful	ei	dec__tful	——	VIII
deceive	ei	dec__ve	——	VIII
decidedly	c	de_idedly	——	IX
decision	c, s	de_i_ion	——	IX
defendants	ants	defend____	——	VIII
defense	se	defen__	——	IX
deferred	rr	defe__ed	——	VIII
definitely	f, i, e	de_in_t_ly	——	VIII
descendant	sc, a	de__end_nt	——	VIII
descent	sc	de__ent	——	IX
describe	es	d__cribe	——	VIII
description	es, p	d__cri_tion	——	VIII
desert	s	de_ert	——	VI
(waste place)				
desirable	e, a	d_sir_ble	——	VIII
despair	e	d_spair	——	VI
desperate	e	desp_rate	——	VIII
despise	e, se	d_spi__	——	VIII
dessert	ss	de__ert	——	VI
destroyed	e, roy	d_st___ed	——	VII
destruction	e	d_struction	——	VII
determined	ined	determ____	——	VIII
development	opm	devel___ent	——	VII
device	ce	devi__	——	IX
dictionary	io, a	dict__n_ry	——	VIII
difference	e, e	diff_r_nce	——	VIII
different	e, e	diff_r_nt	——	VIII
dining	n	di_ing	——	VIII

A. Easy Words	B. Hard Spots	C. Words Minus Hard Spots		D. Chapter to Check
diphtheria	phth	di____eria	——	VII
disappear	s, pp	di_a__ear	——	VIII
disappointed	s, pp	di_a__ointed	——	VIII
disastrous	tr	disas__ous	——	VII
discipline	sci	di___pline	——	IX
disease	i	d_sease	——	VIII
dissatisfied	ss	di__atisfied	——	VIII
divided	i	d_vided	——	VIII
divine	i	d_vine	——	VII
doctor	c, o	do_t_r	——	VIII
doesn't	e, n't	do_s___	——	VII
don't	on't	d____	——	VII
drudgery	dg	dru__ery	——	IX
duplicate	pli	du___cate	——	VIII
dying	yi	d__ng	——	VIII
easily	i	eas_ly	——	VII
economical	n	eco_omical	——	VII
ecstasy	cst, sy	e___a__	——	IX
effects	eff	___ects	——	VIII
eighth	hth	eig___	——	II
eligible	i, ible	el_g____	——	VIII
eliminate	i, ate	el_min___	——	VIII
embarrassment	rr, ss	emba__a__ment	——	VI
eminent	i, e	em_n_nt	——	VII, VIII
emphasize	a, ze	emph_si__	——	VII, VIII
encouraging	ou, a	enc__r_ging	——	IX
endeavor	ea, o	end__v_r	——	IX
enemy	nem	e___y	——	VII
enormous	ous	enorm___	——	VII
environment	ron	envi__ment	——	VI

A. Easy Words	B. Hard Spots	C. Words Minus Hard Spots	D. Chapter to Check
equipment	p	equi_ment	—— VIII
equipped	pp	equi__ed	—— VIII
equivalent	a, e	equiv_l_nt	—— VIII
especially	s, cial	e_pe____ly	—— IX
etiquette	ti, quette	e_____	—— VII
exaggerated	gg	exa__erated	—— IX
exceed	ee	exc__d	—— VIII
exceedingly	ee	exc__dingly	—— VIII
excellent	c, ll	ex_e__ent	—— VIII
exceptional	ce	ex__ptional	—— IX
excitement	e	excit_ment	—— VIII
exercise	x, cise	e_er____	—— VIII
exhausted	h	ex_austed	—— II
exhibition	h	ex_ibition	—— II
existence	x, e	e_ist_nce	—— VIII
expense	se	expen__	—— IX
experience	ie	exper__nce	—— VIII
explanation	a	expl_nation	—— VI
extension	s	exten_ion	—— IX
extraordinary	ao	extr__rdinary	—— VIII
extremely	eme	extr___ly	—— VI
familiar	ia	famil__r	—— VIII
fascinate	s	fa_cinate	—— II
feasible	ea, ible	f__s____	—— VIII, IX
February	ruar	Feb____y	—— VII
feminine	in	fem__ine	—— VII
fiery	ie	f__ry	—— VII
finally	ally	fin____	—— VIII
financial	a, ial	fin_nc___	—— IX
foreigner	eign	for____er	—— VIII

A. Easy Words	B. Hard Spots	C. Words Minus Hard Spots		D. Chapter to Check
forfeit	rfei	fo____t	——	VIII
formally	ll	forma__y	——	VI
formerly	merly	for_____	——	VI
forty	o	f_rty	——	VII
fourth	ou	f__rth	——	VI
freight	ei	fr__ght	——	VIII
freshman	a	freshm_n	——	VII
friend	ie	fr__nd	——	VIII
fundamental	a	fund_mental	——	VII
furniture	ture	furni____	——	VIII
gallantry	lla	ga___ntry	——	IX
generally	e, lly	gen_ra___	——	VIII
genius	ius	gen___	——	IX
gentlemen	le, e	gent__m_n	——	VII
genuine	uine	gen____	——	IX
glimpse	pse	glim___	——	IX
goddess	dd	go__ess	——	VII
governor	er, o	gov__n_r	——	VIII
government	n	gover_ment	——	VII
grammar	a	gramm_r	——	VIII
gratefully	ate	gr___fully	——	IX
grievous	ie, ous	gr__v___	——	VIII
guarantee	ua, a	g__r_ntee	——	II, VII
guard	ua	g__rd	——	II
guardian	ua	g__rdian	——	II
guidance	a	guid_nce	——	VII
handkerchief	d, ie	han_kerch__f	——	VIII
handsome	d	han_some	——	II
harass	r, ss	ha_a__	——	VI
haven't	en't	hav____	——	VI

A. Easy Words	B. Hard Spots	C. Words Minus Hard Spots		D. Chapter to Check
having	v	ha_ing	__	VIII
height	ei	h__ght	__	VIII
heroes	e, e	h_ro_s	__	VI
hoping	p	ho_ing	__	VIII
huge	ge	hu__	__	IX
humorous	o, o	hum_r_us	__	VIII
hundredths	re	hund__dths	__	VII
hungry	gry	hun___	__	VII
hurriedly	ie	hurr__dly	__	VIII
ignorance	n, ance	ig_or____	__	VIII
imaginary	m, ary	i_agin___	__	VIII
imagination	m	i_agination	__	VIII
imagine	m, e	i_agin_	__	VII, VIII
imitate	i	im_tate	__	VII
imitation	i	im_tation	__	VII
immediately	mm, e	i__ediat_ly	__	VII
imminent	mmi	i___nent	__	VII
incidentally	i, all	inc_dent___y	__	VIII
inconvenience	enien	inconv_____ce	__	VIII
independence	e, e, e	ind_p_nd_nce	__	VIII
indispensable	is, a	ind__pens_ble	__	VIII
industrial	trial	indus_____	__	VII
inevitable	i, a	_nevit_ble	__	VIII
influence	lue	inf___nce	__	VI
ingenious	i, io	_ngen__us	__	VII
initial	i, ti	_ni__al	__	VI
inoculate	in	__oculate	__	VIII
instance	ance	inst____	__	VIII
intellectual	ell	int___ectual	__	VIII
intelligence	ll	inte__igence	__	VIII
interested	ere	int___sted	__	VII

A. Easy Words	B. Hard Spots	C. Words Minus Hard Spots		D. Chapter to Check
interesting	ere	int___sting	——	VII
interference	e	interfer_nce	——	VIII
interpreted	pret	inter____ed	——	VII
interrupted	rr	int__upted	——	VIII
intimate	i, a	int_m_te	——	VII
irresistible	e, ible	irr_sist____	——	VIII
it's	t's	i___	——	VII
itself	elf	its___	——	VI
judgment	dg	ju__ment	——	II
kindergarten	t	kindergar_en	——	VIII
knew	k	_new	——	II
knowledge	w, dg	kno_le__e	——	II
laboratory	o	lab_ratory	——	VII
laid	ai	l__d	——	IX
later	at	l__er	——	VII
lavatory	a	lav_tory	——	VII
led	e	l_d	——	IX
leisure	ei	l__sure	——	VIII
lengthen	en	length__	——	VIII
liable	a	li_ble	——	VIII
library	rary	lib____	——	VII
license	c, s	li_en_e	——	IX
lieutenant	ieu	l___tenant	——	VI
lightning	gh	li__tning	——	II
literature	era	lit___ture	——	VII
loneliness	e	lon_liness	——	VII
loose	oo	l__se	——	VI
lose	os	l__e	——	VI
losing	o	l_sing	——	VI, VIII

A. Easy Words	B. Hard Spots	C. Words Minus Hard Spots		D. Chapter to Check
lying	yi	l__ng	——	VIII
maintain	in	ma__tain	——	IX
maintenance	e	maint_nance	——	VII
manufacturer	u, urer	man_fact____	——	VII
marriage	ia	marr__ge	——	VI
mathematics	e	math_matics	——	IX
meant	ea	m__nt	——	IX
medal	e, al	m_d__	——	VII
medicine	icine	med_____	——	IX
menace	ace	men___	——	VIII
messenger	en	mess__ger	——	VII
miniature	ia	min__ture	——	VII
minimum	i, i	m_n_mum	——	VII
minutes	i, u	m_n_tes	——	VI
mischievous	vous	mischie____	——	VI
misspelled	ss, ll	mi__pe__ed	——	VIII
mortgage	rt	mo__gage	——	II
murmuring	u	murm_ring	——	VIII
muscles	sc	mu__les	——	II
museum	eu	mus__m	——	VII
mutual	ua	mut__l	——	VII
mysterious	y, ious	m_ster____	——	IX
naturally	ally	natur____	——	VIII
necessary	c, ss	ne_e__ary	——	VIII
Negroes	es	Negro__	——	VII
nickel	el	nick__	——	VI
niece	iec	n___e	——	VIII
ninety	ety	nin___	——	VII
ninth	nth	ni___	——	VIII
noticeable	e	notic_able	——	VIII
nuisance	uisa	n____nce	——	VI

A. EASY WORDS	B. HARD SPOTS	C. WORDS MINUS HARD SPOTS		D. CHAPTER TO CHECK
obliged	g	obli_ed	___	IX
occasionally	cc, s, lly	o__a_iona___	___	VIII
occur	cc	o__ur	___	VIII
occurred	o, rr	_ccu__ed	___	VIII
occurrence	cc, rr	o__u__ence	___	VIII
o'clock	o'	__clock	___	VII
off	ff	o__	___	VI
omitted	tt	omi__ed	___	VIII
omission	m	o_ission	___	VII
opinion	in	op__ion	___	VII
opponent	pp, e	o__on_nt	___	VIII
opposite	o	opp_site	___	VII
optimistic	i	opt_mistic	___	VII
opportunity	o	opp_rtunity	___	VII
original	rigi	o____nal	___	VIII
originate	rigi	o____nate	___	VIII
outrageous	eo	outrag__us	___	VIII
paid	ai	p__d	___	IX
pamphlet	ph	pam__let	___	IX
parallel	a, l, l	par_l_e_	___	VIII
paralysis	a, y, is	par_l_s__	___	IX
parliament	ia	parl__ment	___	II
partially	ial	part___ly	___	VIII, IX
particularly	ar, lar	p__ticu___ly	___	VIII
partner	tn	par__er	___	VII
pastime	s	pa_time	___	VI
patience	ience	pat_____	___	VI, VIII, IX
patients	ts	patien__	___	VI
peaceable	ea, ea	p__c__ble	___	VIII, IX
peculiar	iar	pecul___	___	VIII

A. Easy Words	B. Hard Spots	C. Words Minus Hard Spots	D. Chapter to Check
perceive	ei	perc__ve	___ VIII
perception	c	per_eption	___ IX
performance	er, a	p__form_nce	___ VIII
perhaps	er	p__haps	___ IX
permanent	a, e	perm_n_nt	___ VII
permissible	ssible	permi_____	___ VIII
perseverance	e, a	pers_ver_nce	___ VIII
personally	o, ally	pers_n____	___ VIII
personnel	nel	person___	___ VI
perspiration	i	persp_ration	___ VII
persuade	er, e	p__suad_	___ IX
physician	y, ian	ph_sic___	___ IX
picnicking	k	picnic_ing	___ VIII
piece	ie	p__ce	___ VIII
planned	nn	pla__ed	___ VIII
pleasant	ea, a	pl__s_nt	___ VIII
pneumonia	p, eu	_n__monia	___ II
politicians	cia	politi___ns	___ IX
possession	ss, ss	po__e__ion	___ VII
possible	ssi	po___ble	___ VIII
practically	al	practic__ly	___ VIII
practice	c, ice	pra_t___	___ VII, IX
prairie	ai, ie	pr__r__	___ VI
precedence	ce	pr__dence	___ VIII
precedents	e, e, ents	pr_c_d____	___ VIII
preceding	ce	pre__ding	___ VIII
preference	e	prefer_nce	___ VIII
preferred	rr	prefe__ed	___ VIII
prejudiced	j	pre_udiced	___ VII
prevalent	al	prev__ent	___ VIII
principal	al	princip__	___ VI

A. EASY WORDS	B. HARD SPOTS	C. WORDS MINUS HARD SPOTS		D. CHAPTER TO CHECK
principle	ple	princi___	—	VI
privilege	i	priv_lege	—	VII
prior	ior	pr___	—	VII, VIII
probably	bab	pro___ly	—	VII
procedure	e	proc_dure	—	VIII
proceeded	ceed	pro____ed	—	VIII
prodigy	i	prod_gy	—	VII
professor	f, sor	pro_es___	—	VIII
pronunciation	u	pron_nciation	—	VII
propaganda	a	prop_ganda	—	VII
prophesy	esy	proph___	—	VI
psychology	ho	psyc__logy	—	II
pursue	u	p_rsue	—	IX
quantity	ti	quan__ty	—	VII
questionnaire	ue, io	q__st__n_aire	—	VI
quiet	ie	qu__t	—	VI
quite	ui	q__te	—	VI
realize	ea	r__lize	—	VII
really	a, ly	re_l__	—	VII
receipt	eip	rec___t	—	II, VIII
received	ei	rec__ved	—	VIII
reciprocate	c, pro	re_i___cate	—	VII
recognize	g	reco_nize	—	VII
recommendation	omm	rec___endation	—	VIII
reference	e	refer_nce	—	VIII
referred	rr	refe__ed	—	VIII
registration	is	reg__tration	—	IX
rehearse	ea	reh__rse	—	IX
relevant	e, ant	r_lev___	—	VIII
religious	ious	relig____	—	IX

A. Easy Words	B. Hard Spots	C. Words Minus Hard Spots	D. Chapter to Check
relief	ief	rel___	___ VIII
repetition	e	rep_tition	___ VII
representatives	a	represent_tives	___ VII
response	se	respon__	___ IX
restaurant	au	rest__rant	___ VI
rheumatism	heu	r___matism	___ II
rhythm	hy	r__thm	___ II, VI
ridiculous	i	r_diculous	___ VII
righteous	ghte	ri____ous	___ IX
sacrifice	i	sacr_fice	___ VII
sacrilegious	i, gi	sacr_le__ous	___ VII
safety	ety	saf___	___ VII
salary	a	sal_ry	___ VII
sandwich	wich	sand____	___ VI
satisfactory	ory	satisfact___	___ VIII
scarcely	cely	scar____	___ IX
scenery	c, ery	s_en___	___ VIII
schedule	sch, ule	___ed___	___ IX
science	ie	sc__nce	___ VII
scissors	c, ss	s_i__ors	___ IX
secretary	re	sec__tary	___ VIII
seems	ee	s__ms	___ IX
seize	ei	s__ze	___ VIII
semester	e	s_mester	___ VII
sense	se	sen__	___ IX
separate	a	sep_rate	___ VI
sergeant	e, ea	s_rg__nt	___ IX
severely	v, e	se_er_ly	___ VII
shining	n	shi_ing	___ VIII
shriek	ie	shr__k	___ VIII

A. Easy Words	B. Hard Spots	C. Words Minus Hard Spots		D. Chapter to Check
siege	ie	s__ge	——	VIII
signature	a	sign_ture	——	VII
similar	ar	simil__	——	VIII
sincerely	ely	sincer___	——	VII
solemn	mn	sole__	——	II
sophomore	o	soph_more	——	VII
souvenirs	e, irs	souv_n___	——	IX
speaks	ea	sp__ks	——	IX
specimen	ci	spe__men	——	VII
speeches	ee	sp__ches	——	IX
spiritual	ua	spirit__l	——	VII
statement	e	stat_ment	——	VII
stationary	ary	station___	——	VIII
stationery	ery	station___	——	VIII
statue	ue	stat__	——	IX
stature	ure	stat___	——	VIII
statute	t	sta_ute	——	VII
stopped	pp	sto__ed	——	VIII
stopping	pp	sto__ing	——	VIII
strengthen	g	stren_then	——	VII
stretch	tch	stre___	——	IX
strictly	ct	stri__ly	——	VII
studying	y	stud_ing	——	VII
succeeds	cee	suc___ds	——	VIII
successfully	ss	succe__fully	——	IX
sufficient	ff, ie	su__ic__nt	——	VIII
suggested	gg	su__ested	——	IX
supersede	sede	super____	——	VIII
superintendent	e	superintend_nt	——	VIII
surely	ely	sur___	——	VII
surprised	ur	s__prised	——	IX

A. Easy Words	B. Hard Spots	C. Words Minus Hard Spots		D. Chapter to Check
syllable	y	s_llable	___	VII
sympathy	a	symp_thy	___	VI
taking	k	ta_ing	___	VIII
tariff	r, ff	ta_i__	___	VI
telegram	e	tel_gram	___	VII
temperament	a	temper_ment	___	VII
temperature	a	temper_ture	___	VII
temporary	o	temp_rary	___	VII
than	a	th_n	___	VI
their	ei	th__r	___	VIII
then	e	th_n	___	VII
there	e	ther_	___	VI
therefore	e	therefor_	___	VI
they're	ey'r	th____e	___	VII
thief	ie	th__f	___	VIII
thoroughly	or	th__oughly	___	VI
thought	ought	th_____	___	VI
till	i	t_ll	___	VI
to	o	t_	___	VI
together	e	tog_ther	___	IX
tomorrow	rr, w	tomo__o_	___	II, IX
too	oo	t__	___	VI
toward	war	to___d	___	II
tragedy	ged	tra___y	___	VII
transferred	rr	transfe__ed	___	VIII
treacherous	ea, er	tr__ch__ous	___	IX
tried	ie	tr__d	___	IX
tries	ie	tr__s	___	IX
trouble	ou	tr__ble	___	IX
truly	ul	tr__y	___	VIII

A. Easy Words	B. Hard Spots	C. Words Minus Hard Spots		D. Chapter to Check
Tuesday	ue	T__sday	___	IX
twelfth	fth	twel___	___	VII
two	wo	t__	___	II, VI
typical	y	t_pical	___	IX
tyranny	yr, nny	t__a___	___	IX
unanimous	nim	una___ous	___	VII
undoubtedly	b, edly	undou_t____	___	II
unnecessary	unn	___ecessary	___	VIII
until	l	unti_	___	VI
using	si	u__ng	___	VIII
usually	lly	usua___	___	VIII
vacuum	cu	va__um	___	VII
valuable	ua	val__ble	___	VIII
vegetable	e	veg_table	___	VIII
vengeance	ea	veng__nce	___	VIII
vigilance	i, ance	v_gil____	___	VIII
villain	ai	vill__n	___	VII
visible	i	vis_ble	___	VIII
weather	ea	w__ther	___	IX
Wednesday	d, e	We_n_sday	___	VII
weird	ei	w__rd	___	VIII
where	h, e	w_er_	___	IX
whether	he	w__ther	___	IX
which	h	w_ich	___	IX
whole	w	_hole	___	II
wholly	w, ll	_ho__y	___	VIII
whose	w, e	_hos_	___	IX
who's	o's	wh___	___	VII
woman	a	wom_n	___	IX

A. Easy Words	B. Hard Spots	C. Words Minus Hard Spots		D. Chapter to Check
women	o, e	w_m_n	___	IX
wretched	ret	w___ched	___	IX
writer	w, t	_ri_er	___	II
writing	w	_riting	___	II
written	tt	wri__en	___	VIII
you're	're	you___	___	VII
yours	rs	you__	___	VII

In this chapter you have become acquainted with over six hundred everyday words that cause many a speller real trouble. You have seen the whole words and the hard part or parts. When you analyzed the errors, you were reviewing word structuring and also associating phonemes with graphemes. You were approaching spelling as an intellectual activity.

In addition you have written each hard word. This is kinesthetic practice, which is very valuable when it is combined with intellectual activity. You are now ready to take a look at an American institution, the National Spelling Bee.

CHAPTER XI

A Nostalgic Touch: The National Spelling Bee

"Do you spell it with a 'V' or a 'W'?" inquired the judge.
"That depends upon the taste and fancy of the speller, my Lord,"
replied Sam.

CHARLES DICKENS
Pickwick Papers

Educators of today, among them the notable spelling authorities Paul and Jean Hanna, maintain that oral spelling exercises of the old-fashioned spelling-bee variety should not be used as a teaching-learning technique in spelling. They say that it is confusing to have pupils vocalize the alphabetical names of letters in spelling the word when a teacher is trying to help a pupil hear the phonemes in a spoken word and translate those phonemes into the correct graphemes for writing purposes.

The authorities have other arguments against the spelling bee. One, that there is little or no relationship between the *sound* of the name of the letter and the *sound* that the letter represents. For example, saying *ef-you-en* isn't too helpful in writing the letters *f, u, n,* when the pupil hears the different sounds of the phonemes in *fun.* There's another fairly strong argument. Oral spelling, they say, is unrealistic. After all, when we have occasion to spell, we write, we do not pronounce. Accordingly, educators of today accept the spell-down as acceptable only as a competitive exercise in sheer recall.

Maybe the picturesque old spelling bee has gone the way of the old oaken bucket. One fact is inescapable, though. The good old-fashioned spelling bee, outmoded though it is, had and still has the virtue of motivating the children to do better work in this subject.

Spelling of yesteryear. The history of the word *spelling* is interesting. The word is derived from the Old English *spell* (meaning *discourse, story*). The Old English form in turn comes from the Old French *espelir, espeller* (meaning "to read out"). Then there's an Old English form *spel* (meaning *news*), which is related to our word *gospel*, which comes from Old English *godspell* ("good news").

The word *spelling,* then, does mean "to tell," that is, "to convey meaning." The invention of the art of printing first brought spelling into the world as a school subject and eventually exalted its companion study, reading, to the first place among the three R's. Before the introduction of printing, the schools taught writing and reading; after printing came in, schools taught reading and writing. "In our own early schools, spelling was the first subject the child was taught. The young learner spelled his way into reading, the order being as follows: first, the alphabet recited in order; then syllables (*ab, ad, etc.*); then words spelled; and finally, reading—spelling one word after another before pronouncing it."

Glancing back into history, we note that the eighteenth-century English reformers—notably Swift, Priestley, and Dr. Johnson—were persistent in their efforts to standardize English spelling. Even though they were inconsistent in their own spelling, and even though the vast majority of changes they proposed were not scientifically sound, they set about to fix, regulate, and standardize English spelling for their own age and for all eternity. Samuel Johnson, author, wit, and philosopher, shared many of the convictions of the grammarians, and in 1755 he published his epoch-making *A Dictionary of the English Language,* which became a universally accepted guide to the mysteries of spelling. Johnson was concerned about fixing the language against corruption, for, as he said in his Preface, "Tongues, like governments, have a natural tendency to degeneration; we have long preserved our constitution, let us make some struggle for our language." He foresaw linguistic deterioration.[1]

This zeal for "right writing" took hold in England. It took hold also in America, where Webster's series of spelling books and dictionaries were a powerful agent in "fixing" the American language. His standard of correctness was the English of the enlightened members of all classes. He did not discriminate in favor of the "polite part" of city society, which he believed consisted largely of city snobs. "General custom must be the rule of speaking," he said; and "it is always better to be *vulgarly* right than *politely* wrong." In those days, Webster, although he was fanatical about his correct spelling, was considered amazingly liberal, even radical, in his approval of popular usage. He approved, for instance, of "Who is he married to?" and "It is me."[2]

Publication of Noah Webster's *Blue-Backed Speller* is one of the greatest success stories in the history of American publishing. In 1807, Webster estimated the annual sale at 200,000 copies; by 1837, he estimated the total sale to date at 15 million. In 1855, D. Appleton and Company took over the plates. On one occasion in 1880, an interviewer asked William H. Appleton about the firm's best-seller. Appleton replied: "Webster's Speller; and it has the largest sale of any book in the world except the Bible. We sell a million copies a year."[3] The best-seller, allegedly, taught millions to read and to spell, and not one to sin.

Our provincial faith and reverence for correct spelling permitted so distinguished a man of letters as Oliver Wendell Holmes to comment that Boston had for one of its distinctions "its correct habit of spelling the English language."

The zeal for the *Blue-Backed Speller* may have cast a spell over the American public and the Appleton company. At the same time, the teaching of spelling cast a spell over American education. With the appearance of Webster's spelling books and others, spelling as a discipline was introduced in America, the only country where spelling is taught as a separate subject. Indeed, Webster's *Blue-Backed Speller* helped make spelling one of the principal subjects in school.

One author writes about Webster's words:[4]

> In one edition of Webster's Elementary Spelling Book, the famous blue-backed speller, are found in the early lessons, presumably easy, such words as sago, copal, and cyst, and in the later lessons, mucilaginous, fugacity, and schismatic.

As a result of this public zeal for right writing, the spell-down, the spelling bee or spelling match became part of American folk culture. Some explanation of its terminology is in order. The term *spelling bee*, defined as a social gathering at which competitive spelling is the chief diversion, came into use considerably later than the term *spelling match*. An 1875 London *Times* article mentioned that the spelling bee, a New England invention, was making rapid strides over the United States.

The spell-down or spelling bee was often used as the Friday afternoon special diversion, looked forward to by the pupils all week. Sometimes the spell-down was a reward for good conduct and progress in studies. And sometimes spelling competition was "the program" at parent-teacher get-togethers to demonstrate the teacher's ability and the pupils' progress. The spelling bees, however, were not limited to the schoolroom. At frontier functions, many a person won prestige and position in the community by spelling down the others. At a box social the crowning event was often a spelling bee. And many a swain romanced and married the schoolmarm by being victorious in a spelling contest. At any rate, the spelling bee became an American institution in the country, town, and city.

The spelling bee in American literature. American literature, especially the literature of frontier life, is replete with references to spelling. Edward Eggleston's work, *The Hoosier School-Master,* marked a distinct advance toward the discovery of literary values in the agricultural West. The Hoosier schoolmaster walked ten miles to get to school in the district, "mentally reviewing his learning at every step he took and trembling lest the committee should find that he did not know enough." One of his pupils is Jim Phillips, the whizz-bang speller, ". . . a tall, lank, stoop-shouldered fellow who had never distinguished himself in any other pursuit than spelling. Except in this one art of spelling, he was of no account." [5]

Then there's Owen Wister's story *The Virginian,* about a cowboy from Virginia and a nicely brought up young woman, Molly Wood, who was from way down East and who turned to teaching school in Wyoming. Molly wanted to teach. Molly's mother, though, wasn't so sure that Molly was qualified. The reason: Molly leaves the u out of *honour.*

The National Spelling Bee. Some educators maintain that the spelling bee is a thing of the past and no longer suited to today's needs. Maybe so, but the National Spelling Bee is alive and well. Begun in 1925 under the sponsorship of the Louisville *Courier-Journal* and nine other newspapers, it has attracted thousands of ambitious boys and girls, driving them to their spelling books, to the study of phonemes, to dictionaries, and eventually into stiff competition. Today the National Spelling Bee is sponsored by Scripps Howard and 218 newspapers.

Some of the excitement found at football games can be found at the National Spelling Bee, a competition "designed to help boys and girls improve their spelling, increase their vocabularies, and develop correct English usage that will benefit them all their lives."

Like some organization operations, the spelling bee is conducted according to established procedures, as you will see when you read the rules for the contest.

Noah Webster gave a fillip to the spelling bee, which he said was "good for the articulation," and so did Benjamin Franklin, who considered it so important that he took the time to set down his version of the rules. For our day, the following are the National Spelling Bee rules, reprinted from *Words of the Champions:*

Contest Rules of the National Spelling Bee

1. City and regional champions participating in the championship finals of the National Spelling Bee in Washington, D.C. must qualify under two basic requirements: (a) they must not have passed beyond the eighth grade at the time of their individual school finals; and (b) they must not reach their 16th birthday on or before the date of the national finals.

2. Contests for classroom, school, district, city or regional championships may be conducted either in writing or orally, or a combination of the two. The national championship finals, however, shall be an oral competition, with eliminations on a "mis-and-out" basis in the traditional Spelling Bee manner.

3. Words used in the national finals shall be selected from the "Words of the Champions" book, from the lists used in the various city and regional contests, and from Webster's Third New International Dictionary.

4. Words shall be pronounced according to the diacritical markings in Webster's Third New International Dictionary, from which in every case the pronouncer shall select the definition or definitions that he gives. With the approval of the judges, he may give a fuller explanation of the meaning of a word to supplement the dictionary definition or definitions quotes.

5. In competition, after the pronouncer gives the contestant a word, the contestant may also pronounce the word before spelling it, after spelling it, or, if he so choose, not at all.

6. The contestant may request the pronouncer to re-pronounce the word, define it, or use it in a sentence. The pronouncer shall grant the request until the judges agree that the word has been made reasonably clear to the contestant. JUDGES MAY DISQUALIFY ANY CONTESTANT WHO IGNORES A REQUEST TO START SPELLING.

7. Having started to spell a word, a contestant shall not be permitted to change letters already pronounced. He may retract from the beginning of the word, provided letters and their sequence are not changed in the retracing. In retracing, if there is any change in the original letters and their sequence, the speller will be disqualified.

8. Upon missing the spelling of a word, the contestant immediately drops out of the contest. The next word on the pronouncer's list is given to the next contestant.

9. When the contestants are reduced to two, the elimination procedure changes. At that point, when one contestant misspells a word, the other contestant shall be given an opportunity to spell that same word. If the second contestant spells that word correctly, plus the next word on the pronouncer's list, then the second contestant shall be declared the champion.

10. If one of the last two spellers misses and the other, after correcting the error, misspells the new word submitted to him, then the misspelled new word shall be referred to the first speller. If the first speller then succeeds in correcting the error and correctly spells the next word on the pronouncer's list, then he shall be declared champion.

11. If both spellers misspell the same word, both shall continue in the contest, and the one who first misspelled the word shall be given a new word to spell. The contest shall then continue under Rules 9 and 10.

12. Webster's *Third New International Dictionary* shall serve as the final authority for the spellings of words in the National finals. If a word has two or more accepted spellings, only the spellings set in boldface type and separated by the word *or,* and in some cases the word *also,* at the beginning of the descriptive matter will be accepted as correct. Words having the labels archaic and obsolete (abbreviated obs) and regional labels (like North, Midland, South, Brit(ish), Irish) will not be accepted as correct.

13. Any question relating to the spelling of a word should be referred to the judges immediately. The deadline for making a protest is before the contestant affected would have received his next word had he stayed in the contest. No protest will be entertained after that word has been given another speller. When only two spellers remain, a protest must be made immediately, that is, before the second speller has started to spell the word given him, or, if both have missed the same word, before the correct spelling is given the audience.

14. The judges are in complete control of the Bee. Their decision shall be final on all questions.

15. Any child having once won a National Spelling Bee championship is ineligible for further competition in the National Spelling Bee.

Winning Words. To paraphrase the Walrus in *Alice in Wonderland,* the time has come to talk of words, words, winning words. The following is a list of the words that won the National Spelling Bee from 1965 to 1988.

1965—eczema	1973—vouchsafe	1981—sarcophagus
1966—ratoon	1974—hydrophyte	1982—psoriasis
1967—chihuahua	1975—incisor	1983—purim
1968—abalone	1976—narcolepsy	1984—luge
1969—interlocutory	1977—cambist	1985—milieu
1970—croissant	1978—deification	1986—odontalgia
1971—shalloon	1979—maculature	1987—staphylococci
1972—macerate	1980—elucubrate	1988—elegiacal

In 1988, before the winner was declared, the finalists had to be able to spell each of the following words correctly. All sixty of the finalists missed at least one word on the list.

ailanthus	indissociable	radicchio
aisling	intussuscept	rectilinearly
aliunde	isopycnic	reglementary
aloisiite	jequirity	siriasis
anaphylaxis	jinete	smaragdine
arrondissement	keratopathy	systole
astichous	lipoprotein	tachyarrhythmia
bilboquet	lithophilous	tektite
coelacanth	mcleod	telencephalon
edulcorate	mitrailleuse	teonanacatl
enchytrae	orchestrelle	terpsichore
endosteal	patronymic	toccata
escritoire	perfidious	troglobiont
ferruginous	periscii	tutoyer
feuilleton	phlogogenic	ventriloquial
firman	phonodeik	ventripotent
gibberellin	pinacotheca	wobbulator
huaco	poliorcetics	wurrung
hyetology	psephology	xerarch
icosahedron	quinquagenary	zugzwang

From all over the nation, young spellers, ranging in age from eleven to fifteen, come to Washington, D.C., for an event-crowded week. Besides the exciting competition, there are handsome rewards. These include a week of sightseeing, entertainment at banquets, receptions by government officials and statesmen, and prizes of more than $5,000 in cash. Some of the spelling celebrities are photographed with their senators and congressmen. For the national champion there's a never-to-be forgotten bonus thrown in—that is, a trip to New York City, some spending money for his or her escort, and perhaps an appearance on national television.

For ammunition on how the younger generation is spelling its way to success, we may find out how youngsters are hurdling tongue-twisting words such as *consanguineous* and *impecunious*. The National Spelling Bee officials agree that each year's contestants are better than the last. Several years ago, at the end of the first day, only seventeen spellers remained of the seventy who had started. The next year thirty-one survived the tense, ten-round competition on opening day.

In the national competition, girls usually far outnumber the boys. Boys contend vigorously, however, and the National Spelling Bee becomes in a way a battle of the sexes. How ever you interpret it, the finalists are the top spellers of more than six million youngsters who competed in local and state bees.

One national champion offered this advice: "Study a lot and look up every word you read and don't know," she said. "The words in Washington are hard."[6]

ANOTHER BREATHER FOR PRACTICE

And so the spelling bee *does* sound exciting. If you feel inclined to compete with the expert youngsters, you might learn your spelling IQ from the following test, which first appeared in an article by the eminent editor T. K. Brown III in the April, 1967, *Esquire*. It presents a list of words, trickily misspelled, and the speller must translate them into dictionary spellings. Try yourself out and then check your work against a dictionary.

uh-kahm-uh-date	lick-wuff-i
ass-uh-9	may-uh-naze
brag-uh-doe-c-o	minnie-school
dessuh-kate	new-moan-yu
eggs-asp-u-ra-shun	rare-uff-i
fees-uh-bull	spatch-uh-luhs
im-pah-stir	stay-shun
i-knock-you-la-shun	tittle-8
in-uh-fish-us	2-mar-o

A score of five rights is average; a score of ten, above average; and a score of fifteen or sixteen possibly puts you on a level with the champions in the National Spelling Bee.

Some secrets for successful spelling. Those who know the secrets of succeeding in spelling without half trying can identify the speller's method of attack. In other words, some spellers rely on visual memory, some on auditory memory. The visualizers read off the word quickly and confidently, and usually correctly. Those who rely on auditory memory spell by syllables. The perceptive listener is aware of the speller's point of uncertainty. Take the confusing word *sacrilegious.* The uncertain speller pronounces *sacri-* and then hesitates about *lig* or *leg.* The visual approach, of course, is more reliable than the auditory.

In the preceding pages, we've taken a nostalgic look at an American tradition, the National Spelling Bee, which has played an important role in our social and literary heritage. We've looked at the present state of our education in the communication process, noting strengths and weaknesses. Using three of Kipling's serving men, we've presented pertinent information on *why* spell, *how* to spell, and *what* words to spell. From time to time we've peeked into the future, trying to predict what young people will be facing in the twenty-first century, and we've tried to relate spelling progress to "future shock." What is this tomorrow? We may answer by saying that there are opening on all sides new frontiers in human knowledge.

A light touch. Some people do go through life spelling with the greatest of ease. There are families whose members all know how to spell. But those who find spelling a hurdle may find consolation in hearing again that there is a low correlation between spelling proficiency and intelligence.

In the professional literature may be found the following selection, which a student has composed in rhymed couplets and which summarizes what we've been saying about the past and the present of communication by spelling.[7]

OUR SPELLING IS A MUESS!
SANDRA LEMAN

Although this comment may be tright,
Our English spelling is a fright!
We should develop some technique

That wouldn't make it quite so blique.
If only we could make some rules
That children, when they go to skules,
Could learn, and wouldn't have to guess,
We might see more effectiveness.
The words would roll right off their tongue,
And they might learn to read quite yongue.
If we would spell with some technique,
They'd learn to read in just one wique!
Yet many people take to heart
The problems that such change would steart.
American printers from ocean to ocean
Would all protest with great commocean;
While changing, adjustments would have to be made—
Teachers would want to be doubly pade.
It might cause a great amount of trouble
To burst this awful spelling bouble.
How did our spelling get in this muess?
There are several reasons why, I guess.
Some borrowed words retained their signs
To show their etymological ligns.
The problem of spelling began to weigh
When words got easier to seigh
And spelling stayed the same as before
This caused a problem, or three or fore.
Printers, spelling's greatest friends,
Started several spelling triends.
Foreign printers printed words
With spellings that were "for the bords."
They changed the spelling of words like ghost;
Then left some words, but altered mhost.
They added letters to save their rows,
Or subtracted some—this caused more wows.
Uneducated printers would
Misspell some words—This wasn't gould.
We owe these printers quite a debt—
Our spelling hasn't recovered yebt!
The vowel shift in men's dialogue
Also helped to make a fogue;
The spelling differences came because
Vowels shifted, and spelling stayed as it wause.
Other spellings also came through

Scholars who wanted to show what they nough
Where words came from (though we doubt
That they were thorough in checking some oubt).
Etymologies often were shown—
This causes modern spellers to grown!
These are some reasons, just a few,
Why spelling may be hard for yew.
But why let old spelling be taught
Instead of changing them, as we aught?
One reason why our spelling's a trial
Is that standard spelling is the stial.
One who from standard spelling is turned
Is classified as being unlurned.
A person who hopes to own a yacht
Must learn to spell, like it or nacht.
Reform would affect a great many people,
From the base of the hill to the top of the steople.
The first reaction will be "No!"
For change is sometimes very slo.
Perhaps someday we'll open our eyes
And maybe we will realyes
The need for change, but until then
We'll have to spell the way we've ben.
But as long as present spelling reigns,
Reading and writing will cause us peigns.

CHAPTER XII

Ten Tests
of Spelling Success

The centipede was happy quite,
Until a toad in fun
Said, "Pray, which leg goes after which?"
That worked her mind to such a pitch,
She lay distracted in a ditch,
Considering how to run.

MRS. EDWARD CRASTER

The centipede in the ditch and the speller at his desk have a problem
in common. The centipede has to know which leg comes after which.
The speller has to know which letter comes after which. This matter
of knowing which letter follows is obviously a difficult job. I believe,
though, that if you have followed the lessons and exercises in this
book carefully, you are now extremely well prepared to solve problems
like the centipede's. The main part of this chapter consists of tests
designed to allow you to show your proficiency. Before we go on
to them, though, let's review a few points that have been made before.
A quick briefing on what we have learned may prove useful:

1. Find and use your own most efficient study technique or combination of techniques.

2. Emphasize particularly the value of clear-cut visual perception
in accurate spelling. Remember that the auditory imagery of pronunciation and the motor imagery of the pronunciation and the writing
of the word are important helps in learning.

207

3. Remember that if you do not visualize words, you may think of them clearly in some other terms. Some spellers recall words in auditory or kinesthetic images which are as clear and distinct as visual images.

4. Beware of shortcomings in speech. Mispronunciation, articulatory defects, dialectical pronunciation, or a foreign language background may be serious obstacles for you. The least excusable of these faults is the slovenly speech behind such bad spellings as *Febuary, athaletics, chimley,* and *reconize.* If you speak carefully, you will never spell *mischievious* for *mischievous, grievious* for *grievous,* *evry* for *every, heighth* for *height, liberry* for *library, sophmore* for *sophomore, suprise* for *surprise,* or *artic* for *arctic.*

5. Remember that success in spelling is heavily dependent upon developing the right attitudes: interest, confidence, a real desire to spell, a spelling conscience, a spelling consciousness, the intention to remember, and an aggressive attack are absolutely essential.

6. Don't allow negative emotions to swamp your attempt to learn. A fear of failure, a distaste for spelling, or the simple frustration of not being able to write well can defeat you from the start. Remember, any person of average intelligence who wants to can learn to spell.

7. Spelling techniques involving phonetics, syllabication, structuring, phonemes, and graphemes have been developed by experts to enable readers and spellers to analyze words for the sounds they symbolize. The same techniques are effective in learning to combine letters into word symbols. Recognition of the sound of a word and of the relation of the sound to its spelling is one of the most important tools in attacking any spelling problem.

8. Go back to the ancient Latin roots, prefixes, and suffixes, and get a good foundation in them. Do learn the roots and employ them as a base for a list of derivative words. Build around single roots you know. The Latin root *fortis,* meaning *strong,* for example, is found in *fort, fortify, fortitude,* and *enforce.*

9. You will find it helpful to relate the suffixes to grammar. Suffix words gain in meaning and usefulness once you learn that the suffix usually classifies the word as a noun, adjective, adverb, or verb. The suffixes *able, al, an, ile, ory, ose,* and *ous,* among others, identify adjectives; *age, ant, icle, eer, ence, ion, ment,* and *ure,* among others, indicate nouns; *fy, ise,* and *ize* signify verbs; and *ly* marks adverbs.

10. Use mnemonic devices to clarify the spelling of homonyms and words that are seemingly inconsistent. The word *principal* may be distinguished from *principle,* for example, if you remember that the *principal* can be a *pal.* Remember that a *complement completes* some-

thing; that there is a *mar* in *grammar*; and that everyone prolongs *dessert*, even in spelling, but hurries through a *desert*.

11. Learn only rules that apply to a large number of words and have a few exceptions. Learn one rule at a time; see how each rule actually works.

12. Don't worry about such quiz kid items as *peripatetic, perspicacity,* or *otolaryngology* when you cannot spell *across* or *benefit*.

13. The dictionary is a speller's best friend. Be kind to it. Observe and learn the syllabic division, pronunciation, derivation, meaning, and use of each word. You will retain an enduring mental picture of the word.

To summarize, a constant and resourceful effort to keep pushing out your horizons can make spelling a vital part of your academic, social, and professional life. Unlike the centipede, who may still be in the ditch wondering which foot to put forward, you should know which letter comes next. When you become competent, you will spell confidently instead of uncertainly, systematically instead of haphazardly, fluently instead of haltingly, and knowingly instead of accidentally.

The real hurdles have now been crossed. Now, like all top-flight word-smiths, you are ready to test your mettle. You may do this by aiming at the series of ten targets below.

If possible, form a team with another person to work on spelling. You can really team up by pronouncing and dictating to each other. The first test is a team test.

TARGET NUMBER ONE
Are you spelling by eye and by ear?

Directions: This spelling test consists of fifty words. Your teammate will announce the number of the word, pronounce the word to be spelled correctly, use the word in a sentence, and pronounce the word again. In each group below four spellings are given for the word pronounced. Select the correct spelling for the word pronounced, underline the answer, and record the number in the parentheses at the right, as shown in the following example:

Number one, friend. He has a *friend. friend.*

(1) frend (2) freind (3) friend (4) firend .... (3)

Of the four spellings, *friend* is, of course, the correct one; so *friend* is underlined. And the spelling is No. 3; so a figure 3 is placed in the parentheses at the end of the dotted line. The answers are on page 223 in the Appendix. Why not ask your partner to read the answers while you check?

(15 minutes)

1. (1) absuence (2) absence (3) absensce (4) absense .... ( )
2. (1) acidentaly (2) accidentaly (3) acidentally
   (4) accidentally .... ( )
3. (1) affect (2) afect (3) affekt (4) afeckt .... ( )
4. (1) amatuer (2) amatur (3) amateur (4) amature .... ( )
5. (1) appriciate (2) apprecate (3) appreciate
   (4) aprecate .... ( )
6. (1) beginning (2) begining (3) biginning
   (4) bigining .... ( )
7. (1) bilieve (2) beleive (3) believ (4) believe .... ( )
8. (1) busness (2) business (3) busines (4) bisnuss .... ( )
9. (1) cemetery (2) cemetary (3) cematery
   (4) cematary .... ( )
10. (1) chaufeur (2) chauffeur (3) chauffuer
    (4) chaufuer .... ( )
11. (1) colum (2) collum (3) colym (4) column .... ( )
12. (1) comittee (2) commitee (3) committee (4) comitte .... ( )
13. (1) critecism (2) criticism (3) critcism
    (4) critusism .... ( )
14. (1) definitly (2) definitely (3) definately
    (4) definatly .... ( )
15. (1) develup (2) devellop (3) develop (4) divelope .... ( )
16. (1) disappoint (2) dissapoint (3) disapoint
    (4) dissappoint .... ( )
17. (1) disapline (2) disiplin (3) disiplun
    (4) discipline.. ( )
18. (1) embarus (2) embarras (3) embarass
    (4) embarrass .... ( )
19. (1) equiped (2) equipped (3) equipt (4) iquipped .... ( )
20. (1) expirence (2) experence (3) experience
    (4) experiense... ( )
21. (1) familiar (2) familar (3) fumiliar (4) familair .... ( )
22. (1) foriegn (2) foreign (3) forein (4) forien .... ( )
23. (1) fuorth (2) fourthe (3) fourth (4) forth .... ( )
24. (1) fundammental (2) fundementel (3) fundemental
    (4) fundamental .... ( )
25. (1) governor (2) guvernor (3) govenor (4) governer .... ( )

Score____

TARGET NUMBER TWO
Are you a word watcher?

The words in the next test are the common staples of conversation. No doubt you've seen the words time and time again in the newspapers, magazines, and advertisements. Now test your powers of recognition by placing the letter of the correct spelling in the blank at the left. When you have finished the test, check your answers with the key in the Appendix, page 224. For practice write in the appropriate space any words about which you are uncertain.

_____ 1. (a) competition   (b) competation   _____

_____ 2. (a) bankruptcy   (b) bankrupcy   _____

_____ 3. (a) negotiability   (b) negotability   _____

_____ 4. (a) suberbanite   (b) suburbanite   _____

_____ 5. (a) contusion   (b) contussion   _____

_____ 6. (a) therepeutic   (b) therapeutic   _____

_____ 7. (a) parady   (b) parody   _____

_____ 8. (a) legecy   (b) legacy   _____

_____ 9. (a) consignement   (b) consignment   _____

_____10. (a) fluctuation   (b) fluctuasion   _____

_____11. (a) delinquents   (b) delinquants   _____

_____12. (a) liability   (b) liabilaty   _____

_____13. (a) inventorie   (b) inventory   _____

_____14. (a) apsolve   (b) absolve   _____

_____15. (a) malignancy   (b) malignency   _____

_____16. (a) accute   (b) acute   _____

_____17. (a) surogate   (b) surrogate   _____

_____18. (a) accomplice   (b) accomplise   _____

_____19. (a) testemant   (b) testament   _____

_____20. (a) cybernetics   (b) cybrenetics   _____

                                                    Score_____

TARGET NUMBER THREE
Is your speech showing?

The following words are often misspelled because they are incorrectly pronounced. They are misspelled here. Display your spelling virtuosity by writing the correct spelling. Consult page 224 in the Appendix for the answers.

1. accidently	11. mathamatics	21. modren
2. atheletics	12. mischievious	22. maintainance
3. canidate	13. probly	23. twelth
4. excape	14. pronounciation	24. Artic
5. dipthong	15. quanity	25. rigamarole
6. diptheria	16. reconize	26. grievious
7. fraility	17. sophmore	27. heighth
8. goverment	18. studing	28. chimley
9. labratory	19. suprise	29. prespiration
10. libary	20. temperment	30. strenth

Score_____

TARGET NUMBER FOUR
Can you correct the other fellow's errors?

Artemus Ward, whose real name was Charles F. Browne, has made many an American laugh by taking words "out of their dictionary clothes." How much joy has been furnished to our exuberant race by the showman's bad spelling can never be known. There are those, however, who have always disliked this sort of easy fun. For a few minutes, then, you are to play the role of one in the latter group and correct the humorist's spelling. Consult page 224 in the Appendix for the misspellings.

Common Skools

A excellent skool sistim is in vogy here. John Slurk, my old pardner, has a little son who has only bin to skool two months, and yet he exhibertid his father's performin Bear in the show all last summer. I hope they pay particular tention to Spelin in those Skools, becaws if a man can't Spel wel he's of no kount.

Score_____

(The total number of different words misspelled is 13.)

TARGET NUMBER FIVE
When the vowel gets lost.

Many spelling errors are made because one vowel is omitted. The following is a list of words with a vowel that often gets lost. See whether you can restore the right one. The answers are found in the Appendix, page 224.

1. bound_ry	10. hist_ry	19. parli_ment
2. choc_late	11. lab_ratory	20. re_lly
3. ever_body	12. li_ble	21. sep_rate
4. envir_nment	13. liter_ture	22. soph_more
5. fact_ry	14. med_eval	23. temp_rature
6. fin_lly	15. mem_ry	24. veg_table
7. gener_lly	16. natur_lly	25. veng_ance
8. g_ography	17. Niag_ra	
9. g_ometry	18. occasion_lly	

Score____

TARGET NUMBER SIX

The pronunciation might be different if . . .

Some words would really be jawbreakers if the silent letters were pronounced. With such words, keep in mind the origin of the word. Visualize the position of the silent letter. Is it at the beginning, the middle, or the end of the word? Now test yourself on this list. Write in the silent letter. If you miss a word, write it in the space at the right. The answers are found in the Appendix, page 224.

1. i_land _____	10. mor_gage _____	
2. bourgeoi_ _____	11. _ry _____	
3. chamoi_ _____	12. su_tle _____	
4. i_le _____	13. dis_ern _____	
5. corp_ _____	14. vi_count _____	
6. indi_tment _____	15. s_ord _____	
7. _salm _____	16. debri_ _____	
8. _tomaine _____	17. arrai_n _____	
9. _sychiatry _____	18. recei_t _____	

19. de_tor   _____   23. _erb   _____

20. hym-   _____   24. r_inoceros   _____

21. vi-tuals   _____   25. r_ythmical   _____

22. colum-   _____

Score___

TARGET NUMBER SEVEN
Can you handle the "sound-alike" words?

Words similar in sound but different in meaning—homonyms—are frequently confused; break and brake are examples. Some words are close enough in sound and appearance—for example, except and accept—to be confusing. The sentences which follow have been taken from student papers. The correct form of the misspelled word has been supplied. Select the correct form and write the word in the space provided. Check your answers with the Appendix, page 224.

1. Mr. Jones is the (principal, principle) of the school. _____

2. The country was under (martial, marital) law. _____

3. The (boarder, border) between the two countries was irregular.

_____

4. One signs a business letter with (Respectfully yours, Respectively yours).   _____

5. The man parked the car at an (angle, angel)._____

6. Canada and the United States were (alleys, allies) in the war.

_____

7. The (cavalry, calvary) made its last march. _____

8. One needs (capital, capitol) for such an investment. _____

9. Some animals have short and furry (tails, tales). _____

10. He couldn't (breath, breathe) because of a cold._____

11. They travel across the Nevada (desert, dessert). _____

12. A (horde, hoard) of adventurers assaulted the castle. _____

13. Some (advice, advise) is free.   _____

14. The dog knows (its, it's) way home.   _____

15. Don't (lose, loose) your gloves.   _____

16. The conductor has (led, lead) the orchestra.   _____

17. The actors rehearsed (their, there) parts.   _____

18. The fortuneteller's (prophecy, prophesy) came true. _____

19. The lesson is (to, too) long.   _____

20. He doesn't know (whether, wheather) he passed or not. _____

21. It's (later, latter) than you think.   _____

22. He joined the police (corps, corpse).   _____

23. The lady received a lovely (complement, compliment) for her singing.   _____

24. The costume is made of (course, coarse) material._____

25. The (assent, ascent) to the mountain was gradual._____

Score_____

TARGET NUMBER EIGHT
When there are two spellings, which do you take?
Some words have two spellings. One is American, called the primary form; and the other is British, called the secondary. Although the British spellings are not incorrect, most American writers prefer the primary form. The twenty-five words below are British spellings. Rewrite the words using the preferred American spelling. If you are not sure of your answers, check with the Appendix, page 224.

1. acknowledgement_____		10. saleable	_____
2. armour	_____	11. judgement	_____
3. calibre	_____	12. labour	_____
4. clamour	_____	13. likeable	_____
5. colour	_____	14. meagre	_____
6. encyclopaedia	_____	15. metre	_____
7. endeavour	_____	16. odour	_____
8. favour	_____	17. parlour	_____
9. flavour	_____	18. programme	_____

19. saviour _____

20. sceptre _____

21. sombre _____

22. splendour _____

23. theatre _____

24. travelled _____

25. vigour _____

Score_____

TARGET NUMBER NINE

Can you unscramble these scrambled words?

Jonathan Swift once defined literary style as "the proper words in the proper places." Spelling might be defined as the proper letters in the proper places. The letters in the following twenty-five words are scrambled. See how successful you are in unscrambling the letters. You can do the exercise alone, or you can team up with someone to see who discovers the word first. You will find the words on page 224 in the Appendix.

1. lyniteifed _____

2. mmaragr _____

3. catedomcoma _____

4. ralimis _____

5. tripponutoy _____

6. iecneccons _____

7. linescipdi _____

8. tingwir _____

9. yfillna _____

10. culeehsd _____

11. gedytar _____

12. ltury _____

13. ginomc _____

14. sytercou _____

15. sopsesions _____

16. palalerl _____

17. asnioux _____

18. werdanes _____

19. sedraip _____

20. hetigh _____

21. lantieuten _____

22. enlobetaic _____

23. cafatiens _____

24. elyrescin _____

25. usliriduco _____

Score_____

TARGET NUMBER TEN (part 1)
Pitting yourself against the experts.

You are ready now to compete with the experts on the list known as the "fateful fifty," words which have decided the fate of fifty contestants in the annual National Spelling Bee. Each of the fifty words is offered in its correct spelling and at least one of its possible misspellings. Write the letter of the form you think is correct. Consult the Appendix, page 224.

_____ 1. (a) pallor   (b) palor

_____ 2. (a) miniatory   (b) minatory

_____ 3. (a) catalist   (b) catalyst

_____ 4. (a) rue   (b) rew

_____ 5. (a) jocose   (b) jococe

_____ 6. (a) urbane   (b) urbain

_____ 7. (a) fishion   (b) fission   (c) fition

_____ 8. (a) aggressor   (b) agressor   (c) agresor

_____ 9. (a) scintilate   (b) scintillate

_____10. (a) insousiant   (b) insouciant

_____11. (a) wainscot   (b) wanescot   (c) wainscott

_____12. (a) assonance   (b) assonence

_____13. (a) concensus   (b) consensus

_____14. (a) herbacious   (b) herbaceous

_____15. (a) meretricious   (b) meretrisious

_____16. (a) pomagranate   (b) pomegranate

_____17. (a) aglomeration   (b) agglomeration

_____18. (a) peraration   (b) peroration

_____19. (a) mannumit   (b) manumit

_____20. (a) febril   (b) febrile

_____21. (a) beir   (b) bier

_____22. (a) aplomb   (b) aplom

_____23. (a) elition   (b) elision

____24. (a) cuizine (b) cuisine

____25. (a) quandery (b) quandary

____26. (a) medalion (b) medallion

____27. (a) airiferous (b) aeriferous (c) ariferous

____28. (a) perepatetic (b) perapatetic (c) peripatetic

____29. (a) curascation (b) coruscation (c) coriscation

____30. (a) exaccerbate (b) exaserbate (c) exacerbate

____31. (a) saponaceous (b) saponacious (c) saponatious

____32. (a) effeminat (b) effemenate (c) effeminate

____33. (a) disputasious (b) disputatious (c) disputashus

____34. (a) requiem (b) requeim (c) requime

____35. (a) arcatype (b) archetype (c) archatype

____36. (a) gutteral (b) guttural (c) gutural

____37. (a) yaul (b) yall (c) yawl

____38. (a) villify (b) villafy (c) vilify

____39. (a) foment (b) fomment

____40. (a) glatial (b) glacial

____41. (a) enoble (b) ennoble

____42. (a) imitator (b) imetator

____43. (a) obbloquy (b) obloquy

____44. (a) imposter (b) impostor

____45. (a) homeletic (b) homiletic

____46. (a) mattok (b) mattock

____47. (a) shellaked (b) shelacked (c) shellacked

____48. (a) emendation (b) emmendation

____49. (a) indisoluble (b) indissoluble

____50. (a) eflorescence (b) efflorescence

TARGET NUMBER TEN (part 2)

It's an old story that our highly trained and technically proficient engineers demonstrate a noticeable deficiency in spelling. Test yourself on the following aerospace misspellings, and check your spelling with the answers in the Appendix, page 224, reprinted from Donald A. Sears' "Engineers Spell Acoustically," in the December, 1969, *College Composition and Communication.*

112 COMMON AEROSPACE MISSPELLINGS [1]

accoustic
accummulator
adversly
alluminum
amature
ammended
analisis
annomaly, anomilies
anotating
apparant
applys
approxamitly, approxamately
argumant

carefull
carrotts (vegetables)
catagory
circumferance
commense
committments
complition
composit
conditian
configueration
critacality
cronological

decible
degredation
derrive
defficient

descision
deveation
diaphram
discribe, discription
docuement

equitorial
erraticaly
exerpts
explanitory
extrapulate

facillity
Farenheidt
flexability

hazzard
hight

imperical
inaccessable
indecated
independant
infanite
injest (to take in)
inquirey
insue
integrety
interferance
interum
irredescent
its'

lead (past tense of "lead")
ledgend
ledgible

magnetude
manualy
manuel
measurments
milage
miscillaneous
mitalic
murge

narritive
nucleor

ocurs
offerred

per say (it itself)
personnal
personell
pesimistic
plotts
pre-mature
preperation
presense
priar
prooved

reaccurence
recomendation

reccomemdation
referance
responce
responsable
retrival, retrive
re-vised

seperate
shreading
(the) significants (of)
sited (for listed)
solinoid
speciman
sub-stantiate
suppliment
suspence
systom

tare (rip)
to (more than one, less than three)
tolerence, tollerance
tubeing
turbulance

uncomprimising
untill

vaccuum
varified
vis-avis
vidio

wheather
wireing

Appendix

ANSWERS

The authority for the answers in the following exercises is the *New World Dictionary of the American Language*, Second College Edition.

CHAPTER III

Reversals. Corrected words are: 9. complete; 11. applied.

Other exercises: *reiteration*.

Exercise 1. *Answers:*   1-d; 2-a; 3-d; 4-d; 5-c; 6-d; 7-b; 8-d; 9-c; 10-a

Exercise 2. *Answers:*   1-a; 2-d; 3-a; 4-d; 5-b; 6-a; 7-d; 8-c; 9-a; 10-c

Exercise 3. *Answers:*   1-b; 2-a; 3-b; 4-a; 5-c; 6-d; 7-d; 8-c; 9-c; 10-d

Recognition and reproduction practice.

Answers: 1-a; 2-a; 3-c; 4-b; 5-b; 6-c; 7-b; 8-c; 9-a; 10-a

CHAPTER VI

Syllabication: Column B: an-thro-poph-a-gous; e-soph-a-gus; Brah-min; per-i-pa-tet-ic; said; sar-coph-a-gus. Column C: 5, 4, 2, 5, 1, 4

Syllabication: 1. ac-com-mo-date; 2. ap-pen-dix; 3. a-wry; 4. ba-sis; 5. cha-rade; 6. cher-ub; 7. cur-ric-u-lum; 8. da-tum; 9. et-i-quette; 10. fo-cus; 11. in-dex; 12. ir-rep-a-ra-ble; 13. nu-cle-us; 14. pref-ace; 15. stim-u-lus; 16. te-di-ous; 17. ter-ri-fy; 18. val-ley; 19. ver-te-brate; 20. val-et.

CHAPTER VIII

Hyphenation: 4. jack-o'-lantern; 5. fly-by-night; 6. will-o'-the-wisp; 7. know-it-all; 8. take-off; 9. go-between; 10. jack-of-all-trades.

Compound Adjectives: 1. thirty-day; 2. forty-nine; 4. silver-plated; 6. percent; 7. childlike; 8. microbiology; 9. one-eyed; 10. six-cylinder.

Special Compounds: 1. self-help; 2. re-cover; 3. anti-Communist; 4. ex-wife; 5. pro-British; 6. re-release.

Latin Roots: 1. aquarium; 2. auditorium; 3. benefit; 4. corporation; 5. mortality; 6. transcribe; 7. attract; 8. televise; 9. solitude; 10. reduction.

Prefix mis: 1. misshape; 2. misspeak; 3. misspell; 4. misspend; 5. misstate; 6. misstep; 7. mistake; 8. mishap; 9. misdemeanors; 10. misconstrue; 11. mischief; 12. misfire; 13. misname; 14. misuse; 15. misunderstand; 16. misprint; 17. mistrust; 18. misfortune; 19. misbehave; 20. mispronounce.

Prefix dis: 1. disappear; 2. disappoint; 3. dissatisfy; 4. dissimilar; 5. dissect; 6. disservice; 7. dissemble; 8. discredit; 9. dispel; 10. dissertation; 11. disentangle;

12. dissuade; 13. dissever; 14. dissension; 15. dissipate; 16. disregard; 17. dissociate; 18. dispose; 19. dissoluble; 20. disturb.

Greek Prefixes: 1. synchronize; 2. periscope; 3. program; 4. diameter; 5. monogamy; 6. prophet; 7. syntax; 8. monotony; 9. antitoxin; 10. apologue.

Suffixes:

2. include, inclusive, inclusively
3. continue, continuous, continuously
4. abominate, abominable, abominably
5. stupefy, stupid, stupidly
6. labor, laborious, laboriously
7. glorify, glorious, gloriously
8. decide, decisive, decisively
9. contend, contentious, contentiously
10. dramatize, dramatic, dramatically
11. conclude, conclusive, conclusively
12. criticise, critical, critically

Suffixes: Vowel + r verb test: *ence.* You should have underlined 1, 2, 5, 6, 9. *ance.* Long *a* test: 1. acceptation; 2. domination; 3. importation; 4. substantiation; 5. jubilation; 6. radiation; 7. observation; 8. signification; 9. toleration; 10. variation.

Suffixes: ise, ize, yze: 1. vulcanize; 2. civilize; 3. alphabetize; 4.amortize; 5. paralogize 6. generalize; 7. harmonize; 8. hypnotize; 9. idolize; 10. comprise; 11. patronize; 12. penalize; 13. organize; 14. pulverize; 15. despise; 16. rationalize; 17. apologize; 18. atomize; 19. authorize; 20. franchise.

Doubling the Consonant: The rule applies to 1, 2, 4, 5, and 10.

Review Exercise I: 1. a; 2. i; 3. i; 4.a; 5. i; 6. a; 7. a; 8. i; 9. a; 10. a; 11. i; 12. a; 13. a; 14. i; 15. i.

Review Exerise II: 1. e; 2. a; 3. a; 4. e; 5. a; 6. e; 7. e; 8. e; 9. a; 10. a; 11. e; 12. e; 13. e; 14. e; 15. a.

Review Exercise III: 1. ar; 2. er; 3. er; 4. ar; 5. er; 6. er; 7. or; 8. or; 9. er; 10. er; 11. ar; 12. or; 13. or; 14. er; 15. or; 16. or; 17. er; 18. or; 19. er; 20. or.

Review Exercise IV: 1. paralyze; 7. analyze; 10. apprise; 17. capitalize.

Review Exercise V: 1. a; 2. e; 3. e; 4. e; 5. a; 6. a; 7. a; 8. a; 9. a; 10. a.

Review Exercise VI: 1. equipped; 4. referred; 6. controlling; 7. compelling.

Review Exercise VII: 1. postscript; 2. catalogue; 3. telephone; 4. symphony; 5. circumnavigate; 6. dissatisfaction; 7. benefit; 8. polytheism; 9. predict; 10. interrupt.

Review Exercise VIII:

1. neither; weird; foreign; counterfeiters; their; leisure; seized; either; heirs; heifers; heights.
2. received; eight; receipts; freight; neighbor.
3. mischievous; belief; cashier; yielded; fierce.
4. chief's; friend; relieved; thief; field.
5. niece; handkerchief; relieve; grief.
6. neighbor; reins; shrieked; sleigh.
7. skeins; weigh; piece.
8. neigh; their; veins.
9. perceive; brief; review.
10. weight; ceiling; deceiving.

Review Exercise IX: 1. video; 2. scribe; 3. pes; 4. deus; 5. aqua.

Review Exercise X: 1. biology; 2. geology; 3. zoology; 4. cosmology; 5. anthropology.

CHAPTER IX

Literature. *Answers:* 1. appendix; 8. fiction; 10. index; 11. librarian; 12. literary; 17. lyric.

Mathematics. *Answers:* 1. bisector; 2. circumference; 4. denominator; 6. diameter; 11. integer; 13. linear; 14. numerator; 15. perimeter; 16. perpendicular.

Medicine. *Answers:* 1. l, s; 2. i, ɔ, k; 3. p, ə, ay; 4. k, s; 5. k, s; 6. k, ə, i; 7. k, s, ow; 8. iy, z; 9. n, k, ʃ; 10. f, i, ʃ; 11. i; 12. uw; 13. ə, m, k; 14. ae, ʃ; 15. d, k.

Nursing. *Answers:* 1. anesthetic; 2. chloroform; 3. clinic; 6. medication; 9. recovery; 12. conscious.

Political Science. *Answers:* 3. congressional; 4. constitution; 6. dictatorship; 8. emigration; 9. fascism; 10. corporation; 11. inauguration; 12. judicial; 14. legislation; 18. reclamation; 20. socialism.

CHAPTER XII

Target One

Answers:

1. *absence.* His *absence* from school was reported. *absence* .... (2)
2. *accidentally.* They met *accidentally. accidentally* .... (4)
3. *affect.* Changes of season *affect* the people very little. *affect*............................. (1)
4. *amateur.* Every artist was at first an *amateur. amateur* .... (3)
5. *appreciate.* Children easily *appreciate* justice. *appreciate* .... (3)
6. *beginning.* They are *beginning* to build a library. *beginning* .... (1)
7. *believe.* Who can *believe* otherwise? *believe* .... (4)
8. *business. Business* is greatly improved throughout the world. *business* .... (2)
9. *cemetery.* A *cemetery* is a place set apart for the burial of the dead. *cemetery*............................. (1)
10. *chauffeur.* A *chauffeur* is familiar with the operation of an automobile. *chauffeur*............................. (2)
11. *column.* A *column* of smoke rises to the sky. *column*............................. (4)
12. *committee.* A *committee* has been appointed. *committee*............................. (3)
13. *criticism.* He reads every *criticism* of a new play. *criticism* .... (2)
14. *definitely.* The nobles were *definitely* conquered by the crown. *definitely*........... (2)
15. *develop.* The seed *develops* into a plant. *develop*............................. (3)
16. *disappoint.* Their companions *disappoint* them. *disappoint* .... (1)
17. *discipline.* The troops were noted for their *discipline. discipline*............................. (4)
18. *embarrass.* The thoughts of his misdeed *embarrass* him. *embarrass* .... (4)
19. *equipped.* The sailors are well *equipped* for the voyage. *equipped*............................. (2)
20. *experience.* Some people know by insight what others learn by *experience. experience*............................. (3)
21. *familiar.* People addressed her in a *familiar,* if not a rude tone. *familiar*........... (1)
22. *foreign.* They depend upon *foreign* trade. *foreign* .... (2)
23. *fourth.* The *Fourth* of July is Independence Day. *fourth*............................. (3)
24. *fundamental.* Readers notice a *fundamental* change in his attitude to life. *fundamental*............................. (4)
25. *governor.* The citizens elected the *governor* of the state. *governor* .... (1)

Target Two

Answers: 1-a; 2-a; 3-a; 4-b; 5-a; 6-b; 7-b; 8-b; 9-b; 10-a; 11-a; 12-a; 13-b; 14-b; 15-a; 16-b; 17-b; 18-a; 19-b; 20-a.

Target Three

Answers: 1. accidentally; 2. athletics; 3. candidate; 4. escape; 5. diphthong; 6. diphtheria; 7. frailty; 8. government; 9. laboratory; 10. library; 11. mathematics; 12. mischievous; 13. probably; 14. pronunciation; 15. quantity; 16. recognize; 17. sophomore; 18. studying; 19. surprise; 20. temperament; 21. modern; 22. maintenance; 23. twelfth; 24. Arctic; 25. rigmarole; 26. grievous; 27. height; 28. chimney; 29. perspiration; 30. strength.

Target Four

Answers: 1. school (four times); 2. system; 3. vogue; 4. partner; 5. been; 6. exhibited; 7. performing; 8. attention; 9. spelling; 10. because; 11. spell; 12. well; 13. account.

Target Five

Answers: 1-a; 2-o; 3-y; 4-o; 5-o; 6-a; 7-a; 8-e; 9-e; 10-o; 11-o; 12-a; 13-a; 14-i; 15-o; 16-a; 17-a; 18-a; 19-a; 20-a; 21-a; 22-o; 23-e; 24-e; 25-e.

Target Six

Answers: 1-s; 2-s; 3-s; 4-s; 5-s; 6-c; 7-p; 8-p; 9-p; 10-t; 11-w; 12-b; 13-c; 14-s; 15-w; 16-s; 17-g; 18-p; 19-b; 20-n; 21-c; 22-n; 23-h; 24-h; 25-h.

Target Seven

Answers: 1. principal; 2. martial; 3. border; 4. Respectfully yours; 5. angle; 6. allies; 7. cavalry; 8. capital; 9. tails; 10. breathe; 11. desert; 12. horde; 13. advice; 14. its; 15. lose; 16. led; 17. their; 18. prophecy; 19. too; 20. whether; 21. later; 22. corps; 23. compliment; 24. coarse; 25. ascent.

Target Eight

Answers: 1. acknowledgment; 2. armor; 3. caliber; 4. clamor; 5. color; 6. encyclopedia; 7. endeavor; 8. favor; 9. flavor; 10. salable; 11. judgment; 12. labor; 13. likable; 14. meager; 15. meter; 16. odor; 17. parlor; 18. program; 19. savior; 20. scepter; 21. somber; 22. splendor; 23. theater; 24. traveled; 25. vigor.

Target Nine

Answers: 1. definitely; 2. grammar; 3. accommodate; 4. similar; 5. opportunity; 6. conscience; 7. discipline; 8. writing; 9. finally; 10. schedule; 11. tragedy; 12. truly; 13. coming; 14. courtesy; 15. possession; 16. parallel; 17. anxious; 18. answered; 19. despair; 20. eighth; 21. lieutenant; 22. noticeable; 23. fascinate; 24. sincerely; 25. ridiculous.

Target Ten (part 1)

Answers: 1-a; 2-b; 3-b; 4-a; 5-a; 6-a; 7-b; 8-a; 9-b; 10-b; 11-a; 12-a; 13-b; 14-b; 15-a; 16-b; 17-b; 18-b; 19-b; 20-b; 21-b; 22-a; 23-b; 24-b; 25-b; 26-b; 27-b; 28-c; 29-b; 30-c; 31-a; 32-c; 33-b; 34-a; 35-b; 36-b; 37-c; 38-c; 39-a; 40-b; 41-b; 42-a; 43-b; 44-b; 45-b; 46-b; 47-c; 48-a; 49-b; 50-b.

Target Ten (part 2)

Answers: 1. acoustic; 2. accumulator; 3. adversely; 4. aluminum; 5. amateur; 6. amended; 7. analysis; 8. anomaly, anomalies; 9. annotating; 10. apparent; 11. applies; 12. approximately; 13. argument; 14. careful; 15. carrots (vegetables);

16. category; 17. circumference; 18. commence; 19. commitments; 20. completion; 21. composite; 22. condition; 23. configuration; 24. criticality; 25. chronological; 26. decibel; 27. degradation; 28. derive; 29. deficient; 30. decision; 31. deviation; 32. diaphragm; 33. describe, description; 34. document; 35. equatorial; 36. erratically; 37. excerpts; 38. explanatory; 39. extrapolate; 40. facility; 41. Fahrenheit; 42. flexibility; 43. hazard; 44. height; 45. empirical; 46. inaccessible; 47. indicated; 48. independent; 49. infinite; 50. ingest (to take in); 51. inquiry; 52. ensue; 53. integrity; 54. interference; 55. interim; 56. iridescent; 57. its (possessive form of it), it's (contraction of it is); 58. led (past tense of "lead"); 59. legend; 60. legible; 61. magnitude; 62. manually; 63. manual; 64. measurements; 65. mileage; 66. miscellaneous; 67. metallic; 68. merge; 69. narrative; 70. nuclear; 71. occurs; 72. offered; 73. per se (in itself); 74. personal; 75. personnel; 76. pessimistic; 77. plots; 78. premature; 79. preparation; 80. presence; 81. prior; 82. proved; 83. reoccurrence; 84. recommendation, recommendation; 85. reference; 86. response; 87. responsible; 88. retrieval, retrieve; 89. revised; 90. separate; 91. shredding; 92. (the) significance (of); 93. cited (for listed); 94. solenoid; 95. specimen; 96. substantiate; 97. supplement; 98. suspense; 99. system; 100. tear (rip); 101. two (more than one, less than three); 102. tolerance; 103. tubing; 104. turbulence; 105. uncompromising; 106. until; 107. vacuum; 108. verified; 109. vis-a-vis; 110. video; 111. whether; 112. wiring.

NOTES

CHAPTER 1

1. Quoted by Joseph Mersand, Spelling Your Way to Success. New York: Barron's Educational Series, Inc., 1959, p. ix.

2. Lord Chesterfield, Letters to His Son, November 19, 1750.

3. Ella Bentley Arthur, "Inscription in a Webster's Collegiate Dictionary: From a Mother to Her Son." From Word Study. Springfield, Mass.: G. & C. Merriam Company, 1946.

4. G E's Answer to Four Why's. Form PRD 45, p. 6.

5. Kenneth B. M. Crooks, "Reading and Science Instruction," The American Biology Teacher, May, 1957.

6. Rollo May, "Language, Symbols, and Violence," Communication, January, 1974.

7. Vance Packard, A Nation of Strangers. New York: David McKay Company, Inc., 1972.

CHAPTER II

1. Harvey Kinsey Boyer, "Why You Can't Spell," Saturday Review, October 2, 1954.

2. Ernest Horn, "Spelling," Encyclopedia of Educational Research. New York: Macmillan Company, 1941.

3. Stuart Robertson, and Frederic G. Cassidy, The Development of Modern English, second edition. Englewood Cliffs, N.J.: Prentice-Hall, 1954.

4. Joseph Mersand, *Spelling Your Way to Success*. New York: Barron's Educational Series, Inc., 1959.

5. Mario Pei, *The Story of English*. Philadelphia: J. B. Lippincott, 1952.

6. Albert C. Baugh, and Thomas Cable, *A History of the English Language*. Englewood Cliffs, N.J.: Prentice-Hall, 1978.

7. Thomas Pyles, *The Origins and Development of the English Language*. New York: Harcourt, Brace & World, Inc., 1964; also Gertrude A. Boyd, *Teaching Communication Skills in the Elementary School*. New York: Van Nostrand Reinhold Company, 1970.

8. Jared Sparks, ed., *The Works of Benjamin Franklin*. Vol. VI. Chicago: Townsend MacCoun, 1882.

9. Robertson and Cassidy, *op. cit.*

10. *Ibid.*

11. Pei, *op. cit.*

12. Thorstein Veblen, *The Theory of the Leisure Class*. New York: B. W. Huebsch, 1919.

13. W. L. Werner, "English for the World," *Saturday Review*, October 4, 1952.

14. Robertson and Cassidy, *op. cit.*

15. Pitman's Initial Teaching Alphabet.

16. The Foundation for a Compatible and Consistent Alphabet.

17. Thomas R. Lounsbury, *English Spelling and Spelling Reform*. New York: Harper and Brothers, 1909.

18. Upton Sinclair, "Letter to the President," *Saturday Review*, August 18, 1962.

19. T. S. Watt, "Brush Up Your English," *Manchester Guardian*, June 21, 1954.

20. Cited by Josef Vachek. *Written Language: General Problems and Problems of English*. The Hague and Paris: Mouton, 1973.

21. Fred Brengelman, "Generative Phonology and the Teaching of Spelling," *English Journal*. November, 1970.

CHAPTER III

1. David A. Sabatino, "The Construction and Assessment of an Experimental Test of Auditory Perception," *Exceptional Children*, May, 1969.

2. John C. Almack and E. H. Staffelbach, "Method in Teaching Spelling." *Elementary School Journal*. November, 1933.

3. Grace M. Fernald, *Remedial Techniques in Basic School Subjects*. New York: McGraw-Hill Company, 1943.

4. Glenn Myers Blair, *Diagnostic and Remedial Teaching in Secondary Schools*. New York: Macmillan Company, 1946.

5. *Ibid.*

6. Gertrude Hildreth, *Teaching Spelling*. New York: Henry Holt and Company, 1955.

7. Fred J. Schonell, "Ability and Disability in Spelling Amongst Educated Adults," *British Journal of Educational Psychology*, June, 1936.

8. Samuel T. Orton, "Word-Blindness in School Children," *Archives of Neurology and Psychiatry*, November, 1925.

———, "Specific Reading Disability: Strephosymbolia," *Journal of the American Medical Association*, April, 1925.

———, "An Impediment to Learning to Read—A Neurological Explanation of the Reading Disability," *School and Society*, September 8, 1928.

9. C. O. Weber, "Strephosymbolia and Reading Disability," *Journal of Abnormal and Social Psychology*, July, 1944. For additional information on reversals, see Helen Kennedy, "Reversals, Reversals, Reversals!" *Journal of Experimental Education*, December, 1954.

CHAPTER IV

1. *Newsweek*, October 8, 1962.

2. William H. Fox and Merrill T. Eaton, *Analysis of the Spelling Proficiency of 82,833 Pupils in Grades 2 to 8 in 3,547 Teaching Units of the City Schools of Indiana*. Bloomington: Division of Research and Field Services, Indiana University, 1946.

3. William H. Fox, *Spelling Proficiency in Township Schools in Indiana*. Bloomington: Division of Research and Field Services, Indiana University, 1947.

4. Fred C. Ayer, "An Evaluation of High-School Spelling," *School Review*, April, 1951.

5. The Denver *Post*, August 31, 1976.

6. *New York Times*, December 4, 1955.

7. *Newsweek*, December 8, 1975.

8. *Ibid.*

9. Tom Talman, "I'd Better Just Whisper It," *Saturday Evening Post*, November 22, 1952.

10. Rudolf Flesch, *Why Johnny Can't Read*. New York: Harper and Brothers, 1955.

11. Ernest Horn, "Spelling," in Chester W. Harris (editor), *Encyclopedia of Educational Research*, third edition. New York: Macmillan Company, 1960.

12. *Newsweek*, March 8, 1965.

13. Gertrude A. Boyd, *Teaching Communication Skills in the Elementary School*. New York: Van Nostrand Reinhold Company, 1970.

14. Copyright 1955, by Holt, Rinehart and Winston, Inc. Reprinted by permission of Holt, Rinehart and Winston.

CHAPTER V

1. Joseph P. Rice, "The Importance of Parent-Teacher Conferences," *Education*, September, 1962.

2. Harold G. Shane and June Grant Shane, "Educating the Youngest for Tomorrow," in Alvin Toffler (editor), *Learning for Tomorrow: The Role of the Future in Education*. New York: Random House, 1974.

3. Eleanor Thomas Pounds. "New Ways to Teach Your Child to Spell." *Parents' Magazine*, February, 1953.

CHAPTER VI

1. Paul R. Hanna and James T. Moore, Jr., "Spelling—From Spoken Word to Written Symbol," *The Elementary School Journal,* February, 1953.

2. Richard L. Venezky, "English Orthography: Its Graphical Structure and Its Relation to Sound," *Reading Research Quarterly,* Spring, 1967.

3. *Ibid.*

4. Abraham H. Lass, *Business Spelling and Word Power.* New York: Donald Publishing Company, Inc., 1961.

5. Adapted from Everett E. Robie, *Word Division, or When to Hyphenate.* Stamford, Connecticut; Stark and Glenbrook Schools, 1951. See also Nebraska Council of Teachers of English, *A Curriculum for English.* Lincoln: Nebraska Curriculum Development Center, University of Nebraska, 1961.

6. Margaret L. Peters, *Spelling: Caught or Taught?* London: Routledge & Kegan Paul, Ltd., 1967.

CHAPTER VII

1. Ernest Weekley, "On Dictionaries," in James Sledd and Wilma R. Ebbitt (editors), *Dictionaries and THAT Dictionary.* Chicago: Scott, Foresman and Company, 1962.

2. Joseph Jordan (editor), *A Handbook for Terrible Spellers; The Backwords Dictionary.* London: Wolfe Publishers, 1964; revised edition by Oliver Stoner, *A Handbook for Terrible Spellers; The Backwords Dictionary.* New York: Spellbinder Division of Innovation Press, 1964.

3. philip b. gove (editor), *the role of the dictionary.* Indianapolis, Indiana: The Bobbs-Merrill Company, Inc., 1967.

4. A. Mervin Tyson, "Exciting New Volume," in Philip Gove, *The Role of the Dictionary.* Indianapolis, Indiana: The Bobbs-Merrill Company, Inc., 1967.

5. Charlton Laird, "Language and the Dictionary," in David B. Guralnik (editor). *Webster's New World Dictionary of the American Language.* Cleveland: Collins and World Publishing Co., Inc., 1974.

6. Warren Weaver, "The Case of Wayward Words," in Jack C. Gray, *Words, Words, and Words about Dictionaries.* San Francisco: Chandler Publishing Company, 1963.

7. *New World Dictionary of the American Language,* Second College Edition. Cleveland, O.: Collins and World Publishing Co., Inc., 1974.

CHAPTER VIII

1. Nebraska Council of Teachers of English, *A Curriculum for English.* Lincoln: University of Nebraska, 1961.

2. W. Powell Jones, *Practical Word Study.* New York: Oxford University Press, 1943.

3. Nebraska Council of Teachers of English, *op. cit.*

4. *Ibid.*

5. *Ibid.*

6. Adapted from C. O. Sylvester Mawson, *The Dictionary Companion.* Garden City,

New York: Doubleday, Doran & Company, Inc., 1932.

7. A. H. Lass, *Business Spelling and Word Power*. New York: Donald Publishing Company, Inc., 1961.

8. *Ibid.*

9. Based upon a discussion of Mawson, *op. cit.*

CHAPTER IX

1. Leonard F. Dean and Kenneth G. Wilson (editors), *Essays on Language and Usage*, second edition. New York: Oxford University Press, 1963.

2. *Ibid.*

3. Mario Pei, *The Story of Language*. New York: New American Library, 1949.

4. Margaret M. Bryant, *Modern English and Its Heritage*. New York: Macmillan Company, 1962.

5. For a comprehensive study of phoneme-grapheme correspondences, see Paul R. Hanna, Jean S. Hanna, Richard E. Hodges, E. Hugh Rudorf, Jr., *Phoneme-Grapheme Correspondences as Cues to Spelling Improvement*. Washington, D.C.: U.S. Department of Health, Education, and Welfare, 1966.

6. The symbols for the vowels follow the system of Henry Lee Smith, Jr., *Linguistic Science and the Teaching of English*. Cambridge, Massachusetts: The Harvard University Press, 1958.

7. The symbols for the consonants are those of the International Phonetic Alphabet, most of them corresponding to the symbols used in English spelling.

8. More nearly complete lists of words commonly misspelled in the special interest areas may be found in Thomas Clark Pollock and Willard D. Baker, *The University Spelling Book*. New York: Prentice-Hall, Inc., 1956.

CHAPTER X

1. Thomas Pollock, "Words Most Commonly Misspelled," *Clearing House*, December, 1964.

2. Paul R. Hanna, Jean S. Hanna, Richard E. Hodges, and E. Hugh Rudorf, Jr., *Phoneme-Grapheme Correspondences as Cues to Spelling Improvement*. Washington, D.C.: U.S. Department of Health, Education, and Welfare, 1966.

3. Richard E. Hodges, "Another Look at Those 'Spelling Demons,' " *Elementary School Journal*, October, 1967. (Cited by Gertrude A. Boyd and E. Gene Talbert, *Spelling in the Elementary School*. Columbus, Ohio: Charles E. Merrill Publishing Company, 1971.

4. Hodges, *op. cit.*

5. Ralph M. Williams, *Phonetic Spelling for College Students*. New York: Oxford University Press, 1960.

6. Wilmer K. Trauger, *Language Arts in Elementary School*. New York: McGraw-Hill, Inc., 1963.

7. Dorothy C. Olson, "A Perfectly Normal Spelling Dilemma," *English Journal,* November, 1969.

8. The following research studies and textbooks are giving attention to hard spots in words:

Edna L. Furness and Gertrude A. Boyd, *Hard Spots in Hard Words for Secondary School Students.* Laramie: Wyoming School Study Council, University of Wyoming, 1958.

Arthur I. Gates, *A List of Spelling Difficulties in 3876 Words.* New York: Teachers College, Columbia University, 1937.

Thomas Clark Pollock, "Spelling Report," *College English,* November, 1954.

J. C. Tressler and Henry I. Christ, *English in Action* (fourth course). Boston; D. C. Heath and Company, 1955.

CHAPTER XI

1. William Morris (editor), *The American Heritage Dictionary of the English Language.* Boston: Houghton Mifflin Company, 1971.

2. *Ibid.*

3. Noah Webster, *American Spelling Book,* with an introductory essay by Henry Steele Commager. New York: Bureau of Publications, Teachers College, Columbia University, 1962.

4. Ernest Horn, *Teaching Spelling.* Washington, D.C.: National Education Association, 1954.

5. Robert L. Coard, "Spelling With a Smile," *Improving College and University Teaching,* Autumn, 1962.

6. For an article by a parent whose children are champion spellers and who have participated in spelling bees, see Marilyn David, "The Spelling Bee Circuit," the Omaha *World-Herald,* April 2, 1967.

7. Included in an article by William R. Linneman, "Our Spelling Is a Muess!" *College Composition and Communication,* May, 1975. Used with the permission of Sandra Leman and the National Council of Teachers of English.

CHAPTER XII

1. Reprinted with the permission of the National Council of Teachers of English.

OTHER DEMON LISTS

APPENDIX A

APPROXIMATE GRADE PLACEMENT OF WORDS IN JONES'S LIST OF 100 SPELLING DEMONS IN THE ENGLISH LANGUAGE*

First and Second Grades

any	here	they
been	know	too
blue	many	two
buy	much	very
could	read	where
dear	said	write
does	some	
every	there	

Third Grade

again	half	shoes
always	having	sure
break	hear	their
can't	heard	tonight
color	hour	used
coming	just	wear
done	knew	week
don't	making	which
early	often	won't
friend	once	would

APPENDIX

Fourth Grade

among	February	ready	tired
answer	forty	says	truly
built	guess	seems	Tuesday
busy	instead	since	Wednesday
choose	laid	sugar	whole
country	none	tear	women
doctor	piece	though	writing
enough	raise	through	wrote

---

*W. F. Jones, *Concrete Investigation of the Material of English Spelling.* Vermillion, South Dakota: University of South Dakota, 1913, p. 24.

Fifth Grade

ache	easy	straight
beginning	loose	trouble
believe	lose	whether
business	meant	
cough	minute	

Sixth Grade

grammar	hoarse	separate

APPENDIX B

FITZGERALD'S MASTER DEMON LIST OF 222 WORDS*

about	can	fun	I'm
address	cannot	getting	in
afternoon	can't	goes	isn't
again	children	going	it
all right	Christmas	good	it's
along	close	good-by	I've
already	come	got	Jan.
always	coming	grade	just
am	couldn't	guess	know
an	cousin	had	lessons
and	daddy	Halloween	letter
answer	day	handkerchiefs	like
anything	Dec.	has	likes
anyway	didn't	have	little
April	dog	haven't	lots
are	don't	having	loving
arithmetic	down	he	made
aunt	Easter	hear	make
awhile	every	hello	Mar.
baby	everybody	her	maybe
balloon	father	here	me
basketball	Feb.	him	Miss
because	fine	his	morning
been	first	home	mother
before	football	hope	Mr.
birthday	for	hospital	Mrs.
bought	fourth	house	much
boy	Friday	how	my
boys	friend	how's	name
brother	friends	I	nice
brought	from	I'll	Nov.

*James A. Fitzgerald, "A Crucial Core Vocabulary in Elementary School Language and Spelling," *American School Board Journal,* 103: 22-24, July, 1941. Used with permission of the American School Board Association. All rights reserved.

now	Santa Claus	teacher's	until
nowadays	Saturday	Thanksgiving	vacation
o'clock	saw	that's	very
Oct.	school	the	want
off	schoolhouse	their	was
on	send	them	we
once	sent	then	weather
one	sincerely	there	well
our	snow	there's	went
out	snowman	they	were
outside	some	they're	we're
party	something	think	when
people	sometime	thought	white
play	sometimes	through	will
played	soon	time	with
plays	stationery	to	won't
please	store	today	would
pretty	studying	together	write
quit	summer	tomorrow	writing
quite	Sunday	tonight	you
receive	suppose	too	your
received	sure	toys	you're
remember	surely	train	yours
right	swimming	truly	
said	teacher	two	

APPENDIX C

THE REMINGTON RAND LIST OF WORDS MOST FREQUENTLY MISSPELLED BY ADULTS *

A	ac-quaint-ance	al-lege	as-phalt
ab-rupt	ac-qui-esce	al-lot-ment	as-sign-ment
ab-sorb-ent	ac-quire	al-lot-ted	as-sist-ance
ab-sorp-tion	ac-quit-tal	al-ready	as-ter-isk
abun-dance	a-cross	alu-mi-num	ath-let-ics
ac-cede	ad-journ-ment	amend-ment	at-tend-ance
ac-cel-er-ate	ad-mis-si-ble	a-nal-y-sis	at-tor-neys
ac-cept-a-ble	ad-mit-tance	ana-lyze	auc-tion-eer
ac-ces-si-ble	ad-van-ta-geous	an-ec-dote	au-di-ble
ac-ces-sory	ad-ver-tise-ment	apos-tro-phe	au-thor-i-ty
ac-ci-den-tally	af-fect	ap-pa-ra-tus	aux-il-iary
ac-com-mo-date	(verb—to influence)	ap-par-ent	
ac-com-mo-da-tion	af-fil-i-ate	ap-pear-ance	B
ac-com-pa-ny-ing	ag-gres-sive	ap-point-ment	bache-lor
ac-cu-mu-late	air-plane	ap-pro-pri-ate	bal-lot
achieve-ment	align-ment	ar-chi-tect	bank-ruptcy
ac-knowl-edg-ment	all right	ar-range-ment	ban-quet

* Remington Rand Corporation

bar-ba-rous
bas-i-cal-ly
bat-tal-ion
bat-tery
be-hav-ior
be-liev-able
bene-fi-cial
bene-fited
bi-cy-cle
bound-a-ry
bril-liant
bro-chure
budget
bul-le-tin
bu-reaus
busi-ness

C
cal-en-dar
cam-paign
can-celed
can-cel-la-tion
can-di-date
can-vas (noun)
can-vass (verb)
ca-reer
care-ful
cash-ier
ceil-ing
cem-e-ter-y
cen-sus
change-able
char-ac-ter
cli-en-tele
col-lat-eral
col-lege
co-los-sal
com-mit-ment
com-mit-tee
com-peti-tor
con-cede
con-ceiv-a-ble
con-demn
con-fi-dent
con-science
con-sci-en-tious
con-scious
con-secu-tively
con-spicu-ous
con-tin-u-ous

con-trib-ute
con-trol
con-trol-ling
con-tro-versy
con-ven-ience
cor-re-spond-ent
coun-cil
   (an assembly)
coun-sel
   (noun—advice;
   verb—to give
   advice)
criti-cism
criti-cize
cu-ri-ous
cyl-in-der

D
de-ceive
de-ci-sion
de-fend-ant
de-ferred
de-fi-cient
defi-cit
defi-nite
dele-gate
de-lin-quent
de-pend-ent
de-scribe
de-scrip-tion
de-sir-a-bil-ity
de-velop
de-vel-op-ment
di-ag-no-sis
dif-fer-ent
dis-ap-pear
dis-ap-point
dis-burse-ment
dis-crep-ancy
dis-sat-is-fied
dis-tinct
di-vine
domi-nance

E
ec-stasy
ef-fect
   (verb—to bring
      to pass;
   noun—result)

ef-fi-cient
eli-gi-ble
elimi-nate
em-bar-rass
emi-nent
en-cy-clo-pe-dia
en-dorse-ment
en-ter-prise
en-velop (verb)
en-vel-op-ment
en-vi-ron-ment
e-quipped
er-ro-ne-ous
es-pe-cial-ly
evi-dently
ex-ag-ger-ate
ex-ceed
ex-cel-lent
ex-haust
ex-hi-bi-tion
ex-ist-ence
ex-pe-ri-ence
ex-or-bi-tant
ex-pla-na-tion
ex-tem-po-ra-ne-ous
ex-ten-sion
ex-traor-di-nary

F
fac-sim-ile
fal-la-cy
fa-mil-iar
fas-ci-nate
fea-si-ble
Feb-ru-ary
fi-nal-ly
fi-nan-cial-ly
flexi-ble
flu-o-res-cent
for-ci-ble
for-eign
forth-right
forty
fran-chise
ful-fill
fun-da-men-tal

G
gauge
gen-u-ine

ges-ture
gi-gan-tic
gnaw-ing
gor-geous
gov-ern-ment
gov-er-nor
gram-mar
gra-tu-ity
gro-cery
grudge
guar-an-tee
guid-ance

H
hand-ker-chief
hand-some
hap-haz-ard
heart-rending
heav-ily
hec-tic
height
hin-drance
homely
ho-mo-gen-ize
hy-giene

I
il-le-gal
il-legi-ble
il-lit-er-ate
im-ag-ine
imi-ta-tion
im-me-di-ately
im-mi-grant
in-au-gu-rate
in-ci-den-tally
in-deli-ble
in-de-pend-ence
in-dis-pen-sa-ble
in-flam-ma-ble
in-hab-it-ant
in-stal-la-tion
in-te-grate
in-ter-cede
in-ter-est
in-ter-fere
in-ter-fered
in-ter-pre-ta-tion
in-ter-rupt
ir-rele-vant

ir-re-sisti-ble
ir-revo-ca-ble
is-suing
its (possessive)
it's (contraction)

J

jeop-ard-ize
jew-elry
jour-ney
judg-ment
jus-ti-fi-able
jus-ti-fied

K

khaki
ki-mono
knowl-edge

L

la-bel-ing
labo-ra-tory
lac-quer
led (past of lead)
ledger
le-giti-mate
lei-sure
li-ai-son
li-brary
li-cense
lien
lik-able
lis-ten
live-li-hood
lone-li-ness
loose
  (adj.—free)
lose (verb)
lovely
lux-u-ry

M

mag-nif-i-cent
main-te-nance
man-age-able
man-age-ment
ma-neu-ver
man-ual
manu-fac-turer
manu-script

mathe-mat-ics
me-di-ocre
mile-age
mis-cel-la-ne-ous
mis-spell
mod-ern
mo-rale
mort-gage
mov-able
mur-mur

N

nec-es-sary
ne-ces-sity
nickel
niece
nine-teenth
ninety
ninth
no-tice-able
now-a-days
nui-sance

O

oblige
oc-ca-sion
oc-ca-sion-ally
oc-curred
oc-cur-rence
omis-sion
omit-ted
one-self
op-er-ate
op-po-nent
op-por-tu-ni-ty
op-pose
op-po-site
op-ti-mism
or-di-nance (law
  or regulation)
ord-nance (military
  supplies)

P

pam-phlet
par-al-lel
par-cel
par-tial
par-tic-u-lar
pas-teur-ize

peace-able
pe-cul-iar
peni-cil-lin
per-ceive
per-form-ance
per-ma-nent
per-mis-si-ble
per-se-ver-ance
per-sist-ent
per-son-ally
per-son-nel
per-suade
Phil-ip-pine
phi-los-o-phy
phy-si-cian
Pitts-burgh (Pa.)
planned
play-wright
pos-ses-sion
prac-ti-cal
prai-rie
pre-cede
pre-ced-ing
pre-cious
pre-fer
pref-er-able
pre-limi-nary
pre-sump-tu-ous
preva-lent
prin-ci-pal (chief
  or main)
prin-ci-ple (rule
  or method)
privi-lege
prob-a-bly
pro-ce-dure
pro-ceed
pro-fes-sion
pro-fes-sor
promi-nent
prom-is-sory
pro-nun-ci-a-tion
pro-pel-ler
proph-e-cy (noun,
  prediction)
proph-e-sy (verb,
  to predict)
psy-chol-ogy
pub-licly
pur-sue

pur-su-ing

Q

quan-tity
ques-tion-naire

R

re-al-ize
re-ceipt
re-ceive
re-cipi-ent
rec-om-mend
rec-om-men-da-tion
rec-on-cile
re-cur-rence
ref-er-ence
re-ferred
rele-vant
re-lief
re-lieve
rem-i-nisce
rep-e-ti-tion
re-pel-lent
re-nown
re-plies
res-tau-rant
re-veal
rhu-barb
rhyme
rhythm
ri-dicu-lous
ro-tary

S

safety
sal-able
scho-las-tic
scis-sors
sec-re-tary
seize
sen-si-ble
sepa-rate
se-rial
shep-herd
ship-ment
siege
sig-nif-i-cance
simi-lar
si-mul-ta-ne-ous
since

siz-able	sur-vey	tying	war-ranty
skep-ti-cal	sus-cep-ti-ble	tyr-anny	weather
sneak	sus-pi-cious		Wednes-day
sou-ve-nir	sym-bol	**U**	wel-fare
sov-er-eign		u-nan-i-mous	whether
spe-cifi-cally	**T**	un-doubt-edly	
speech	tai-lor	unique	**X**
split-ting	tan-gi-ble	un-u-su-al	X ray (noun)
sta-tion-ary (fixed)	tar-iff	us-able	X-ray (adj. and verb)
sta-tion-ery (paper)	tech-ni-cal	use-ful	xy-lo-phone
sta-tis-tics	tech-nique	us-ing	
strength	tele-vise		**Y**
strictly	tele-vi-sion	**V**	yacht
sub-sidy	tem-per-a-ment	vac-ci-nate	yes-ter-day
sub-stan-tial	tem-po-ra-ry	vac-uum (preferable	yield
suc-ceed	ten-ant	not to syllabicate)	young-ster
suc-cess	tend-ency	var-ies	you're (contraction)
suc-ces-sor	ter-ri-ble	vege-ta-ble	youth
suf-fi-cient	ter-ri-tory	visi-ble	
sum-ma-ry	their (possessive)	visi-tor	**Z**
su-ing	theory	vi-ta-min	
su-per-in-tend-ent	there-fore	vol-ume	zeal-ous
super-sede	too (also)		ze-nith
sur-geon	trans-ferred	**W**	zephyr
sur-prise	tri-umph	waiver	zo-ol-ogy

APPENDIX D

FURNESS-BOYD LIST OF 335 REAL SPELLING DEMONS FOR COLLEGE STUDENTS*

absence	altogether	around	business
absorption	amateur	arouse	calendar
accidentally	among	arrangement	careful
accommodate	analysis	article	carrying
accomplish	analyze	ascend	ceiling
achievement	angel	athlete	cemetery
acquire	annual	athletic	certain
across	answer	author	changeable
advise	apparatus	auxiliary	chief
affect	apparent	beginning	choose
against	appearance	believe	chose
all right	appropriate	benefit	clothes
almost	Arctic	benefited	column
already	arguing	breathe	coming
although	argument	brilliant	committed

*Edna L. Furness and Gertrude A. Boyd, "335 Real Spelling Demons for College Students," *College English*, 20: 294-295, March, 1959. Copyright by the National Council of Teachers of English. Reprinted with permission.

committee
comparatively
conceive
conceivable
conscience
conscientious
conscious
consistent
continuous
control
controlled
convenience
counsel
criticism
criticize
curiosity
cylinder
dealt
decide
decision
definite
desirable
despair
destroy
develop
development
difference
different
dining
disappear
disappoint
disastrous
discipline
disease
dissatisfied
distinction
divide
divine
easily
effect
efficient
eligible
embarrass
enemy
environment
equipped
especially
etc.
exaggerate
excellent

except
exercise
existence
expense
experience
experiment
explanation
extremely
familiar
fascinate
February
finally
financier
foreign
foresee
forty
fourth
friend
fundamental
further
generally
government
governor
grammar
grateful
guarantee
guard
guidance
height
heroes
heroine
hoping
humorous
imaginary
imagination
immediately
incidentally
independence
independent
indispensable
influential
intellectual
intelligence
intelligent
interest
interfere
irrelevant
island
it's
its

jealous
judgment
kindergarten
knowledge
laboratory
laid
larynx
later
led
leisure
length
library
license
likelihood
likely
livelihood
loneliness
lose
magazine
maintenance
maneuver
many
marriage
mathematics
meant
medicine
miniature
morale
muscle
naturally
necessary
· neighbor
neither
nickel
niece
ninety
ninth
noticeable
obstacle
occasion
occasionally
occur
occurred
occurrence
official
omit
omitted
opinion
opportunity
optimism

origin
original
paid
parallel
particularly
pastime
peaceable
peculiar
perceive
perform
permanent
personal
perspiration
persuade
pertain
piece
planned
playwright
pleasant
poison
politician
possess
possession
possible
practical
precede
prefer
preferred
prejudice
preparation
prepare
prevalent
primitive
principal
principle
privilege
probably
procedure
proceed
professor
prove
psychology
pursue
pursuit
quantity
quiet
realize
receipt
receive
recognize

recommend	shoulder	temperature	using
regard	significant	tendency	usually
relieve	similar	than	vacuum
religious	simile	their	vegetable
repetition	sophomore	then	vengeance
resistance	specimen	there	villain
rhythm	speech	therefore	weather
ridiculous	stopped	they're	Wednesday
safety	straight	thorough	weird
scene	strength	thought	where
schedule	strenuous	through	whether
science	stretch	together	wholly
seize	studying	too	whose
sense	succeed	tragedy	woman
separate	suppress	tries	women
sergeant	surprise	truly	writing
several	syllable	undoubtedly	written
shepherd	symmetrical	until	you're
shining	temperament	unusual	

APPENDIX E

For teachers who lack confidence in teaching spelling, or who are deficient in knowledge of linguistics, here is a list, reprinted from Carlton E. Beck's "When Teachers Misspell," *Improving College and University Teaching*, Spring, 1965, which may renew seriousness of attitude and generate teacher competence in spelling.

A SPELLING LIST FOR TEACHERS*

accept	behavior	co-ordinator	distraction
achievement	bookkeeping	correspondence	distribute
address	boundaries	corridor	district
adequate	building	counselor	diverts
adjust	business	courteous	effect
administrator	cafeteria	criticism	elementary
adolescents	calendar	curriculum	entrance
affect	Catholic	decision	epileptic
aggressive	census	deficient	everything
algebra	certain	delinquency	excellent
alternative	channels	democratic	exception
anonymous	children	despite	exercise
anxiety	choir	destructive	experiment
applies	climbing	detention	extension
argument	commercial	different	faculty
arithmetic	community	diploma	field
assignment	comparative	disastrous	foreign
assistant	complaints	discipline	genius
attitude	compulsory	discrimination	grammar
audio-visual	conference	discussion	government

* Used with the permission of Oregon State University Press, Corvallis, Oregon.

group
guidance
guilty
gymnasium
handicapped
hectic
height
heterogeneous
history
homogeneous
honorary
illiterate
immature
incidentally
independently
innocent
instructor
insurance
integration
intelligence
irate
irritated
journal
janitor
judgment

laid
languages
leisure
library
license
lounge
luncheon
Lutheran
mathematics
mischievous
motivated
municipal
negative
necessary
Negroes
observant
opportunities
orchestra
parental
parochial
perform
physics
pieces
plumbing
practically

practice
preference
prejudice
premises
preparatory
principal
professor
projector
psychiatric
quiet
quit
quite
receive
recess
recognize
reference
repetition
reprimand
requirements
responsible
salary
secondary
secretary
segregation
sensitive

significant
sincerely
smoking
sophomore
status
strength
student
suburban
successful
superintendent
supervisor
technology
tenure
theories
tried
truly
typical
ultimately
usually
vacancy
violent
vocational
(plus names of
local businesses,
streets, etc.)

References

The following books and articles are very helpful to a person who wants to know more about spelling, language, and linguistics:

Anderson, Paul S., (editor), *Linguistics in the Elementary School Classroom.* New York: The Macmillan Company, 1971, pp. 209-257.

Barnett, Lincoln, "The English Language," Life, 52: 74-83, March 2, 1962.

Brain, Joseph J., *The Blue Book of Spelling.* New York: Regents Publishing Company, Inc., 1960.

Causey, Oscar S., *The Reading Teacher's Reader.* New York: The Ronald Press, 1958, pp. 129-31; 173-205.

Chomsky, Noam, and Morris Hale, *The Sound Pattern in English.* New York: Harper & Row, 1968.

Dewey, Godfrey, *English Spelling: Roadblock to Reading.* New York: Bureau of Publications, Teachers College, Columbia University, 1971.

Funk, Hal D., and DeWayne Triplett (editors), *Language Arts in the Elementary School.* J. B. Lippincott Company, 1972, pp. 423-442.

Furness, Edna L., "Spelling Is Serious Stuff," Delta Kappa Gamma *Bulletin*, 45:37-40, fall, 1978.

Goldstein, Miriam B., *The Teaching of Language in Our Schools.* New York: The Macmillan Company, 1966.

Hall, Robert A., Jr., *Sound and Spelling in English.* Philadelphia: Chilton Company, 1961.

Hinrichs, R. W., "Spelling Lists: Old but Valid Procedure," Elementary English, 52: 249-252, February, 1975.

Holmes, Jack A., *Personality and Spelling Ability.* Berkeley, California: University of California Press, 1959.

Hunnicutt, C. W., and William J. Iverson, *Research in the Three R's.* New York: Harper & Brothers, 1958, pp. 286-315.
Contains discussions on such topics as "Self Study in Spelling," "What Methods are Better?" and "Why Some Children are Better Spellers."

Johnson, Falk S., *A Self-Improvement Guide to Spelling.* New York: Holt, Rinehart and Winston, 1965.

MacCracken, Mary, *Turnabout Children: Overcoming Dyslexia and Other Learning Disabilities.* Boston: Little, Brown and Company, 1986.

Magary, James F., and John R. Eichorn, *The Exceptional Child.* New York: Holt, Rinehart and Winston, Inc., 1960, pp. 410-44.

Malone, John R., "The Larger Aspects of Spelling Reform," Elementary English, 39: 435-445, May, 1962.

McCrum, Robert, William Cram, and Robert MacNeil, *The Story of English*. New York: Viking Penguin, Inc., 1986.

Monson, J., "Is Spelling Spelled Rut, Routine, or Revitalized?" *Elementary English*, 52: 223-224, February, 1975.

Owens, Ralph Dornfield, "Those Spelling Deemuns," *Journal of Business Education*, 36: 339-41, May, 1961.

Pyles, Thomas, *The Origins and Development of the English Language*, New York: Harcourt Brace Jovanovich, 1971.

Scragg, D.G., *A History of English Spelling*. New York: Barnes and Noble, 1974.

Shaw, Harry, *Spell It Right!* New York: Barnes & Noble, Inc., 1963.

Sledd, James, and Wilma R. Ebbitt, *Dictionaries and That Dictionary*. Chicago: Scott, Foresman and Company, 1962.

"Spelling: Encoding English; symposium," *Elementary English*, 52: 221 +, February, 1975.

Tiedt, Iris M., *Spelling Strategies*. San Jose, California: Contemporary Press, 1975.

Vachek, Josef, *Written Language: General Problems and Problems of English*. The Hague: Mouton, 1973.

Wallace, Gerald, and Stephen C. Larsen. *Educational Assessment of Learning Problems: Testing for Teaching*. Boston: Allyn and Bacon, 1978.

Williams, Ralph M., *Phonetic Spelling for College Students*. New York: Oxford University Press, 1960.

Glossary

Accent. The vocal prominence given to a particular syllable of a word by greater intensity (stress accent), or by variation of pitch or tone (pitch accent). In dictionaries, marks show the kind of emphasis required. For example, in the word, *alphabet,* the first syllable has primary (strong) stress, or accent: al´pha bet.´ The final syllable has secondary (light) stress. *Accent* is often considered a synonym for *stress.*

Adjective. A word that modifies or describes a noun or noun equivalent: *one* house, *beautiful* eyes.

Adverb. A word that modifies a verb, an adjective, or another adverb; answers the questions *how, when,* or *where:* The teacher who *really* teaches explains the lesson *clearly* (how), answers the questions *daily* (when), and meets the class *there* (where). Some adverbs qualify a complete statement: *Therefore,* teachers *really* teach.

Affix. A word element—a prefix or suffix—that is attached to a base, root, or stem. *Af* is a prefix derived from Latin *ad,* which by assimilation becomes *af.* See Assimilation

Agglutination. In linguistics, the systematic combining or compounding of independent words that retain their original forms and meanings with little change during the combination process: *landowner, farmhouse.*

Analogy. A process by which new or less familiar forms are produced, conforming to the pattern of older or more familiar ones: past tense of *climb* changed from *clomb* to *climbed* by analogy with weak verbs like *rhyme* (those which add -*ed*); *energize* from *energy; finalize* from *final.*

Articulatory phonetics. The study of speech sounds; the manner of production, the points points of articulation, and the relationship to classification of speech sounds.

Assimilation. The linguistic process by which a sound is modified to resemble an adjacent sound. For example, the prefix *sub* in *suffix* becomes *suf*- in *suffix* by assimilation.

Compound. A word composed of two or more base *morphemes,* written either as one word or hyphenated. Compounds are characterized by reduced stress on one of the elements and by changes in meaning: *bluebird, blue bird; greenhouse, green house; grandfather, grand father.*

Configuration. According to Gestalt psychology, a physical or symbolic form or figure is determined by the arrangement of parts: [tag] [hat].

Consonant. A "hard" letter. As contrasted with vowel sounds, which are produced with less constriction and with fuller resonance, the consonants are produced by partial or complete obstruction of the breath stream by various constrictions of the speech organs. A sudden stopping and releasing of the air stream produces *b, p, t, d, k, g.* Forcing the air through a narrow channel produces *f, v, s, z.* Obstructing the air in one area and releasing it in another produces *m, n, l, r.* Consonants produced with the voice are voiced: *b, d, g, v;* those not produced with the voice are voiceless: *p, t, k, f.*

Derivation. A linguistic and morphological process of forming new words from existing words by adding one or more affixes to roots, stems, or words: prefix *un* + prefix *pre* + root *dict* + suffix *-able* = unpredictable.

Diacritical mark. A mark, such as a macron or cedilla, added to a letter or symbol to show its pronunciation. For example, the macron in *lāte* indicates that the *a* has a long sound. The cedilla in the French word *français* indicates that the *c* has a sibilant value (s).

Digraph. A combination of two letters to spell a single sound: h*ea*t, s*ee*d, *ei*ther, p*ie*ce, b*oo*k, c*oa*t, y*ou*, *ph*ysics, *th*en.

Dyslexia. See Strephosymbolia.

Etymology. In historical and comparative linguistics, the study of the history of a word: the origin and analysis of the development of the word from its earliest form, through various changes, to its present form and meaning.

Eye-dialect. False phonetic respelling of words to show nonstandard pronunciation and to burlesque the words of the speaker. In reality, eye-dialect represents the standard English pronunciation of the words spelled: *cum, enuff, lissen, ruff, sez, wuz.*

Grapheme. A written or printed alphabetic character, a letter, a unit of visual shape, or a symbol. The twenty-six letters of the alphabet are our basic graphemes.

Homograph. A word spelled the same as another but with a different meaning and origin, sometimes with a different pronunciation: *bow* of a ship, bend a *bow;* having wound a bandage around the *wound.*

Homonym. Homophone or homograph.

Homophone. A word pronounced like another but different in spelling, origin, and meaning: *to, two, too; so, sew, sow; plain, plane; beet, beat; sum, some; hear, here; their, there; all, awl; altar, alter; our, hour.*

Hyphen. A mark (-) used between the parts of a compound word or the syllables of a word, especially of a word divided at the end of a line of writing.

Imagery. Mental images which are visual, auditory, or kinesthetic, and which are produced by memory or imagination.

Lexicography. A branch of the discipline of linguistics concerned with the writing or compiling of a dictionary or dictionaries.

Linguistics. The systematic study of language, and, more particularly, of the aspects of individual language, including phonology, morphology, syntax, and semantics. The discipline is subdivided into descriptive linguistics, historical linguistics, psycholinguistics, comparative linguistics, geographical linguistics, dialectology, and lexicography.
 English linguistics, of course, is the study or analysis of details of the English language.

Macron. A short, straight mark (-) placed horizontally above a vowel to indicate a long sound in pronunciation: *a* in the words c*a*ge, c*a*pe.

Mnemonics. A technique or system using mottoes, formulas, or rhymes as an aid to improve the memory.

Monosyllable. A word of one syllable: *spell, word.*

Morpheme. The smallest meaningful unit in the language. A morpheme consists of one or more phonemes. The simple word *hut* is a morpheme. So are prefixes like *de-* in *derive* or *per-* in *perfect,* and suffixes like *-dom* in *kingdom* and *-ent* in *excellent.*

Morphology. The scientific and linguistic study of internal structure, of the forms of words, and of the way in which morphemes are classified, arranged, and connected to each other.

Neologism. A newly coined word, as opposed to one that enters a language by the process of language development. Many originally *coined* words have been accepted: *telephone, kodak.* Neologisms coined by a commercial firm include *Nabisco* (National Biscuit Company).

Noun. A word naming a person, place, thing, quality, idea, or action: *Gregory, yard, pencil, strength, honesty, inscription.*

Orthography. A branch of linguistics concerned with translating the sounds of a spoken word into alphabetic symbols. A synonym for *spelling.*

Parts of speech. Words are nouns, pronouns, verbs, adverbs, adjectives, prepositions, conjunctions, determiners *(a, an, the),* expletives *(it, there),* or exclamations *(ouch!).* Sometimes the part of speech can be told only by seeing how the word is used—whether it names, whether it describes, or whether it joins.

Patois. A hybrid language or special jargon, which differs considerably from the accepted standard.

Perception. Mental awareness of symbols, comprehension, insight, intuitive judgment, or understanding acquired by means of the senses.

Phoneme. The smallest practical unit of speech sound. The word *boat* has three phonemes, which are represented by the pronunciation symbols, *b-o-t.*

Phonemics. An important or significant sound. Each language has a limited number of phonemes, or important message-transmitting sounds. The behavioral principles of phonemes are known as phonemics or collectively as the phonemic principle.

Phonetics. The branch of linguistics that gives attention to the speech sounds—their formation, production, combination, description, and the exact representation of pronunciation by phonetic symbols.

Phonics. A simplified version of phonetic knowledge. Phonics is a method of teaching beginners to read, to spell, or to pronounce by learning the accepted sounds of letters or combinations of letters.

Phonology. The science of speech sounds (including phonetics and phonemics), that considers the sounds of language, their formation, and the exact representation of pronunciation by phonetic symbols.

Prefix. An affix or morpheme that is united with and placed *before* a word to alter its meaning or to create a new word: *adverb, supermarket,*

Pronunciation. The act or manner of enunciating words with reference to the production of sounds, the placement of accents, the accuracy of pitch or intonation.

Root. In morphology, a base or linguistic form to which an affix (prefix or suffix) can be added: known, unknown; class, classify, classification.

Schwa. An obscure vowel sound (ə) found in more than 5,000 polysyllabic words in the 10,000 most common English words. It can be heard in the initial syllable of *aside,* in the second syllable of *derivation,* and in the final syllable of *dyslexia.*

Security segment. A core of the most commonly used words.

Sesquipedalian words. From Latin *sesquipedalis,* of a foot and a half in length. Long, ponderous, and polysyllabic (many-syllables) words.

Sibilant. A consonant which is produced by the tongue touching the palate, and which is characterized by a hissing sound. Sibilants are s(six), z(zero), sh (shop), zh (rouge), ch (chunk), j (joy).

Stem. See Root.

Strephosymbolia (twisted symbols). A term used to designate the tendency that certain individuals have to reverse letters, parts of words, or even whole words, especially in reading and spelling: *mazagine* for *magazine; 710* for *OIL.*

Stress. See Accent.

Syllable. A unit of pronunciation that consists of a single vowel or a vowel combined with one or more consonants: one syllable, *a, an;* two syllables, *writ-ing, spell-ing.*

Suffix. An affix or morpheme added after the end of a word or word base to change its meaning, to alter its grammatical function, or to form a new word: *gentle, gentleness* (noun from adjective); *govern, government* (noun from verb); *act, active* (adjective from noun); *social, socialize* (verb from adjective); *origin, originate* (verb from noun).

Synonym. A word that has a meaning similar or nearly similar to that of another word in the same language.

Verb. A word expressing action or a condition: Ann, Kristine, and Jack *study* the words, I *am* certain.

Vowel. A speech sound articulated so that the breath passes through the middle of the mouth and is relatively unobstructed by the speech organs. The vowels in English are *a, e, i. o, u* and sometimes *w* and *y: vowel, hymn.*

Index

A

Abbreviations, 116
Ability and speech sounds,
    spelling, 80
ABLE suffix, 134
Accentuation, 108
    exercises in, 109
Adjective suffixes, 132
Adjectives, compound, 122
Adverb suffixes, 132
Aerospace misspellings, 220
Age and spelling, 47
Agriculture, words in, 162
Alphabet
    history of the, 157
    importance of the, 159
    instruction and spelling, 61
    reform, 34
    shortcomings of the, 158
    single-sound, 34
    suitability of the, 159
Alphabetology, 159
American Philological
    Association, 33
American spellings, 30, 216
Analysis, methods of word, 208
ANCE suffix, 138, 141
ANT suffix, 138
Approach to spelling
    psychological, 43
    using auditory, 208
    using kinesthetic, 208
    visual, 204, 207

AR suffix, 142
Art, words in, 163
ARY suffix, 141
Association of ideas, 90
ATION suffix, 139
Attitude toward spelling, 60
    mental, 22
    and proficiency, 208
    reform, 25
    of students, 63
    of teachers, 62
    to teachers, 58
Auditory
    approach, using, 208
    imagery, 46, 87
    perception, 44

B

Bad spelling
    effect of, 17
    See also Poor spelling.
Basis for English spelling, 37
Bee, National Spelling, 196
Bees
    advantages of spelling, 196
    arguments against spelling, 196
    in literature, spelling, 199
    practice exercises for, 203
Biology, words in, 163
Books, educational importance
    of spelling, 198
British spellings, 216
Business world and spelling, 19

C

Capitalization, rules of, 115
Careers and spelling, 19
Causes of poor language skills, 58
Caxton, William, influence of, 31
CEDE suffix, 145
CEED suffix, 145
Cerebral dominance and reversals, 48
Changes in spelling, rate of evolution of, 31
Chemistry words, 164
Child, learning patterns in the, 44
Children, parent help for, 74
Chinese writing, 157
Communication and spelling, 17, 20
Compound
  adjectives, 122
  nouns, 122
  words, 121
  words, special, 123
Compounding
  by affixing, 124
  word formulation by, 121
Consonants
  doubling, 148
  and phonemes, 161
  spelling, 81
Crucial core words, 172

D

Deaf, spelling ability of the, 80
Definition of spelling, 18
Definitions of words, 113
Demon words, 172
  categories of, 173
  grade placement of, 231
  lists of, 174, 231
  reasons for, 173
Dentistry, words in, 165
Derivations of words, 111
Dewey, John, educational influence of, 55
Diacritical marks, 105
Dictionaries
  abridged, 101
  modern, 100
  types of, 101
Dictionary
  development of the, 99
  entry words in, 104
  finding unknown words in, 103
  future dilemma of the, 103
  and guessing, 103
  guide words in, 104
  importance of the, 97, 209
  reliance on, 97
  as a spelling reference, 102
  as a tool, 99
  using the, 103
  using a picture, 77
Digraphs, 160
Dislike of spelling, 63
Doubling the consonant, 148
Drill lack as cause of poor language skills, 59
Dyslexia, 48

E

E, rule of the final, 147
Ear and eye, spelling by, 209
Education
  and John Dewey, 55
  and the home, 75
  role of spelling in, 198
  words in, 165

Educational
  decline, modern, 56, 57
  status and spelling, 19
EFY suffix, 144
Egyptians and the alphabet, 157
EI-IE words, testing, 146
EI rule, 145
Elimination process for National
  Spelling Bee, 202
Emotions and spelling, 208
ENCE suffix, 138
Engineering, words in, 166
English
  history of, 25
  irregularity of spelling, 25
  language, contributions to, 26
  and phonetics, 25
  spelling, basis for, 37
  spelling, problems of, 24
ENT suffix, 138
Entry words in dictionary, 104
Environment and spelling, 75
ER suffix, 142
Errors, correcting, 212
ERY suffix, 141
Etymology
  exercises, 112
  of words, 111
Eye-dialect, 19
Eye and ear, spelling by, 209

F

Final E, rule of the, 147
Fitzgerald's Master Demon List,
  232
Flesch, Rudolf, 60
Foreign sounds, dictionary, 107
Form and spelling, 17
Formulation of words, 120
Foundation for a Compatible
  and Consistent Alphabet, 34

Franklin, Benjamin, and
  phonetic alphabet, 30
French, unphonetic nature of, 25
Furness-Boyd List of 335 Real
  Spelling Demons for College
  Students, 236

G

Gates, A. I., influence of, 80
Geology, words in, 166
Grade placement of spelling
  demons, 231
Grammar
  importance of, 208
  and suffixes, correlation of,
  208
Graphemes, 157, 159
  and phoneme correlation, 160,
  173
Greek
  influence on alphabet, 157
  prefixes, knowing, 129
  words, 26
Guide words in dictionary, 104

H

Habit, spelling as a
  sensory-motor, 45
Hanna, Paul R., and spelling
  research, 173
Hard words, 102
  handling, 22
Hearing and spelling, 18
Help
  home, 75
  parents and spelling, 77
  school, 78
  in spelling, self, 22
Historical spelling, 26
History of English, 25

Home
  educational approach of the, 75
  importance of the, 75
  spelling help at, 75
Homographs, evolution of, 102
Homonyms
  misspelling and, 174
  problems of, 214
Hyphenation formulation of words, 121

I

IBLE suffix, 134
Ideas, association of, 90
IE rule, 145
IE-EI words, testing, 146
IFY suffix, 144
Imagery, 45, 87
  age variations in, 45
Imitation, formulation of words by, 120
Importance of spelling, 17, 21
Improving spelling instruction, 64
Influences on spelling, 32
Intelligence and spelling, 46, 47, 204
Inversions, spelling, 47
ISE suffix, 143
Iterative formation of words, 120
IZE suffix, 143

J

Johnson, Dr. Samuel
  and dictionary, 100
  and spelling reform, 29
Jones's List of Spelling Demons, 231
Journalism, words in, 167

K

Kinesthetic
  approach, using, 208
  imagery, 46
  practice, importance of, 195
Kinetic reversal, 48

L

Language
  contributions to English, 26
  skills, causes of poor, 58
  skills, decline in, 57
  skills and drill, 59
  skills, teaching, 58
Latin
  prefixes, knowing, 126
  roots, importance of, 124, 208
  words, 26
Law, words in, 168
Learning
  patterns in the child, 44
  to spell, steps in, 21
  spelling rules, 209
Letters, silent, 213
Linguists and spelling, 159
Listening, use of, 22
Literacy, spelling as a sign of, 18
Literature
  spelling bee in, 199
  words in, 168

M

Manchester Guardian, 37
Mann, Horace, influence of, 61
Match, spelling, 198
Mathematics, words in, 169
Medicine, words in, 170
Memory and Spelling, 22
Mental
  attitude to spelling, 22

qualifications to spell, 21
Method
  mnemonic, 79, 90
  multisensory, 49
  sight-sound, 83
  structuring, 120
Methods
  basic spelling, 79
  conflict in reading and
    spelling, 60
Misspellings, aerospace, 220
Mnemonic
  devices, exercises on, 96
  method of spelling, 79, 90
  use of, 208
Morphology of words, 110
Multisensory method of spelling,
  49

N

National Spelling Bee, 196, 199
  elimination process for, 202
  rewards of, 203
  rules of, 200
Nature of spelling, 45
Noun suffixes, 130
Nouns, compound, 122
Number
  of words in common use, 101
  of words to learn, 67
Nursing, words in, 170

O

Observation, use of, 22
OR suffix, 142
Origin, spelling according to
  word, 29

P

Parents
  child-help from, 74

educational action by, 73
school participation by, 72
self-evaluation of, 71
and spelling help, 77
spelling as problem of, 70
teacher help for, 74
and teachers, cooperation of,
  73
Participation by parents, school,
  72
Parts of speech, 110
Patterns, spelling, 159
Perception
  auditory, 44
  visual, 44
Permanence of spelling, 24
Phonemes, 157, 159
  and grapheme correlation, 160,
    173
  spelling variations of, 25
  use of, 158
Phonetic
  alphabet and Franklin, 30
  spelling, exercises in, 108
  spelling, use of, 18
Phonetics, 80
  and English, 25, 81
  exercises, 83
  and French, 25
  and reading, 81
  and sight-sound method, 83
  and spelling, 81
Physical nature of spelling, 45
Picture dictionary, help from, 77
Political science, words in, 171
Pollock, Thomas, research of,
  172
Poor
  language skills, drill lack as
    cause of, 59
  spelling, increase in, 21
  spelling, prevalence of, 172
  spelling, problems of, 56
  spelling, reasons for, 24

spelling, remediation for, 65
Popularity of spelling, 62
Preferred spelling, exercises in, 114
Prefixes
  exercises for, 127
  knowing Greek, 129
  knowing Latin, 126
Prestige of spelling, lack of, 63
Primary spellings, 216
Principles, importance of spelling, 37, 38
Printers and spelling standardization, 31
Printing and traditional spelling, 158
Professional words, 163
Proficiency and attitude, spelling, 208
  tests of spelling, 207
Pronunciation
  importance of, 208
  key, 105
  key, dictionary, 106
  key, exercises in, 108
  and spelling, 18, 211
  and spelling, differences between, 28
Psychological
  approach to spelling, 43
  nature of spelling, 45
  problems and spelling, 76
Psychologists and spelling, 21
Psychology and spelling, 43

R

Reading
  and spelling, correlation in teaching, 60
  and spelling methods, conflict in, 60
Recall and spelling, 18
Recognition
  exercises for, 53
  and spelling, 50
Reform, spelling, 36
  attitude toward, 25
  rate of, 33
  resistance to, 37
Reformers, spelling, 29, 197
Reiteration, exercises on, 50
Remediation for poor spelling, 65
Remington Rand List of Words Most Frequently Misspelled by Adults, 233
Reproduction
  exercises for, 53
  of letters and spelling, 18
  spelling by, 52
Research, spelling, 64
Reversals
  causes of, 48
  help for, 48, 49
  spelling, 47
  types of, 48
Roots
  of English, language, 26
  importance of Latin, 208
Rules
  learning spelling, 209
  of the National Spelling Bee, 199
  special language, 145

S

School
  action by parents, 73
  participation by parents, 72
  spelling help from, 78
Science and spelling, 20
Scrambled words, 217
Secondary spellings, 216
Secrets of spelling success, 204
SEDE suffix, 145
Self-help in spelling, 22

Sensory-motor habit, spelling as a, 45
Sight, spelling by, 79
Sight-sound method, 79
  exercises, 88
  and phonetics, 83
  research on, 87
Silent letters, knowledge of origins of, 213
Simpler Spelling Association, 34
Simplified Spelling Board, 33
Simplified Spelling Society, 34
Single-sound alphabet, 34
SION suffix, 140
Social
  influence of spelling, 198
  status and spelling, 18
Society, spelling and, 198
Sound
  spelling by, 80
  See also Sight-sound method.
Specialist, help from the school, 78
Speech
  parts of, 110
  See also Pronunciation.
Spell-down, 198
Spelling
  history of word, 197
  match, 198
Spelling Reform Board, 33
Standardization
  of spelling and printers, 31
  of spelling words, 197
Standardized English spelling, 28
Static reversal, 48
Strephosymbolia. See Dyslexia, Reversals.
Structuring, spelling by, 120
Students, attitude of, 63
Study
  importance of, 23

techniques, 207
Suffixes
  adding, 134
  adjective, 132
  adverb, 132
  and grammar, correlation of, 208
  meanings of, 130
  noun, 130
  verb, 132
Syllabication, 84
  chart, 85
  exercises, 86
  importance of, 87
Synonyms, 114

T

Teachers
  attitude of, 62
  attitude to, 58
  helping spelling, 65
  improving spelling of, 238
  parent-help from, 74
  and parents, cooperation of, 73
Teaching
  language skills, problems of, 58
  reading and spelling, correlation between, 60
  spelling, 55
  spelling, changes in, 67
  spelling, improving, 64, 65
  spelling, responsibility for, 61
Tests of spelling success, 207
Thorndike, Edward L., and dictionary, 101
TION suffix, 139
Traditional spelling and printing, 158
Transposition reversal, 48

V

Variant spelling, 114
Verb suffixes, 132
Visual
   approach, importance of, 204,
      207
   imagery, 46, 87
   perception, 44
Vowel irregularities, 82
Vowels
   omission of, 212
   and phonemes, 160
   spelling, 82

W

Webster, Noah
   and Americanization of
      spelling, 30
   and dictionary, 100
   influence of, 198
Word, words
   agricultural, 162
   analysis, methods of, 208
   art, 163
   biology, 163
   chemistry, 164
   in common use, number of,
      101
   crucial core, 172
   defining, 102
   definitions of, 113
   demon, 174

dentistry, 165
derivations of, 111
in dictionary, entry, 104
in dictionary, guide, 104
differentiation of, 102
in education, 165
in engineering, 166
formulation of, 120
frequently used, 102
in geology, 166
grade placement of demon,
   231
Greek, 26
hard, 102
in journalism, 167
Latin, 26
to learn, number, 67
legal, 168
in literature, 168
lists, demon, 231
in mathematics, 169
in medicine, 170
morphology of, 110
in nursing, 170
in political science, 171
professional, 163
scrambled, 217
spelling, history of, 197
watching, importance of, 211
Writing and spelling, 18

Y

YZE suffix, 143

NTC LANGUAGE ARTS BOOKS

Business Communication
Business Communication Today! *Thomas & Fryar*
Handbook for Business Writing, *Baugh, Fryar, & Thomas*
Meetings, *Pohl*

Essential Skills
Building Real Life English Skills, *Starkey & Penn*
English 93, *Reynolds, Steet, & Guillory*
English Survival Series, *Maggs*
Essential Life Skills
Essentials of Reading and Writing English Series
How to Improve Your Study Skills, *Coman & Heavers*
303 Dumb Spelling Mistakes, *Downing*
Vocabulary by Doing, *Beckert*

Genre Literature
Another Tomorrow: A Science Fiction Anthology, *Hollister*
The Detective Story, *Schwartz*
The Short Story & You, *Simmons & Stern*
You and Science Fiction, *Hollister*

Journalism
Getting Started in Journalism, *Harkrider*
Journalism Today! *Ferguson & Patten*

Language, Literature, and Composition
An Anthology for Young Writers, *Meredith*
The Art of Composition, *Meredith*
Creative Writing, *Mueller & Reynolds*
Literature by Doing, *Tchudi & Yesner*
Lively Writing, *Schrank*
Look, Think & Write, *Leavitt & Sohn*
The Writer's Handbook, *Karls & Szymanski*
Writing by Doing, *Sohn & Enger*
Writing in Action, *Meredith*

Media
Photography in Focus, *Jacobs & Kokrda*
Television Production Today! *Kirkham*
Understanding Mass Media, *Schrank*
Understanding the Film, *Johnson & Bone*

Mythology
Mythology and You, *Rosenberg & Baker*
Welcome to Ancient Greece, *Millard*
Welcome to Ancient Rome, *Millard*
World Mythology, *Rosenberg*

Reading
Reading by Doing, *Simmons & Palmer*

Speech
The Basics of Speech, *Galvin, Cooper, & Gordon*
Contemporary Speech, *HopKins & Whitaker*
Creative Speaking, *Buys et al.*
Creative Speaking Series
Dynamics of Speech, *Myers & Herndon*
Getting Started in Public Speaking, *Prentice & Payne*
Listening by Doing, *Galvin*
Literature Alive! *Gamble & Gamble*
Meetings, *Pohl*
Person to Person, *Galvin & Book*
Public Speaking Today! *Prentice & Payne*
Speaking by Doing, *Buys, Sills, & Beck*

Theatre
The Book of Cuttings for Acting & Directing, *Cassady*
The Book of Scenes for Acting Practice, *Cassady*
The Dynamics of Acting, *Snyder & Drumstra*
An Introduction to Theatre and Drama,
    Cassady & Cassady
Play Production Today! *Beck et al.*

For a current catalog and information about our complete line
of language arts books, write:
National Textbook Company,
a division of NTC Publishing Group
4255 West Touhy Avenue
Lincolnwood (Chicago), Illinois 60646-1975 U.S.A.